GOOD COMPANY

GOOD COMPANY

A Mining Family in Fairbanks, Alaska

SARAH CRAWFORD ISTO

For my dear friend Joanne with whom I share so many treasured memories in Fairbanks.

Sally Crawford

UNIVERSITY OF ALASKA PRESS
Fairbanks

Sarah Crawford Isto

Printed in the United States

This publication was printed on paper that meets the minimum requirements
for ANSI/NISO Z39.48-1992 (Permanence of Paper).

Library of Congress Cataloging-in-Publication Data

Isto, Sarah A.
Good company : a mining family in Fairbanks, Alaska / Sarah Isto.
p. cm.
Includes bibliographical references and index.
ISBN-13: 978-1-889963-88-4 (pbk. : alk. paper)
ISBN-10: 1-889963-88-7 (pbk. : alk. paper)
1. Crawford family. 2. Isto, Sarah A.—Childhood and youth. 3. Crawford, Jim,
1904–1994—Family. 4. Mining engineering—Alaska. 5. Alaska—Biography. I. Title.
CT274.C73I77 2007
979.8'600922—dc22

2006013892

Cover design: Dixon Jones, Rasmuson Library Graphics

Cover photos: Jim and Alta Crawford in 1930 (top); Fairbanks Dredge No. 3 (bottom).

Back cover: View of Second Avenue, Fairbanks, ca. 1948. Courtesy Jane Crawford Tallman.

CONTENTS

Introduction   ix

SETTLING INTO THE COUNTRY

1 An Emigrant from the South: James Crawford   3
2 Emigrants from the West: Alta Tanner and the Stanfield Girls   19
3 Marriage   35
4 Hunkering Down in the Depression   47
5 Adoption and War Jitters   59
6 War, Birth, and Exile   73

POSTWAR ON GARDEN ISLAND

7 Dredge Superintendent   91
8 Alta's Domain   103
9 Kids at Play in the Compound   119
10 Sister Jane   125

DOWNTOWN FAIRBANKS AT MIDCENTURY

11 Fairbanks Operations Manager   139
12 The Town Through Schoolgirl Eyes   151

LIFE IN THE WHITE HOUSE

13 General Manager for Alaska   167
14 Hosting Company   179
15 Schoolgirls on the Creeks   191
16 New Lathrop High School   197
17 Into Statehood and Off to the University of Alaska   211
18 Leaving Alaska   221

Endnotes   229
Works Cited   243
Index   247

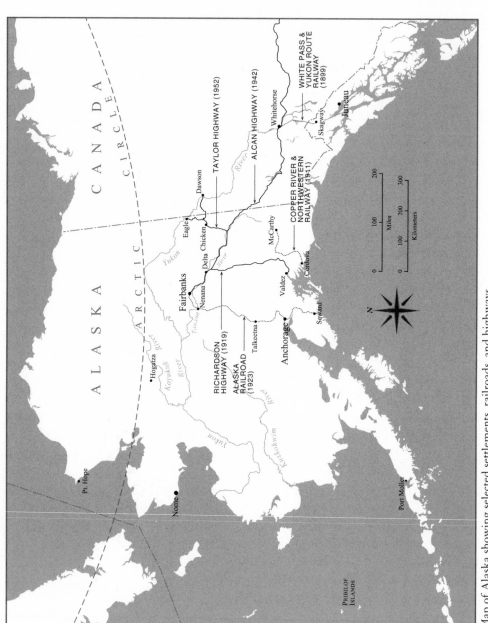

Map of Alaska showing selected settlements, railroads, and highways.

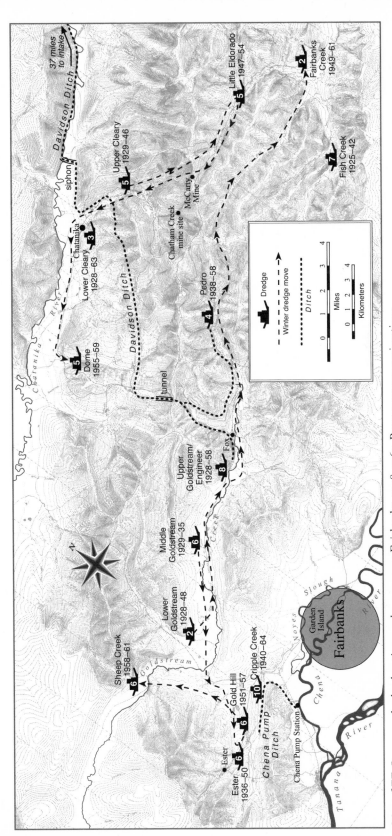

Map of FE Company dredge locations and moves near Fairbanks, 1928–1964. Routes are approximations.

INTRODUCTION

MY PARENTS, Jim Crawford and Alta Tanner, were citizens of the twentieth century. Born respectively in Missouri in 1904 and Montana in 1902 and dying in Washington in 1994 and 2001, they each remembered the first time they saw an airplane, a television, a dial telephone, and a satellite streaking below the stars. They were children during a decade of great optimism about technology. Their parents and teachers believed that man's mastery of mechanics and electricity would bring world prosperity, health, and freedom. As teenagers they were reassured that the Great War in Europe was the war to end all wars. But as adults they lost relatives and friends in World War II, Korea, and Vietnam. They understood the atomic dread that underlay the cold war. They lived through the Farm Depression, the Great Depression, and polio epidemics. But by the end of the century, they looked back on lives of greater prosperity and geographic scope than their parents'. Jim had become an expert in the technology of gold dredges, the American economy had thrived, and Alta had become a consummate homemaker and active community volunteer. As the decades passed, Jim and Alta held to the optimism imbued when the century was new, and they saw most of the benefits of modernity touted in 1910 realized in their part of the world.

In my parents' lives the triumphs and mishaps of the twentieth century were filtered and modified by a special geography. Jim and Alta were, in a sense, expatriates from the continental United States, spending their productive adult lives in the Territory and State of Alaska. They raised two daughters, who still remember a child's perspective on Fairbanks, the town where their parents chose to live.

Like others in my mother's extended family, my parents each settled in Fairbanks to earn a livelihood. They left nearly forty years later, when Jim's employment terminated. But until they were debilitated by age, they returned to Alaska yearly to visit second- and third-generation family members. They continued to think of themselves as Alaskans—retired Alaskans. Their conversations were filled with reminiscences of the North, where national and international events were played out on a wide natural stage by a small local cast.

This book is an attempt to describe that time and place and to tell that family story.

ACKNOWLEDGMENTS

THE AUTHOR THANKS all those who shared photos, family manuscripts, and information. These generous people include Nancy Earling Allen, Mike Busby, Tom Campbell, Jeff Cook, Christine MacDonald, Barbara Hale, Jule Hurley Loftus, Dee Longenbaugh, Vieve Metcalfe, John Reeves, Joan Adler Tollefson, Oscar Tweiten, Gale Weatherell, Ted Wiegert, Judie Tweiten Wischman, Ann Loftus Younger, and the librarians and archivists of the State Historical Library and University of Alaska Archives.

With special appreciation to my sister, Jane Crawford Tallman, for her corrections and clear memories.

And, finally, with gratitude to my husband, Gordon Harrison, for his keen reading and exceeding patience.

SETTLING INTO
THE COUNTRY

Jim Crawford, mining engineer, evaluating a claim for sale in Alaska.
Author's collection.

{1}

AN EMIGRANT FROM THE SOUTH

James Crawford

MY FATHER, JAMES DONALD CRAWFORD, was from the time of his birth in Missouri intense about his interests and irritable when thwarted. When he was three, the woman who knew him best, the hired and loved Mammy with whom he spent his waking hours, pierced his ears "to let the devil out," but his body and spirit resisted her intervention. The piercings healed, and his native temperament persisted. It was a temperament that led him far north, through trouble and success.

In grade school, Jimmy, skinny and small for his age, thrilled to the realization that hidden in the earth in the midst of dirt and ordinary stones were rocks of value—ore riddled with silver and gold that were minted into the silver dollars and $10 gold eagles that his father earned working for Wells Fargo Express. He dreamed of a future unearthing these shining minerals. His family lived on the outskirts of St. Louis in semirural Webster Groves. In the summer he wandered along local streams trapping muskrats and catching crayfish, frogs, and catfish. He relished being outdoors, but he did not dream of a future as a prospector tramping through the outback with shovel and gold pan. He was a modern boy, born in 1904, the year that the great St. Louis World's Fair, featuring newfangled automobiles and a seven-acre Palace of Electricity, announced to the nation that the twentieth century was to be an era of invention and progress. My father and his generation would apply science and engineering to human endeavors, including mining. The world was changing.

Pearle Crawford and her older children, Toni and Jim, 1904 (two
years before the birth of her youngest, Gus). *Author's collection.*

Certainly life in Missouri was changing. My grandfather James Marion
Crawford (our family tree is replete with James Crawfords distinguished only by
middle name and generation) worked in the center of St. Louis, then the fourth-
largest city in the country. He had begun adulthood as a stagecoach driver for
Wells Fargo & Company in Texas. By 1915 he was in charge of Wells Fargo's
express office next to the great St. Louis train station where steam engines, some
capable of traveling 100 miles per hour, arrived and departed constantly, hauling
steel freight cars, passenger cars, and luxurious Pullman sleepers. And in Rolla,
forty miles to the southwest, the state had established the Missouri School of
Mines and Metallurgy, dedicated to training engineers in modern technology.
James Marion Crawford's son, my father, was determined to enroll in this institution of higher learning.

In 1920 only one other member of Jimmy's family had attended college, and
she was considered an anomaly, a character in a proud family with a conservative

view of women. Katharine Anthony, his mother's sister, had not only graduated from the University of Chicago and studied at the University of Heidelberg, but had become a prolific biographer of famous women (such as Margaret Fuller, Catherine the Great, and Susan B. Anthony), living with a female partner in New York City in a milieu of intellectual suffragists. In contrast, her sister, my grandmother Pearle, aside from one or two early adventures riding shotgun on the stagecoach for her husband, devoted herself to making her modest home gracious. Pearle was the family beauty and managed to remain distant from the rumpus of her three children by hiring Mammy to care for them. She was an active member of the Daughters of the American Revolution, tracing family back through a tree featuring several first-cousin marriages and a string of impressive given names—Griffith, Hershel, America, Bryce, Augustus, and Asenath. She was also a partisan for Southern gentility and the defeated Confederacy. As late as World War II she admonished her granddaughters for such unladylike behavior as smoking, wearing slacks, or performing household tasks properly allotted to the males of the family.

Grandmother Pearle's marriage was sometimes cited by the family as an example of the attraction of opposites. No one now can quite recall how she met her husband, or what the two of them recognized in each other that would lead to a successful sixty-three-year union. Pearle's husband, James Marion Crawford, came from a family of relatively recent immigrants, a family deeply committed to self-education and the Union cause. The American founder of the Crawford line, Henry Crawford, at age fourteen had been indentured in Scotland to a weaver after his family had been forced off the land when the laird replaced tenant farmers with sheep. By the time Henry immigrated to the United States in 1839 with his widowed mother and seven siblings, he had educated himself sufficiently to become a schoolteacher and poet. Henry had strong views on slavery formed by his family's near-serfdom in Scotland. When he established his own farm in Illinois, it became a stop on the Underground Railway. His son, my great-grandfather James Garvin Crawford, also went to work after a few years of grammar school but was fully literate, writing letters home from the Union Army complaining about Lincoln's slowness in declaring the Emancipation Proclamation and regretting that a more radical candidate had not been elected president. Later in life, my father wryly observed that "the battles of the Civil War were recapitulated daily" in the Webster Groves house.

But there was no conflict at home about my father's desire to attend college to learn to be a mining engineer. Both parents shared his optimism about technology and progress. In 1922 they sent him to Rolla with tuition money in his inside coat pocket. He thrived at the Missouri School of Mines and Metallurgy. Jim was diligent and received good grades. Like his mother, he tended to be slightly proud and distant with new acquaintances, but he joined a fraternity and took pleasure in its social life. Slim and just five feet four, he was nonetheless strong and competitive, wrestling in the lightweight division for the college team. When he was a senior, his brother, Gus (Ernest Augustus), also enrolled at Rolla.

In 1926 Jim graduated triumphantly, ready to take the role of a modern American mining engineer, an engineer like Herbert Hoover, whose name was already being circulated as a presidential nominee. The bull stock market was making rich men out of speculators, but few Americans realized that the inflated stock prices did not mean that mining companies (or other companies, for that matter) were actually making money. To his dismay, Jim discovered that hiring was tight and that the only job he could get was a minor post with Standard Oil. He became foreman of a crew installing oil tanks and burners in the Westchester County suburbs of New York City.

During the two years that he (in his joking phrase) "worked in oil," Jim applied diligently, perhaps desperately, for engineering work with one mining company after another. Geography was unimportant. He was prepared to work wherever there was a professional opportunity. He finally received a job offer from the Seattle office of a gold mine in Alaska's Chisana (Shushana) District. Unfortunately, by the time he gave his two weeks' notice to the oil company and used his final paycheck to cross the continent by train, he arrived to discover that the job had been given to another man while he was en route. Temporarily, in his words, "stymied in Seattle," he gave no thought to returning to Westchester County or to St. Louis. He found a room in a boardinghouse and a job to pay his rent.

Early every morning he went to Kristoferson's Dairy to grease, maintain, and gas up milk trucks for the day's deliveries. Every afternoon he walked the rounds of offices that hired mining engineers, stopping first at the office that had offered him the job in the Chisana. Finally the representative, possibly to get rid of the annoyance and daily guilt of his visits, offered him a job as an underground miner—a mucker-trammer (translation: shoveler and ore-car pusher)—at the Kennecott Copper Mine. The wage was $4.50 per day, less $1.45 for board and 8¢ for hospital insurance.* Jim understood the reason for the latter deduction. He may not have known the exact statistics, but he had a pretty good grasp of the occupational risks of underground mining. Moreover he was green; he had

---

* Explanatory material (such as comparisons of 1930s and 2000 dollars), additional anecdotes, and citations of sources can be found in the Endnotes.

never mucked or trammed. But he was a young man desperate to break into his profession. Surely he would be closer to engineering opportunities in a tunnel near McCarthy, Alaska, than in the dairy's garage. In a leap of hope, he signed up for the job.

Jim bought a steerage ticket on the Alaska Steamship Line to Cordova. There he boarded the Copper River and Northwestern Railroad, which carried passengers and equipment from the coast to the mine and carried ore concentrate from the mine to the coast. The concentrate was loaded onto freighters bound for a Tacoma smelter that, like the railroad, the freighters, and the mine itself, was owned by Guggenheim-Morgan interests. The passengers on the Copper River and Northwestern Railroad, however, were not just monopolists or miners. The railroad was renowned among intrepid and independent tourists. The autumn scenery passing the train windows was unlike the Missouri Ozarks, the New York Adirondacks, and even unlike the Rockies, over which Jim had passed on his way to Seattle. Above the railroad's unpopulated valley route rose 14,000-to-16,000-foot peaks: Mounts Sanford, Regal, Wrangell, and Blackburn. A four-span "million-dollar bridge" carried the train past the facing snouts of Miles and Childs glaciers. After twisting north through the Copper River Canyon to Chitina, the railroad turned easterly sixty miles to McCarthy and the Kennecott Mine. Jim was tantalized rather than intimidated by the barrenness and beauty of the land through which he passed. He was moved by the red of the alpine tundra, the yellow of valley willows, and the great bare sweep of visible geology above them. But he was also pressingly distracted as he tried to remember what he knew, to use his phrase, "about the nuts and bolts of underground mining." His firsthand underground experience had consisted entirely of watching miners at work during college field trips.

Jim describes himself as arriving at Kennecott Mine in 1928 "like a typical cheechako, with a steamer trunk." The mine was built on a slope so steep that the bunkhouses were supported by long front pilings and fastened to the mountainside with cables. The bright-red mine buildings could only be reached by aerial tram. Jim had to abandon his trunk, buy used duffle bags, and repack his possessions—presenting "something of a problem for me and entertainment for spectators." He provided further amusement by arriving in leather boots instead of the standard footgear of the working North—shoepacs, whose rubberized lower halves keep feet dry and whose spacious leather uppers can be laced to adjust for insoles or layers of socks. To experienced miners he was probably an unprepossessing sight: a fair Southerner of slight build, incipient baldness visible through thinning hair. But college wrestling had given him strength for arduous

Kennecott mine. *University of Alaska Archives, John McAnerney Collection, box 9, folder 56.*

work. He shoveled, shoved trams, and survived moderate bunkhouse hazing from miners of, by his count, nine different nationalities—none of whom were impressed by his college degree and lack of underground experience. Then, a few weeks after his arrival, his hopes for advancement were suddenly rewarded when first a surveyor and then the assayer abruptly quit and, in the Alaskan phrase, "left the country" for warmer and less insect-ridden climes "Outside."

Jim, age twenty-four, transferred from mucking to surveying to assaying with enthusiasm, eager to use his professional training and to earn more money. As assayer he made twice as much as a mucker-trammer—$175 per month, minus deductions—and he was assigned a small private bedroom in the attic of the staff house. His job advancement was a relief to him and probably also to the miners on his shift, whose safety depended in part on the skill and experience of fellow workers. In the assay office he consulted manuals and worked alone, checking and rechecking results, learning through trial and error details not taught in college. Twenty-six years later, when I returned with him to the closed ghost mine, I was thrilled to find that his story of an early mishap in the assay office was confirmed by an acid stain on the dusty floor where he said it would be.

Like the assayer before him, however, Jim remained a Kennecott employee for less than a year. Aware that copper was selling for seventeen cents a pound, and that the mine might have to close (as it finally did in 1938), he began looking for another job, preferably in gold mining. The price of copper fluctuated with the market, but the price of gold was fixed by the U.S. government at $20.67 per troy ounce. (Gold is measured in troy ounces, which are slightly heavier than regular ounces.) Gold was stable and not subject to job-threatening devaluation. Jim's résumé had improved at Kennecott; he could now list professional work experience. In May 1929 he applied for an engineering job with a gold-mining company farther north and was promptly accepted. Two weeks later he boarded the train, leaving behind isolated McCarthy for the larger, more sophisticated town of Fairbanks.

Gold mining in Fairbanks was unlike copper mining at Kennecott. Kennecott was a hard-rock mine with tunnels bored into a mountain veined with copper. Most of the gold in Fairbanks was in the form of dust and small nuggets eroded from mountains of earlier geologic times and deposited in ancient gravel river-beds overlying impermeable bedrock. Placer miners washed this gold-containing gravel and sand through sluice boxes with riffles that separated the heavy gold from lighter dirt and stones. The difficulty that Fairbanks miners faced was that, except where modern streams had cut deeply into the earth, most of the ancient river bottoms were covered by a layer of permanently frozen "muck"—a fine silt-like material windblown from retreating glaciers at the end of the last great Ice Age. Moreover, beneath the 30-to-130-foot-thick muck layer, the gold-bearing gravel overlying bedrock was also frozen.

Between 1902 and 1924 prospectors staked claims and mined on "the Creeks," the common name for the Fairbanks goldfields. During the winter these early miners drove shafts through the frozen muck by thawing the ground with fires and digging it out with hand tools. The shafts were cribbed with logs and descended to the gold-bearing gravel overlying bedrock. This "paydirt" was thawed with steam and hoisted in buckets to the surface, where it was stockpiled. In the summer when running water was available, the accumulated mound of paydirt was washed through sluice boxes. Responsible for a few personal fortunes and many personal failures, this inefficient process left large areas of paydirt untouched—some of it too deep for early miners, some left in frozen pillars needed for support, some simply never drilled and discovered. In 1910, at the height of the initial mining boom, Fairbanks had 3,500 residents. Ten years later so many miners had given up that the population had shrunk to 1,150.

In the following decade, mining companies realized that it might be possible to dredge the Fairbanks goldfields. The largest of these was the firm that hired my father to move from Kennecott to Fairbanks—the United States Smelting, Refining and Mining Company, known to its employees as USSR&M or simply

Operation of United States Smelting Refining and Mining Com[...]

STRIPPING

Muck Overburden

THAWING

Gold Bearing Gravel

Bedrock

Stripping, thawing, and dredging. *Drawing (enhanced) from Gold Dredging in Fairbanks District Alaska, USSR&M pamphlet, ca. 1951.*

the Company. In the 1920s the Company was already mining gold in Mexico, copper and coal in Utah, and iron in New Mexico, and refining lead in Illinois. It had sufficient capital to carry it through the necessary two to three years of preparation for dredging. Dredging was an offspring of the industrial revolution that made it feasible to mine large placer fields, even if the concentration of gold was too low for older methods to make a profit. As early as 1911, a partnership of Fairbanks miners had imported (by river steamer) a little wood-burning, wooden-hulled dredge from the Stewart River in Canada to mine a shallow area of naturally thawed paydirt on Fairbanks Creek. The operation ended when the small dredge ran out of thawed ground.

The big, modern, steel-hulled dredges that USSR&M used were powered by electricity. They were rectangular, ungainly boats that floated in man-made ponds. They could dig into paydirt sixty feet beneath the water's surface. The typical dredge had a chain of about one hundred nine-cubic-foot buckets that, like the stairs of an escalator, continuously circled a digging ladder. The buckets scooped away paydirt forming the front bank of the pond. The fine materials from the buckets were washed over gold-saving riffles inside the dredge while stones and rocks were diverted out the rear stacker as "tailings" that filled in the back of the pond, causing the pond and its dredge to move slowly across a gold-field, leaving ridges of waste rock in its wake. But these huge steel dredges, like the small wood-hulled ones that preceded them, could only dig thawed ground.

The concentration of placer gold in Fairbanks and Nome was many times that in California where dredging was active. However, removing the frozen

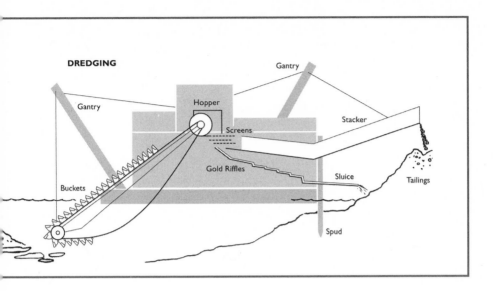

muck that overlay the paydirt gravel and then thawing the gravel itself was costly. By 1920, miners had learned to strip off the overlying layer of frozen muck using pressurized water sprayed from giant nozzles. And in 1918 John Miles, an engineer, began experimenting with cold-water thawing as an alternative to the expensive hot-water or steam methods previously tried. He patented his process in 1920 and three years later licensed it to Hammon Consolidated Gold Fields (later purchased by USSR&M) in Nome. The process required a decade of refinement, but it made dredging in areas of permafrost economically feasible as long as sufficient water was available for removing muck, thawing paydirt, and filling dredge ponds.

At the time USSR&M was considering dredging the Fairbanks goldfields, the Company faced two main barriers. The first was obtaining an adequate supply of water. Interior Alaska is semi-arid, with only eleven inches of precipitation per year, and the rich goldfield did not lie along the banks of a river. The second barrier was delivering the dredges to the goldfields. The typical USSR&M dredge weighed about a thousand tons. The usual sea route for freight from Seattle—across the ocean to St. Michael then up the Yukon, Tanana, and Chena rivers to Fairbanks—was not practical for transporting the heavy modern dredges. But both the problem of water and the problem of transportation were solved in 1924.

The water problem was solved by George Davidson, a consulting engineer who designed a ninety-mile-long water conduit from the Chatanika River across rolling, permafrost-ridden hills to the Fairbanks goldfields. Known as the

Davidson Ditch, it consisted in some areas of an open twelve-foot-wide ditch, in other areas of an elevated pipeline, fifty-four inches in diameter. The sinuous route included two tunnels and fifteen valley-crossing siphons that were up to a mile and a half long. The Davidson Ditch would supply all the dredging areas north of town. Ester and Cripple Creek to the west would be served by Chena River water through a pipeline pressurized by ten large pumps at the Chena pump station.

The transportation problem was solved by the United States government. Worldwide, the early 1900s were the palmy years of railroads. Tracks criss-crossed not only most of Europe and North America, but barely industrialized nations in Asia, Africa, and South America. The U.S. Congress found it somewhat scandalous that its Alaska Territory, rich in undeveloped resources, had only a few short, mainly narrow-gauge railroads—several of which had already gone bankrupt by 1915. The navy was eager to have Alaska coal from the Territory's Interior delivered to tidewater to fuel its northern steamship patrols. Mining entrepreneurs and even a few agricultural enthusiasts lobbied for a railroad to "open up the country." No private railroad company was willing to undertake the risk of building the five-hundred-mile track to the Interior. The proposed railroad would have to snake by glaciers, bridge river canyons, tunnel through mountains, span marshes, and cross plains of frozen soil, where the railbed would have to be insulated with a pad of gravel thick enough that underlying permafrost would not melt and collapse. It was a daunting task, but Congress had at its disposal money from the U.S. Treasury and surplus construction equipment from the recently completed Panama Canal. Among this equipment was wide-gauge rolling stock from the temporary, construction-related Panama Railroad. These cars could be modified for use on the standard-gauge railway planned for Alaska. In 1914 Congress appropriated $35 million for the project with the route to be determined by the president, based on options listed in the report of an engineering commission. Fairbanks held a torchlight parade anticipating good times ahead.

President Wilson selected the commission's western route, which began at tidewater in Seward, passed near the Chickaloon and Healy Coal Fields, reached the navigable Tanana River at Nenana, and continued to Fairbanks with its goldfields. His choice was influenced by his deep distrust of the powerful Guggenheim-Morgan interests. He wanted nothing to do with the eastern route, which would have incorporated Copper River and Northwestern tracks. Government officials expected the building of the government railway to take five years.

Fairbanks Dredge No. 3. Assembled 1928—Ceased work, 1963. *Author's collection.*

Delayed by the manpower shortage during World War I and influenced by wartime inflation, the Alaska Railroad eventually took eight years and $70 million to complete. In July 1923 President Harding hammered in the symbolic golden spike at Nenana. The completion of the tracks failed to produce the flood of miners and farmers anticipated by politicians, but the railroad did make it feasible in 1924 for USSR&M to move large equipment to the Fairbanks goldfields in preparation for dredging. The *Fairbanks Daily News-Miner* celebrated the end of hard times: "After many long years Fairbanks has been re-DISCOVERED. 'Big Money' has discovered that this District is One Good Bet.... Strangers have SHOWN US that there is merit in our ground."

USSR&M staked some gold claims and bought others. Company crews ran Keystone drilling rigs to obtain the core assay samples needed to delineate the areas to be prepared for dredging. USSR&M rapidly became the town's largest employer. In 1926 the winter population of Fairbanks was 1,725 people; that summer the Company wrote paychecks to 1,372 men. Among the Company's first projects was construction of the Davidson Ditch. Prior excavations in Fairbanks had used horse-drawn equipment. The Ditch was dug by self-propelled steam shovels surplused from Panama Canal construction. The Ditch took three summers to complete and remained in use for forty-two years.

Steam shovels were also busy digging dredge ponds—one at Chatanika and one at Fox. In 1927 two new dredges were shipped in sections on the Alaska Steamship Line from Seattle to Seward. There the parts were loaded on to more than a hundred gondolas and flatcars to travel the length of the Alaska Railroad to Fairbanks. In Fairbanks they were transferred to the narrow-gauge Tanana Valley Railway and its temporary spurs that led to the dredge-pond excavations where the boats were to be reassembled. Over the next thirteen years the Company added six more dredges to its Fairbanks fleet.

USSR&M was a private corporation based in Boston. Perhaps sensitive to Alaskans' tendency to scorn effete Easterners, it named its local operations the Fairbanks Exploration Company. Although some of its equipment was stenciled "USSR&M Co." (occasionally confusing and exciting Communist haters during the cold war), nearly everyone in Fairbanks, including the telephone book, called it the FE Company.

In May 1929, when my father arrived, the FE Company was well established with offices on Garden Island across the Chena River from Fairbanks. Garden Island was formed by Noyes Slough, which, in a manner typical of the braided rivers of the north, made a wide arc leaving the main channel of the Chena then rejoining it downstream. The south side of the island had once been the home-stead of a locally renowned woman truck farmer. By 1929 it held the hospital, the railway station, and a few pioneer businesses that, in the first couple of decades, had avoided city taxes by vigorously resisting annexation. They finally yielded in 1922, and Garden Island was incorporated into the city limits. The north side of the island had originally been the seventy-four-acre site of Fred Noyes's sawmill, the largest in the Tanana Valley. This land now held the impressive headquarters of the FE Company. The Company's fenced yard included a power plant, a rail siding for coal delivery, warehouses, workshops, garages, a foundry, an assay office, a small smelter, and the old sawmill modernized to handle large Doug-las fir logs imported from Washington. (The local spruce not only had more knots but had already been logged off near town for construction and fuel.) The centerpiece of the yard was the two-story corniced office building, constructed from concrete blocks locally cast to resemble hewn stone. The FE office, the first concrete-block building in Fairbanks, was exotic and impressive in a town made up almost entirely of wood buildings hastily erected with a sense of transience. Near the fenced headquarters several three-bedroom homes, surrounded by lawns and transplanted trees, had been constructed for upper-echelon employ-ees. Still in the planning stage was a colonial-style manager's residence that, like the mortared office building, would betray the Brahmin background of the Company's owners. The FE Company may have been on the northern frontier, but it was thoroughly modern. Jim Crawford was impressed.

My father joined several other young engineers charged with overseeing the complex system for dredging frozen goldfields. Jim's title was assistant engineer.

His assignment was supervising the thawing of paydirt for the dredge at Chatanika. His work had been preceded by that of an engineer in charge of stripping, whose crews had used giant hydraulic nozzles to clear away the muck "overburden." Now all that remained was gold-bearing gravel some thirty to forty feet deep that had to be thawed before it could be dug up and washed by the dredges. My father's task was to keep the thawing crews moving as efficiently as possible without leaving any frozen ground behind to ruin the dredge buckets. Moreover, he needed to plan so that one year's worth, but not more than one year's worth, of ground would be thawed at all times. A year provided adequate reserve in case the dredge moved more rapidly than expected. In one winter thawed gravel refroze shallowly and could be melted in the spring with a few steam points. But if gravel had two winters to freeze deeply, the Company was forced to rethaw the ground fully.

Jim's crews used what his letters home described as the "arm and hammer" method of thawing ground. Men raised and dropped twenty-five-pound sliding hammers to gradually drive hollow steel pipes (called points) into the upper layer of gravel. Low-pressure creek water ran through the points to melt the surrounding ice, typically at a rate of nine inches per day. Each day the points were again driven through the newly thawed layer to the frozen gravel below. The points were placed at precise intervals based on the depth of the gravel. The thaw field looked like a young forest of steel saplings on barren ground.

Thawing was not a subject discussed by Jim's professors in Missouri. It took pioneer engineering to put into action the patented cold-water process. Jim was working on novel questions: What was the ideal distance between points? Was it economical to sun-warm the water? Could wastewater be recovered and reused? Could a machine for driving points replace strong young men? What was the best method for determining the moment when the last corner of permafrost had melted and the points could be moved? My father was being challenged, and he was enthusiastic about his new job. If he worked for the FE Company for two years, he could gain enough engineering experience to get a job with one of the mining companies in the States that had rejected his application when he was a new college graduate.

My father was also enthusiastic about Fairbanks, even though he spent little time in town during his first summer. Chatanika was the most distant of the FE Company's camps, which were all built in a similar pattern and dominated by the same material—gray corrugated iron. Each camp had a bunkhouse, cabins for married supervisors, a laundry and shower, a boiler house, machine and blacksmith shops, and garages. The mess house was the heart of the camp. The FE

Company correctly understood that good food in ample quantities was essential to retain workers. Ever attentive to detail, the Company had even calculated the average number of calories consumed by the hard workers at Chatanika—3,900 calories per person per day. They employed both cooks and bakers to serve these hearty eaters. My father, who enjoyed eating but not cooking, consumed meat, locally grown vegetables, and fresh bread and pies with the miners at the mess house six days a week.

On his Sundays off Jim would catch a ride into town. At the time Chatanika was served both by road and by the Tanana Valley Railway, which zigzagged thirty miles north from Fairbanks through Fox, Goldstream, Pedro, Gilmore, Dome, Vault, and Olnes before reaching Chatanika. Taking the road was faster and cheaper, a fact that accounted for the demise of the railroad a few years later.

My father did not rank high enough to be assigned a Company truck, but hitching a ride to town with another employee was simple. Fairbanks bore little resemblance to St. Louis or New York City or Seattle, but Jim liked what he saw. It was true that some sourdoughs still referred to Fairbanks as "the camp," a reminder that its existence might be transient. Scattered boarded-up buildings and empty cabins were a reminder that the population of Fairbanks in 1930 was less than two-thirds of its population in 1910. Noteworthy towns had already come and gone from Alaska maps: Treadwell, Koserefsky, Chena, and Katalla. But to Jim, Fairbanks looked like a permanent town. The Steese Highway from Chatanika and other camps northeast of the city cut across the middle of Garden Island to the arching steel bridge that spanned the swirling, silty, unswimmable Chena River. Boats dotted the waterfront, which was navigated by small river steamers from the Tanana. The business district and most of the residences were clustered on the south bank of the Chena across from the island. The wooden Main School on Eighth Avenue, the concrete Empress Movie Theater on Second Avenue, and the Northern Commercial Company store, power plant, and warehouses facing the river were the town's most prominent landmarks. The two thousand inhabitants came from diverse backgrounds—Americans from the States, immigrant Europeans, local Athabascan Indians, and Eskimos from the coast. The town was cosmopolitan, rough, and small enough for the post office to deliver a letter from Jim's grandfather, James Garvin Crawford, simply addressed "Mr. J. D. Crawford, Fairbanks, Alaska" with "Mining Engineer" noted in the lower left-hand corner. Although Jim was a new resident, the letter from his Civil War veteran grandfather reached him promptly, in transit no longer than the usual two weeks.

Fairbanks may have been tiny compared to St. Louis, but it was large compared to McCarthy. The 1930 census taker in McCarthy, even when the bunkhouses at the mine were included, counted only 332 people. Even more important than total population was the ratio of men to "respectable" women. In Fairbanks it was three to one. According to my father, this represented a major social improvement over McCarthy, where he estimated the ratio at thirteen to one. Jim used some of his wages to buy a suit and dancing shoes. When mining at Chatanika closed in the fall, he moved into town to work in the office. Soon he began appearing regularly at the dances, plays, and "socials" that Fairbanksans contrived to divert themselves from the long winter.

Alta Tanner on river-steamer day trip near Fairbanks, 1928. *Author's collection.*

{2}

EMIGRANTS FROM THE WEST

Alta Tanner and the Stanfield Girls

B Y THE TIME JIM CRAWFORD arrived in Fairbanks, already among the town's women were my mother, Alta Tanner, and her lively first cousins, Audrey and Claire Stanfield. The Tanner sisters and the Stanfield sisters had been raised on neighboring ranches in northeast Montana. Between them, the two families had seven girls, who often played together as children, but reversals in their families' fortunes separated them as teenagers.

The Stanfield family lost their ranch after the father, aptly named Romeo, abruptly left home with one of his amours, a woman younger than three of his children. Romeo was not only a wandering but also an abusive husband. His exit was hastened by his twenty-three-year-old daughter Norma, who interrupted him in the act of slapping her mother by heaving a heavy chair over her head, saying, "Go ahead! Hit her once more." Romeo looked at Norma (the only one of his daughters to inherit his strapping build), left the house, and never returned—an emotional relief but an economic disaster for mother Leslie and her four daughters still living at home.

Two years after the divorce, Norma moved out to marry Dick Dellage. Leslie, a woman with great fortitude but less than an eighth-grade education, also moved, taking Claire (fifteen), Elma (thirteen), and Audrey (eleven) to Oregon, where they struggled to make a living. In the summers they tented on Goodpasture Island in the Willamette River, working as pickers in local farms and orchards. In the winter they lived in rented rooms in Eugene, where Leslie had a job cooking at the university. Elma left home at sixteen to marry Sid Stiers. Claire graduated

Alta's mother, Lillian Tanner, in divided skirt
astride "Judge," 1908. *Author's collection.*

from high school that same year and began to dream of escaping from hard summer picking work and dull winter jobs by traveling to the Far North. It was not
long before Audrey was swept into this dream. The sisters read every magazine
story and every book about Alaska that they could find. Claire traveled north in
1924 and quickly found a job. The following summer she sent money for railroad
tickets and passage on the steamship *Admiral Watson* to her mother and to Audrey,
who had just finished high school. Leslie's ticket to visit and inspect the home that
Claire had chosen was round-trip; Audrey's was one-way. By fall the sisters were
on their own, employed and alert to adventure in Fairbanks, the last stop on the
newly completed Alaska Railroad.

My mother's family had also lost their ranch. In their case, the cause was the
Farm Depression of 1921, an economic disaster forgotten when it was eclipsed
by the Great Depression of 1929. The Tanner ranch had been established by my
mother's father, Frederick Tanner. In the 1870s, Frederick, the fifth of eight children, had left the crowded New York tenement of his German immigrant parents with an older brother to seek his fortune in the West. Frederick was eleven;
his brother was fourteen. They found work building fences and herding cattle.
His brother persisted in a cowboy life, but after several years my grandfather settled on Montana land near the Canadian border and built a sod-roofed house of
cottonwood logs. He planted wheat and raised cattle. When the eight-hundred-
acre ranch began to make a profit, he married Lillian Hurley, whose parents and

Isaiah and Sarah Hurley with their grandchildren, ca. 1914.
FRONT: Elma Stanfield, Frances Tanner, Audrey Stanfield, Alta
Tanner, Claire Stanfield. BACK: Pearl, Norma, John Stanfield.
Author's collection.

married sister, Leslie Stanfield, lived nearby. After the death in infancy of a son, Lillian and Frederick raised two daughters, Alta and Frances. The family rose temporarily into the middle class with a spacious two-story house in the nearby town of Hinsdale, where the daughters attended school and received piano lessons. Alta, the elder, was energetic, capable, optimistic, and bright enough to skip a grade in school. After high school, her parents sent her to the University of Oregon, where she demonstrated during her freshman year that she could earn good grades, have an active social life, and be a star on the women's rifle team. Then came the crash—the Farm Depression of 1921. The ranch and the town house went to the bank, and my mother went to work.

Alta's first job was teaching in a one-room school, living with a rural Montana family whose idea of evening entertainment, she said, was eavesdropping on the telephone party line. The school's regular teacher had resigned to attend college, so Alta substituted during the second semester, which ran from August to November. (The rural school year began in February and ended in November to avoid student travel during Montana's severe winters.) Each day she saddled a horse provided by the school district and rode to the schoolhouse, where she was responsible for starting and stoking the wood stove and educating fifteen assorted pupils—some just starting to read; some intellectually curious; and some, already taller and stronger than she, just biding time until they could start work as full-time adults in rugged ranch jobs.

Alta was parsimonious. When the semester was over she had saved enough money to pay for a business course in typing, shorthand, and bookkeeping. With these new skills, she returned to the University of Oregon to work in the bursar's office. She lived with her mother, whose marriage, never strong, had dissolved in discouragement and unproductive infidelities during the demise of the ranch. Photographs from this time show Alta smiling—a short, slim, confident office worker, hemline a few conservative inches below flapper level, but with her dark hair arranged in a chic helmet-shaped bob. Years later, she admitted to the pain of watching young women her age going to classes, carrying books from the library, and relaxing on the lawn in front of her office window.

By the summer of 1928 my mother had accumulated a month's vacation from her university job. When Audrey and Claire invited her to come to Fairbanks for a visit, she accepted immediately. She was eager to see Alaska and to meet Claire and Audrey's new husbands, the brothers Theodore (Ted) and Jule Loftus. The notion of sisters marrying brothers was no surprise to my mother or her cousins. Their grandmother, Sarah Frances, was one of three Holston sisters who married three Hurley brothers. A frequently told family story is that when Cinderella Belle Holston, the youngest sister, announced her intention to marry the youngest Hurley brother, Eleven, her mother responded that she refused to have one more Hurley son-in-law. To prevent the match she burned Cinderella Belle's only Sunday dress. Cinderella Belle, nicknamed "Dill" (perhaps for her perseverance and lack of humor), was equally adamant and matched her mother's dramatic gesture by getting married in a faded cotton work dress. In contrast to my Holston great-grandmother, Leslie Stanfield had welcomed the Loftus brothers into her family, and anecdotes about the good-humored brothers-in-law had already reached my mother.

Audrey and Claire's husbands had come north with a third brother, Arthur. Ted, Jule, and Art were siblings from a Tomahawk, Wisconsin, farm due to be inherited by an elder brother. Far from being depressed by their birth-order fate in the matter of land inheritance, they relished the adventure of escaping the farm and finding their way in the world. As best I can understand, they selected the most distant point on the U.S. map for their destination.

Art, a World War I navy veteran and the oldest of the three, was the first to arrive in the Territory. In 1920 he decided to make money fishing cod in the Bering Sea. He snatched rides on freight trains from Wisconsin to Seattle and signed on to a two-masted schooner, the *Maid of Orleans*, captained by J. J. "Codfish" Kelly. Art was green; his crewmates taught him to handle sails and to fish. Each morning that weather permitted, he rowed a fourteen-foot dory away from the schooner at

Ted, Art, and Jule Loftus, ca. 1922.
University of Alaska Archives, Dorothy Loftus Collection, 80-84-128.

5 AM, set anchor, and dropped two lines of baited hooks just off the bottom. He had a windlass for pulling the anchor, but he pulled the tarred cotton fish lines by hand. He brought in twenty-pound cod, one at a time, slit their throats, and distributed them in open bins so that the dory remained balanced. At noon he rowed, sometimes assisted by a small sail, back to the schooner; pitched his catch on board for the dress gang to count, split, and salt; ate dinner; and returned to fishing for the afternoon. A good day's catch totaled three thousand to four thousand pounds, and the fishermen fell into their bunks as soon as they finished supper. Sometimes the men in dories found themselves not only out of sight of land and each other, but unable to see the mast of the mother ship because of distance or fog. One evening Art failed to find *Maid of Orleans*. He spent an unnerving night at sea in his tiny boat before locating the ship at daybreak. Art's naval wartime experience had been limited to the Great Lakes on coal-burning ships. Cod fishing under sail in the Bering Sea was hard work and dangerous by comparison.

Art netted $350 for his five months at sea—thirteen weeks catching cod and seven weeks working as a sailor on the schooner's trip out and back. He touched Alaska's land only once, when the ship docked at Port Moller to pick up a machine part, but the Territory attracted him. He used his fishing money to learn a skill useful on land, enrolling in a six-week automobile engine repair course in Kansas City. As soon as this schooling was over, he and middle brother Jule (whose wallet was empty after one semester at the University of Wisconsin) started for the North. The two economized their way to Seattle, jumping freights and living on jelly rolls and canned milk. In Seattle they signed up for jobs with the Alaska Engineering Commission, which was building the new government railroad from Seward to Fairbanks. Jule wired for repayment of a loan he had made to a college roommate to buy the brothers steerage tickets to Seward on the Alaska Pacific Steamship *Admiral Watson*.

The Alaska Engineering Commission was the largest employer in Alaska, seasonally employing some four thousand men billeted in camps studding the route. The construction camps were temporary but substantial, with machine shops, small sawmills, log-cabin headquarters, wall-tent warehouses, and bunk-houses divided into four-foot-tall, honeycomb-like sleeping quarters nicknamed muzzleloaders. The track was built in sections under separate contracts, with the result that one crew would have many Italians, the next Greeks, the next Swedes—all with cooks who made the kind of food their crews liked. For a dollar an hour plus three daily fifty-cent meal tickets usable at camps or roadhouses, Jule did an assortment of jobs. He unloaded freight cars, shoveled snow to make way for more track "at the end of steel," and ate ethnic food in various camps.

Based on his six weeks at Sweeney's Auto School, Art got a plum job—hauling gravel behind a Caterpillar tractor up a steep, twisting trail to the site where a 920-foot steel bridge was being built high across Hurricane Gulch. After the bridge (a "marvel of engineering," everyone said) was completed in the spring of 1921, Art hauled freight for the railroad with Jule as his helper until the construction season ended. In the fall they bought dog teams and became commercial sheep hunters supplying the Canyon Roadhouse. The winter was spent trapping on the Yanert Fork of the Nenana River, where Ted, the youngest brother, joined them in March 1922.

Claire and Audrey were easy to recognize as sisters; they resembled each other—tall, slim brunettes who were quickly amused into low-pitched laughter. Art, Jule, and Ted also shared traits: they possessed practical skills, worked hard, stuck together, and had confidence in their ability to learn anything. But even though they were like-minded and came from the same tall Norwegian stock, they were sufficiently different in appearance and personality to be hard to recognize as brothers. Jule was dark-haired, round-faced, and merry; he had a quick eye for the absurd. Ted was lean, blond, athletic, and more reserved than his older brothers. Art was broad-shouldered and known for his uncommon strength among the men building the Alaska Railroad.

The new standard-gauge railroad incorporated the southern portion of the Tanana Valley Railroad, a bankrupt narrow-gauge line originating in Fairbanks. The narrow-gauge tracks were not replaced until near the end of construction, so for a time supplies had to be transferred from cars of one gauge to another. For a year or two the transfer point was Nenana on the south bank of the Tanana River. Until a bridge was built across the river and the entire line converted to standard gauge, the narrow-gauge tracks were extended across the river ice each winter to reach Nenana. Art recalled one occasion when he shoveled seventy-two tons of coal, at forty cents per ton, from standard-gauge cars into two narrow-gauge cars in a single, fourteen-hour day. On another occasion he achieved brief local fame by single-handedly unloading a flatcar of railroad ties faster than the three-man crew competing with him. He collected a modest monetary bet but achingly swore he would never again make such a wager.

Wages for railroad laborers and commercial hunters were not munificent. Nevertheless, Ted, Art, and Jule made enough each summer to live frugally through the winter, working odd jobs and subsisting on sourdough pancakes, rice, rabbits, and mountain sheep from fall hunts. By the fall of 1922, when they reunited in Fairbanks, the brothers had saved a combined grubstake of $85.

In Fairbanks Art met his landlord's daughter, lively Dorothy Roth, and was instantly charmed. Dorothy was about to enroll at the Alaska Agricultural College and School of Mines. The college, located on a hill outside Fairbanks, was beginning its first year, and Art suddenly found himself interested in higher education. Jule also liked the idea of picking up where he had left off at the University of Wisconsin. The $2 registration fee (there was no tuition) fit the three brothers' winter budget. They enrolled along with Dorothy and eight other students to take courses from the school's six professors in the single classroom building surrounded by a campus partially cleared of willows. The Loftuses made up three-fifths of the first basketball team. Since the other two starters were the McComb twins, the team was jocularly called "the full house squad"—a pair and three of a kind. The team won the "Alaska Championship" in 1923 by beating high school and city teams from Fairbanks and Anchorage.

The following summer Jule staked—and because he was also a World War I army veteran, gained immediate patent on—a 173-acre homestead on Jennie M. Slough in the flats just below College Hill. The brothers cut and peeled logs to build a twenty-by-twenty-two-foot cabin within easy snowshoeing and walking distance of the college—"down the hill...along the [railroad] tracks...through the spruce by a trail we blazed ourselves." Art described the cabin as a "jolly frat house, without the bother of Greek letters on the door, or the nuisance of house rules." Interior photos show the three-bed, one-table frat house lit with a gasoline lantern, heated by a Yukon stove, and decorated with a bearskin on the wall. The Jennie M. Slough supplied their water, the spruce grove offered firewood, and willow patches nurtured dinner entrées: grouse and rabbits. The frat house was satisfactory in other ways: "It is uncommonly pleasant...in the dark Winter days to follow the narrow path overhung with the peaceful, snow-laden trees, and to emerge at last upon a primitive clearing that is all the result of our own labor, and that might from its appearance, be a thousand miles from college or from civilization."

Ted eventually earned degrees in geology (1927) and mining engineering (1928) and went to work for the FE Company. Jule's interests were animal rather than mineral. The summer before he started at the college, he and Ted had a job for biologist Olaus Murie corralling wild caribou from a herd near McKinley Park. The wranglers waited until caribou wandered by to feed along one of the fences that led to the corral. The men would then spring out of hiding, yelling and waving to force the animals into the corral. Young bulls from the herd were lassoed, thrown, trussed, and dehorned before being transported several miles down the railroad. The goal was to breed these bulls to domestic reindeer pastured near the railroad in an effort to produce hardier and heavier offspring. According to Jule, male calves from the spring of that year, even through they had to be hand-fed Eagle Brand milk, were preferable to adult bulls, which had a reputation for charging without warning. Jule eventually transferred from the college in Fairbanks to Colorado to pursue a veterinary degree. He returned to Alaska in 1930 to work for the next decade—first as territorial veterinarian in Juneau, then as director of the Cooperative Extension Service in the Matanuska Valley where farming colonists had settled, and finally as director of the Extension Service experimental fox farm near Petersburg.

Art, who claimed his impetus for enrollment was being fired as a Caterpillar driver by the road commission, attended classes for five years but did not graduate. The 1927 yearbook issue of *The Farthest-North Collegian* includes a handsome studio photograph of him in cap and gown as student-body president and member of the eight-person graduating class. But in his last semester he stumbled on analytic geometry and ended up three credits short of joining his fiancée, Dorothy Roth, on the platform. Art never looked back. Instead he combined his university training, economic good sense, and easy grasp of mechanics and construction to become a successful jack-of-all-trades.

LEFT: Dorothy Roth.
*University of Alaska Archives, Dorothy
Loftus Collection, 80-84-289N.*

RIGHT: Florence Roth, modeling
eider duck parka. *Author's collection.*

Students like the Loftus brothers and Roth sisters who needed to support themselves at the Alaska Agricultural College and School of Mines had plenty of opportunity to add to their practical skills. The college's sole administrator, President Charles Bunnell, hired them to cut cordwood from campus property to heat buildings; to plant birches in the areas they denuded; and to dig sewers, waterlines, and cesspools. Art declared that he learned finance through repeated personal loans from the sympathetic president and by running the "To-and-Fro Taxi" that served a route between town and college. A letter from Jule to President Bunnell in 1933 was accompanied by a check for $202.75, repayment of a personal student loan with interest. In a reply Bunnell expressed reluctance to accept the interest; he had never received nor expected interest on loans to students.

As part-time workers, college students, and new Alaskans, the three Loftus brothers thrived. All married soon after leaving the college. In the log Episcopal Church fronting the Chena River, Jule married Claire in 1926, Ted married Audrey in 1927, Art married Dorothy Roth in 1928, and Florence Roth married another new graduate, Charles "Tommy" Thompson, in 1930.

The Roth sisters, both students at the college, grew up in Fairbanks. Dorothy, the elder, was a singer, pianist, and omnivorous reader. Florence was beautiful, smart, and athletic. Their mother, Ada Roth, caught pneumonia and died suddenly a few months after Dorothy enrolled in college. Rinehart, their father, was a district attorney chronically infected with gold fever, perhaps because his brother-in-law had in just a few seasons made a fortune at Cleary Creek and had retired to California. Rinehart exhausted most of his salary on an unsuccessful gold mine at Skoogie Gulch, not far from Cleary. By the time his wife died, he had given up on gold and become enthusiastic about a coal claim near Healy. Six months a widower, he packed a pigskin steamer trunk with black samples from his claim and left the Territory to raise money for this new venture. But he found no investors. After Alaskan coal, it was Californian oil. Rinehart never made his fortune, never returned to Fairbanks, and never saw his daughters again, although he sent sporadic, optimistic letters.

Dorothy, age eighteen, and Florence, fifteen, continued to live meagerly in the family house in town. Concerned neighbors frequently dropped off an "extra" loaf of bread or some "surplus" moose steaks. Dorothy taught piano students half-time and attended college half-time. The girls saved money by eating ketchup sandwiches for lunch. When Florence graduated from high school and joined Dorothy at the college, they often walked the five miles to campus to save the twenty-five-cent round-trip fare charged by the "Toonerville Trolley" that provided transportation between town and campus.

The four young couples that met at the college—sisters, brothers, in-laws, and in-laws of in-laws—formed an extended family. As with many frontier families, it was constructed spontaneously with scant attention to bloodlines. When I was born in the 1940s, the four couples from the College—these "shirttail relatives" and cousins once or twice removed—were my "aunts" and "uncles." And when my mother arrived in Fairbanks in June 1928, she was met at the train station by not just Claire and Audrey, but a crowd of new relations.

Alta had been traveling for a week—five days on an Alaska Steamship Company vessel, the SS *Aleutian,* and two days on the Alaska Railroad from the port of Seward—but she had not been lonely. Within a few hours of boarding the steamship, she discovered that strangers—old, young, men, and women—greeted her on the observation deck and started conversations, pointed out landmarks, and offered advice on seasickness. Many of the passengers returning to Fairbanks knew her cousins. My mother, who had never before been aboard ship, was bemused by the egalitarian familiarity of her fellow passengers. Her vacation was a journey into new territory, socially as well as geographically. She was intrigued by Ketchikan, Juneau, and the other little port towns where the ship docked as it steamed north along the Inside Passage. The weather across the Gulf of Alaska was unusually calm during the voyage. It was not until subsequent and more typical trips across the gulf that she came to understand passengers' intense interest in seasickness remedies.

Like most of her shipmates Alta boarded the train at Seward. She'd had more experience with trains than with ships. She had ridden the Union Pacific from Oregon to Washington and had crossed Montana more than once on the straight tracks of the Great Northern. But the moving view from the windows of the Alaska Railroad was rousingly different from prairies or northwest coast. Tripods of rough poles carried telephone and telegraph lines alongside the track. For many miles these wires and the train track were the only signs of human life. Glaciers curved down mountainsides, the spruces became stubbier and scrawnier as the train wound north, and at 10 PM the sun still hung high in the northwest. The route was twisting and the railbed far from level. The train's maximum speed was thirty-five miles per hour, and it often slowed to sway through a series of turns. Fifty miles out of Seward the train canted sideways as it spiraled upward around the 360-degree five-trestle "Loop" that detoured Bartlett Glacier. Only the station houses looked familiar. They were modern shingled buildings constructed on a pattern used throughout the West. Their hip roofs jutted out over the platform to shelter waiting passengers. Their interiors contained a waiting room with wood benches, wainscoted walls, a ticket cage, and a pen for baggage carts. Alta stepped onto the platform at Fairbanks, the last stop, with enthusiasm for Alaska, a suitcase of summer clothes, a return ticket, and $50. She and the town that awaited her were both twenty-six years old.

Alta's vacation was brief. Within fourteen hours of arrival, her shorthand and typing skills were properly acknowledged by the offer of a summer job as secretary for the Alaska Road Commission. The salary was almost triple her Oregon wages. If she took the job, she would no longer have to live with her mother to save money, no longer have to watch lucky coeds stroll by her office window. She did not hesitate. She posted a businesslike letter of resignation to the bursar and a cheerful letter of independence to her mother. At 8 AM the next day she reported for work. When the Road Commission job ended in the fall, she became deputy clerk of the Fourth Division District Court and settled into Fairbanks life.

She found an amiable roommate, Gladys Welch. Together they rented a tiny log cabin on the riverbank near the ice house. It was equipped with a wood furnace, a kerosene cookstove, and electric lights but lacked plumbing. They signed up for water services provided by three local businessmen: Frank Musjerd of Blue Crystal Wells, Murray Smith of Smith's Ice Service, and Mr. Webb, whose business name was never mentioned by my family. He was simply called the "scavenger" or the honey-bucket man.

Permafrost made it hard to dig private wells and to set up septic tanks in Fairbanks. The Northern Commercial Company piped water and steam heat to businesses and homes in the center of town, pairing water and steam pipes to prevent freezing. However, many people, like Alta and Gladys, lived beyond the piped water grid. They had to purchase their water from Blue Crystal Wells. In the 1920s even families with piped water often patronized Blue Crystal Wells because NC Company water—like that of many private wells—stained wash-basins, spaghetti, and clothing a locally famous shade of orange.

Alta and Gladys hung a placard with a large "W" in their window to signal Mr. Musjerd to stop his truck (which in winter contained a stove to keep his product liquid) to fill their buckets with clear water from his deep well outside town. The price was one dollar for eight five-gallon buckets. Although today's inflated dollar makes this invaluable liquid sound cheap, my mother and her roommate were careful with the water they bought. They consumed a fraction of the one hundred gallons per person per day typical for indoor use in modern homes. Saturday-night bathwater in the galvanized washtub near the kitchen stove was reused to scrub the kitchen floor. In the summer purchased water was supplemented by a rain barrel, whose "soft" water was favored for washing hair. However, melting snow in winter to supplement Mr. Musjerd's deliveries was not practical; not only is the water content of cold-weather snow low, but the city snow contained ash, soot, and dog unmentionables.

Human unmentionables were another problem. The rental house was equipped with an outhouse. But in winter a mottled ice stalagmite began to rise in the shaft below the chilly seat (its cold ameliorated by a caribou-fur cover), and the dark walk down the narrow path shoveled to "the little house" began to seem long. Like most of their neighbors, Alta and Gladys then employed the ser-vices of Mr. Webb. Every two or three days he would come to remove the honey bucket and to replace it with a clean one. The toilet seat under which the bucket rested was in an unheated shedlike back room. The "chemical toilet," as it was termed in polite company, was an improvement in convenience, but not necessar-ily in odor. It was abandoned for the airy outhouse when summer returned.

In contrast to Mr. Webb, whose services were needed in winter, the product sold by Mr. Smith was in demand in the summer. The ice seller's work began in March. By that time of year the Chena River ice was usually six or seven feet deep. Using a handsaw, pry bar, and winch, he and his assistant removed blocks of ice and hauled them to his large warehouse on First Avenue, where he stored them insulated with sawdust. Mr. Smith sold the ice to chill the iceboxes and summer drinks of early twentieth-century Fairbanks. In the warm months he would drive through town three times a week. At the home of each of his regular customers he would cut a block of ice to the size needed and, seizing it with tongs, carry it inside to the icebox. My sister remembers that in the 1930s on hot summer days, children followed his canvas-covered truck through the neighborhood as if it were the ice-cream truck of the 1950s. Whenever Mr. Smith chopped a household's block from a larger cake, he would hand out broken slivers of ice for children to suck. Although the river was silty, my sister remembers this treat as being clear and delicious. When home refrigerators operated by electricity were introduced, Smith's Ice Service succumbed to the new technology.

Mr. Webb's business was also ruined by technology. In the 1930s, the NC Company expanded its downtown steam, water, and sewer pipes, and the FE Company provided services to a portion of Garden Island. With the expansion of utilities, outhouses rapidly disappeared from town. Except for cabins on the Creeks or at Harding Lake, my mother never again had to walk the path to the little house out back.

But at the time, Alta, raised on a rural ranch, was not put off by outhouses or other small inconveniences of living in Fairbanks. She rapidly came to enjoy life in her new hometown. Her job at the courthouse, in addition to paying well, introduced her to people and to ideas that would otherwise have been foreign to her. During court trials she recorded, in neat shorthand, testimony about larceny, assaults, and bootlegging. Alaska had gotten a four-year jump on Prohibition when Congress in 1916 passed the Bone Dry Law for the Territory. Bone Dry was no more effective for Alaska than the subsequent Volstead Act was for the rest of the country. Alaska's populace and authorities were relatively tolerant of frequent liquor misdemeanors. The usual punishment for still owners was prompt destruction of discovered and usually disavowed equipment. Bootleggers were not particularly interesting to Alta. Perhaps because she was a carefully raised young woman, the defendants she thought about the most were the prostitutes. She found herself feeling some sympathy for the beautifully dressed "girls of the line," who offered company and gratification for miners and men of the growing town.

The federal courthouse where my mother worked was only two blocks from the town's red-light district. At one time twelve-foot wood fences across Fourth Avenue at Cushman and Barnett Streets barricaded this area from public view. Customers entering through pedestrian doors in the fences were treated to a row of narrow cabins with large front windows where the "girls" displayed themselves attractively when available for company. The city fathers erected the fences in 1906, supposedly to protect respectable citizens from the sight of sexuality publicly flaunted to attract single men and ensnare husbands. The barriers, of course, also protected the privacy of male clients and allowed the police to patrol the area, collect monthly "fines," and enforce health inspections. This quasi-legal "restricted district" was a socially progressive idea in that it allowed prostitutes to own their cribs, releasing them from bondage to pimps. My mother did not approve of prostitution, but she understood that, as one of the community matriarchs explained it, "the prostitutes…are pioneers too—independent, on their own, with no husband, no family, and with no other training."

Fairbanks had norms of tolerance that served both prostitutes and respectable citizens well. Personal privacy is necessarily limited in isolated frontier towns. Fairbanksans had a fair notion about the standing arguments between businessmen, about which families in the town suffered the grief of alcoholism, and about who had arrived in Alaska with an invisible past. The *Fairbanks Daily News-Miner* regularly published the names of patients in the hospital, the registers of local hotels, and the passenger lists of the Alaska Railroad and the Alaska Steamship Line. The telephone operator who placed local calls did not require a telephone number to find Miss Tanner. The woman answering to "Central" already knew everyone's phone number; moreover, she often knew whether Miss Tanner was at home or at her cousin's house using the sewing machine. Most people dealt with this transparency by limiting speculation and expressions of disapproval to private moments, and by placing high value on restraint and tolerance in public. Eventually Alaska's state constitution even contained wording not found in the U.S. Constitution: "The right of privacy is recognized and shall not be infringed." When, as was not uncommon, a prostitute married into respectability, her past became invisible, a benefit to several founding families.

But what appealed most to my mother about Fairbanks was not her job, nor her new relatives, but her social life. Alta was fond of parties, picnics, and dances. She had always had fun in groups, but she had never had a serious beau. Her sister Frances, six years younger, was already married. Alta was over twenty-five. Despite her aunt's and her mother's experiences with marriage, she was an optimist and an idealist. By the time she came to Fairbanks, she had probably developed some concern about spinsterhood. But Fairbanks was heartening: the ratio of men to women was in her favor, and her cousins had each married within two years of stepping off the train.

Winter, not summer, was the social season in Fairbanks. During the short summer, the local population scattered to placer mines on the Creeks. Men— permanent residents and summer transients alike—worked long daylight hours in muck and gravel stream bottoms. A few were accompanied by wives who tended gardens, children, and summer cabins that lacked amenities such as electricity. In the winter, Fairbanks regrouped. Almost every chimney in town had a straight plume of smoke rising into the windless air. It was a leisurely time for miners—a time for repairing equipment and making plans for next summer. Women's gardens were buried under snow, and their older children were out of the house and in school. Chores were lighter than on the Creeks. Water was delivered by the waterman, cordwood by the woodcutter, and coal by the Healy River Coal Company. Everyone had electric lights for the dark days. Fairbanksans relaxed, and the cabin-fever-defeating social season began.

Alta was not prone to cabin fever. Fundamentally cheerful and raised on a Montana ranch often isolated by snow, she knew how to use her energy during cold, dusky days. On weekends she attended skating parties on the river, and she learned to make stem turns on waxed hickory skis at Cleary Summit fifteen years before Fairbanks got its first rope tow. "Twenty minutes up, two minutes down" was her summary. Her ski teacher was the well-known dog musher Leonhard Seppala. He willingly gave her a ride with his team, and she sent her mother a photo of herself enveloped in a fur parka and seated in a dogsled.

Skiing and skating were informal daytime social occasions. Formal events— most of which were dances—were scheduled on Saturday nights several times each winter. In those days, the Elks, the Moose, the American Legion, and the Masons all owned buildings with ballrooms. They sponsored formal dances with sedate live music. Many of these balls were fund-raisers for worthy causes. They included door prizes, an entry fee for couples and single men, but free admission for respectable single women. When these latter desirable guests arrived, each was handed a little decorated dance card with a tiny pencil. The dance cards had thirty or so numbered blanks, each representing a dance. Popular women would write in the names of partners who requested the next free dance. Given the ratio of eligible women to men, all single women were popular, and the system worked well to reduce conflicts among the men.

Attire for these occasions was elaborate and required hours of preparation. At least it was elaborate for women, dark suits being the ne plus ultra for men.

Women wore long dresses and high-heeled shoes with thin straps. In the winter, the ladies' cloakroom next to the ballroom of the Odd Fellows Hall, the Masonic Lodge, or the Elks Club was the scene of intricate dressing changes. Women removed parkas, mittens, and wool scarves. They wiggled out of the long johns or snow pants they had been wearing under satin skirts, straightened the seams in their silk stockings, and changed from snow boots to ostentatiously impractical shoes carried in homemade velveteen sacks with drawstrings. The women's magical transformations as they entered the ballroom denied not only the weather but also coal stoves, frozen plumbing, power outages, and the amount of time required to create an impression of cultured leisure.

During the week prior to one of these events, my mother and her cousins would try on their dresses over restrictive girdles and brassieres designed to flatten their figures into a stylish "flapper" shape. From the girdles hung garters to which their stockings, carefully checked for runs, would attach. Gowns for formal balls could be store-bought from Fairbanks dress shops at a considerable cost, or from a dressmaker at an even greater cost. My mother and her cousins usually bought from neither, adopting the alternative open to rural young women properly trained by their mothers—making their own. Audrey owned a treadle sewing machine, and Fairbanks supported several stores that sold patterns and fabrics, including elegant bolts of velvet, satin, and chiffon. Fortunately, the styles of the 1920s featured simple lines. Most women wore each ball dress on several occasions, cleverly modifying it with different accessories. For those who could afford it, locally made brooches and bracelets of nugget, jade, and ivory were popular.

By the time Jim Crawford reached Fairbanks in May 1929, my mother had danced, skied, or skated with most of the eligible men in town and had a full social calendar. Her brief vacation was starting to stretch into what would eventually become thirty-eight years of residence—not because of job opportunities, but because of romance.

{3}

MARRIAGE

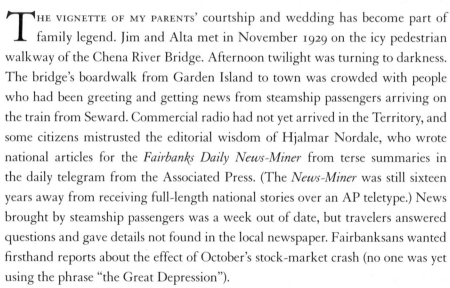

THE VIGNETTE OF MY PARENTS' courtship and wedding has become part of family legend. Jim and Alta met in November 1929 on the icy pedestrian walkway of the Chena River Bridge. Afternoon twilight was turning to darkness. The bridge's boardwalk from Garden Island to town was crowded with people who had been greeting and getting news from steamship passengers arriving on the train from Seward. Commercial radio had not yet arrived in the Territory, and some citizens mistrusted the editorial wisdom of Hjalmar Nordale, who wrote national articles for the *Fairbanks Daily News-Miner* from terse summaries in the daily telegram from the Associated Press. (The *News-Miner* was still sixteen years away from receiving full-length national stories over an AP teletype.) News brought by steamship passengers was a week out of date, but travelers answered questions and gave details not found in the local newspaper. Fairbanksans wanted firsthand reports about the effect of October's stock-market crash (no one was yet using the phrase "the Great Depression").

Jim's mind, however, was not on economics. For several weeks he had been watching for an opportunity to meet the dark-haired deputy clerk of court, but she always seemed to be surrounded by friends—possibly beaus—waltzing at a ball, watching a silent movie at the Empress Theater, or accompanying singers on the popular portable instrument of the day—a banjo ukulele. On the Chena River Bridge, Lady Chance tossed Jim a favor. Alta was walking just ahead of him. He deftly blundered into her, then with apologies and Southern courtesy

Jim and Alta Crawford, 1930. *Author's collection.*

helped her up after she fell. Solicitously, he walked her home, and managed to make a date for the next Saturday to hunt ptarmigan.

Neither he nor she owned a car, but Saturday's weather was mild, well above zero, and there were good hunting areas an hour's walk from town. He borrowed an extra .22 rifle, and when they arrived at the upper reaches of a small creek, he carefully instructed her in its use. She listened attentively and charmingly. They worked their way quietly up the creek until they found a covey of the ground-feeding birds. Alta couldn't resist the challenge they presented. Carefully lining up a standing shot, she killed two birds with a single shell, a coup even for a former member of the University of Oregon rifle team. My father had the wit to realize immediately that the shot was not a lucky accident. Deeply smitten by her combination of beauty, modesty, and competence, he willingly resigned himself to being the second-best hunter in the family if he could persuade her to marry him.

Jim had been promoted from supervising the gravel-thawing operations at Chatanika to the main FE office. His assignment was to refine and streamline the Company's muck-stripping and thawing methods. Despite worrisome economic news from the rest of the nation, the FE Company showed no signs of slowdown. The price of gold was steady; Fairbanks was still thriving. My father, confident he could support a wife, courted Alta assiduously for the next four months.

Alta found Jim's enthusiastic courtship heartwarming. She noted that, unlike her father whose disastrous speculation in wheat futures had lost the Montana ranch, Jim was a professional man, conservative with money and careful about his behavior. Events at work had already caused him to abandon, or nearly abandon, two vices. The first was smoking. One day, looking up from a blueprint, he confronted three cigarettes burning in his ashtray—each lit and abandoned in his concentration. He decided that he could not afford cigarettes as incense and quit buying them, although he continued to smoke an occasional cigar or pipe after dinner. A more serious incident had caused him to become cautious in drinking. One morning during his first month at headquarters, he arrived for work on time but still smelling of beer from a previous night's party. The general manager—an upright man, possibly even a teetotaler who supported Prohibition—dismissed him and sent him home. Jim was mortified and deeply apprehensive, recalling his painful hiatus of underemployment between college and the Kennecott assaying job. To be fired in 1929 from his valued position as assistant engineer for research and operations would be a devastating blow. The next day he returned to earnestly petition his boss and was relieved to be reinstated at his desk. Thereafter he rarely drank more than two glasses, even on New Year's Eve. Remembering her parents' divorce, Alta noticed that even if he did have one drink, he spent no time flirting with other women. But it was not her rational assessment of Jim's good character that charmed my mother; it was his Southern gallantry and his humor. He may not have been a practical joker or even a hearty laugher, but he was willing to don costumes and act a comic part at masquerades. His humor was wry and self-deprecating; in his first-person stories, he was usually the butt of an amusing situation.

Jim had one powerful rival for my mother's affection, his coworker Jack Boswell, a recent graduate of the Alaska Agricultural College and School of Mines. But Jack had left town for the winter without proposing, and my father, with his usual intensity for important projects, devoted considerable energy to persuading Alta to be his wife. He took her skiing; he took her to church. He made minor repairs to the house that she and Gladys rented. Two days before Christmas he took the roommates out to the hills to select a Christmas tree. The scraggly black spruce of Interior Alaska were not as lush as the pines of Oregon and Missouri, so the women chose two and Jim drilled holes in the trunk of the best one to insert supplemental branches cut from the second. Even though the tree began to audibly rain needles a few days later, the experiment was such a success that it wasn't until late in my childhood that I learned most Christmas trees are not constructed in the garage on Christmas Eve. Jim's devotion and wholehearted admiration lighted Alta's heart. In January, to his delight, she accepted his proposal for a March wedding.

Soon after their engagement was announced, Jack Boswell returned to town. Dismayed at my father's success in his absence, Jack sent Tommy Thompson to visit Alta as his belated advocate. My mother, who had experienced no shortage of admirers since coming to Fairbanks, briskly replied that if Jack had been sincerely interested, he would have been wise to propose before leaving. Tommy, who later became a career foreign service officer, described his brief experience as go-between as his most uncomfortable diplomatic mission. Jack acted with more alacrity when he fell in love with Jewel Booth, whom he married, and the Crawfords and Boswells settled into being longtime neighbors and friends.

My father was aware that his own mother in Missouri might be mildly disapproving of his chosen bride. Alta had a pleasing graciousness, but not the bloodlines, reserve, or fragility of a Southern lady. Jim's mother was not likely to be as impressed as he was by Alta's sharpshooting, speedy shorthand, prize-winning spelling, and pleasant ukulele playing. Pearle Crawford already openly mourned the loss of her son to geographic distance and wild country. A wife from Alaska might be hard for her to embrace. My father was not deterred. Like some Athabascans of his generation, but for different reasons, he felt dislocated from the culture of his parents. This sense of separation from relatives in the States produced in immigrant Alaskans both pride and insecurity—the pride of "taming" a frontier, a revered American virtue, and the insecurity of plunging into a cultural backwater, far from the elegance of the Eastern elite or the sophistication of jazz, flappers, and silent-film stars. The truth is that neither Jim nor Alta would have partaken deeply of these cultures in their hometowns. For them pride outweighed insecurity. My father wrote home describing Alta's charm and competence, and announcing the good news of his upcoming wedding. He was neither surprised nor dismayed when no one in his family could attend.

It was probably fortunate that Pearle Crawford never had the opportunity to observe the lack of amenities in modest Fairbanks homes, and also that she missed her chance to meet Alta's mother, Lillian Tanner, who traveled from Oregon to Fairbanks for the wedding. I have a favorite photograph of each of my grandmothers. Pearle is posed for a professional photographer in a lace-trimmed bodice, grave and beautiful, her head held high. Lillian and her sister Leslie are walking through knee-high prairie grass, their cotton dresses blown back by the wind, heads also high, implacable matriarchs striding through the West. Lillian took two weeks' leave from her job as a cook and arrived in Fairbanks several days before the wedding to meet her new son-in-law and to help with last-minute sewing. In accordance with family custom, she did not come for the purpose of offering her daughter information or advice about the intimate aspects of marriage. In rural Montana where Lillian and Alta were raised, such subjects were not discussed; couples raised on ranches surrounded by farm animals were assumed to be competent to work out the details for themselves.

Although the bride-to-be worked at the courthouse, the engaged couple never considered a civil ceremony. Alta, a confirmed Episcopalian, wanted to be married in St. Matthew's Episcopal Church, where Audrey, Claire, and Dorothy had married the Loftus brothers and where Florence Roth would marry Tommy Thompson in the fall. The log church on First Avenue had been constructed just two years after Fairbanks was established. At slightly over a quarter of a century old, it was a venerable, solid institution. Jim, although a baptized Christian, did not accept as true every story in the New Testament, but he certainly believed in the sacrament of matrimony. Printed wedding invitations were issued for March 23, 1930, at 7:15 AM. On March 18, the day Lillian arrived, the groom broke out in measles. The ceremony was postponed almost a week to allow Jim time to recuperate. Lillian hastily wrote a letter to her boss, explaining that she would be a week late in returning; she hoped the post office could deliver this urgent news before the day she was expected back in the kitchen.

On March 27 the early-morning ceremony was finally held. It was not a fancy wedding. Tuxedos, bridesmaids in matching dresses, and a floor-length bridal gown did not fit the young couple's budget. The bride and groom, their guests, and their two attendants (Gladys Welch and Bill Holt) wore Sunday best for the church ceremony. There was no photographer with a flashbulb camera, so there is no picture of my mother's wedding dress. She described it to me, however, as an "afternoon dress," custom-made by one of the local dressmakers and fashionably up-to-date—based on the weekly illustration in the *Fairbanks Daily News-Miner* titled "Modes of the Moment!" With the onset of the Depression, waistlines had reappeared and hems (having risen from ankle in 1923 to knee-cap in 1927) had abruptly dropped to midcalf, rendering rolled stockings, the flat-chested flapper look, and many young women's wardrobes passé. Knowing my mother's tastes, I suspect her modish, midlength wedding dress was pastel, trimmed out with the traditional "something old, something new, something borrowed, something blue."

The breakfast-hour timing of the wedding was chosen so that the newlyweds could depart on the 8 AM train for their honeymoon. The reason that Jim and Alta did not take pity on their friends and get married the evening before the train's departure had to do with my father's desire to forestall an embarrassing shivaree. This custom involved high-spirited friends arriving with merriment and home brew just as the bride and groom were settling in for their wedding night. My father was probably right to be wary. His new in-laws, the Loftus brothers, enjoyed jollity and practical jokes. Jule's wedding night had been marked by (1) the stovepipe outside the cabin being blocked by rags, forcing smoke into the house, (2) a racket loud enough to wake the neighborhood when he went out to unblock the pipe and crashed into the gunnysacks of tin cans piled in front of his door, and (3) someone trying to force a house cat to leap abruptly into the cabin through the eight-inch wall vent in the kitchen area.

After the short morning ceremony, the new Mr. and Mrs. James Crawford bundled into a sheepskin coat (him) and a fur parka (her) to be chauffeured by the best man to the nearby train depot. Between Prohibition and the early hour, no one proposed a toast to the bride and groom. Instead their game, early-rising wedding guests showered them with rice as they climbed aboard a train headed for the Curry Railroad Hotel, 220 miles and ten hours down the tracks. This luxurious two-story hotel, subsidized by the federal government, was a required overnight stop for railroad passengers. The steam-powered trains needed two days to travel between Fairbanks and Seward, and the railroad owned no Pullman sleeping cars. In 1922 the railroad builders realized that the approximate midpoint of this journey, where the overnight hotel would be built, was a collection of cabins called Deadhorse Hill. Recognizing that this name lacked cachet, the builders renamed the spot after railroad supporter Representative Charles Curry of California. Two evenings a week the north and southbound trains both pulled onto the siding next to the Curry Hotel. The passengers disembarked to eat and spend the night. The following morning the travelers departed on their respective trains. Train crews also spent the night, but they changed trains, making a U-turn back to their home bases—either Fairbanks or Seward (in later years replaced by Anchorage as the southern base).

But the seventy-five-room Curry Hotel was not only a required overnight; it was also a destination for honeymooners and vacationers. Its accommodations ranged from fifty-cent-a-night dormitory beds to three-dollar-a-night luxury rooms with

Train arriving at Curry Hotel.
University of Alaska Archives, Reuel Griffin Collection, 59-845-415.

attached baths featuring long claw-footed tubs. The better rooms included niceties such as ashtrays and matches, brass cuspidors, and shoeshine kits. In the dining room a maître d' seated up to forty-five guests at white-linened tables, and the chef—notified of the passenger count a few hours before the trains arrived—offered multicourse meals with a choice of entrées. In summer, the courses included locally fattened beef or pork, greenhouse salads, garden vegetables, wild berries, and hotel-made jams. The "resort hotel," as it was called in railroad brochures, looked out on a narrow, rapid stretch of the Susitna River. Its grounds sported a tennis court, a three-hole golf course, and an outdoor swimming pool.

On the occasion of my parents' stay, the tennis court and swimming pool were buried under snow, but the days just after the spring equinox were sunny, barely freezing. The newlyweds spent their days in shoepacs, wool jodhpurs, and plaid wool shirts, hiking along the tracks, watching the foxes at a nearby fur farm, and crossing the suspension footbridge over the river to tramp the snow-packed trail to Lookout Ridge for a view of Mount McKinley. Like most of the guests, they upheld the standards of civilization by dressing for dinner. My father donned his dark blue wedding suit and a tie. My mother wore high heels, silk stockings, and either her wedding dress or one of the other three dresses she had brought for the four-day honeymoon.

Among those dresses was one that, unlike her wedding dress, Alta did not discard when it went out of fashion. This treasured item was a dinner dress in

1928 style that almost revealed her kneecaps—a sleeveless brown lace shift with a decorative hip-level satin belt that did not interfere with the dress's perfectly straight lines. She must have looked smashing in it with her dark shoulder-length hair swept smoothly away from her face in marcelled waves. My father titled himself "spellbound" on a photo of her taken during the honeymoon. Although short skirts were already out of style in the States, fashion changed more slowly in Alaska, creating in the Territory a six-month grace period for favorite, outdated dresses. By the fall of 1930 my mother had to give up the lace dress, but she took care to preserve it—probably out of affection rather than out of prescience that the fashion wheel would turn sufficiently for me to wear it on special occasions in the 1960s.

Handsomely dressed dinner guests were few after the trains pulled out, but their number swelled again three days later when the trains returned. On their third morning at Curry, my parents climbed aboard the northbound train with the other passengers, but their ride was unexpectedly foreshortened. During the night, wet snow had swept down a steep hillside five miles north of the hotel and covered the tracks. The engine, equipped with a plow, tried to force its way through, but the plow jumped the tracks and the whole train had to be pulled back to Curry. A maintenance crew and more equipment were requested from Anchorage while the northbound passengers settled back into their rooms at the hotel. The Anchorage maintenance crew and the railroad's chief, Colonel Otto Ohlsen, arrived in the afternoon and worked into the night. The next morning the train made a full ten miles before having to back up again.

The March train travelers, experienced in the vagaries of northern weather, responded to their enforced two-day vacation by entertaining themselves. During daylight, the hearty spent their time outdoors enjoying the warm, avalanche-promoting weather, while indoor enthusiasts started bridge tournaments and exchanged reading material. In the evenings after dinner (which gradually declined to bread, corned beef, and canned peas), the strandees mounted impromptu entertainment in front of the huge fireplace in the salon. One man played the banjo and sang mournful songs in a Swedish accent. Others told jokes, put on comic skits, or recited poetry. (Alta, with her encyclopedic memory for amusing poems, may have done the latter.) The most popular entertainer, however, was Judge James Wickersham, who, after a decade away from politics, was again campaigning for territorial delegate to Congress. Wickersham was an accomplished raconteur. His experiences in Alaska, including an attempt on Mount McKinley, provided him with an extensive fund of stories. According to my parents, he was easily prevailed upon to tell a story on each night of the delay. When the snow was finally removed from the tracks, my parents boarded the train to Fairbanks, satisfied with their honeymoon adventure.

In Fairbanks, Jim and Alta rented a downtown three-room cottage, which had no running water but did have cockroaches—an exotic species in the North where normally only silverfish scuttled across the floor in winter. Each day my father dressed for the weather and made the three-quarter-mile walk to FE headquarters, where he shared a large office with three other engineers. There he continued to devise cheaper and more efficient ways to thaw frozen ground. He designed collection ponds to reuse water from the thaw points. He made preliminary drawings for a mechanical point-driving machine, although it wasn't until 1944 that others in the Company (master mechanic Ralph Norris, master electrician Bob Clark, and engineers Roy Earling and Jack Boswell) invented a successful prototype that could replace muscular young men lifting and dropping sliding hammers onto the crossbars of the points. Ironically, Jim also worked out a method for refreezing thawed ground along the sides of a dredge pond to prevent the banks from sloughing into the water. The design called for a liquid with a low freezing point to circulate through vertical pipes placed at intervals along the bank. In winter the liquid could be cooled to ambient air temperature using Caterpillar tractor radiators; during the summer, standard refrigeration units would maintain the freeze. Deeply interested in the questions he was trying to answer, Jim began the habit of bringing office tasks home when the six o'clock whistle from the FE powerhouse signaled the end of the workday. As a sign that he was now a serious married man, or perhaps just to compensate for thinning hair, he grew a small brown moustache that resembled his father's larger white one.

My mother, as expected in those days, resigned her job at the district court for employment more suitable to a married woman, substitute teaching at the high school (Latin, shorthand, and typing). Alta willingly set out to learn her new role—wife of a provident man, an engineer likely to rise in the mining company. In the summer Jim was stationed at Gilmore Creek or Pedro Creek, where he instituted thawing modifications developed during the winter. Alta moved with him to the Creeks to make a home in a Company cabin with three rooms and running cold water in the kitchen. Her wifely duties in these cabins perched on rocky dredge tailings were similar to tasks she had learned on the Montana ranch—cooking, mending, washing clothes, and making friends with neighboring women. Tutored by gatherer-wives, she became adept at picking

The Crawfords' summer quarters, Gilmore Creek. Family car on left. *Author's collection.*

and preserving berries. She learned to find highbush cranberries by their aroma, to defer picking lingonberries until after the first frost, and to pick blueberries by hand instead of using a berry scoop with tines that captured so many leaves that the task of cleaning took longer than the picking. In later years she told with amusement about a berry-cleaning lesson she received from Fannie Quigley, a locally famous woman, who mined, hunted, and maintained a camp with her husband in the Kantishna District. On Alta's kitchen table, Fanny draped a damp dish towel over a breadboard and propped one end of the board on a box to create a sloping surface. Then she called for a ptarmigan wing to gently roll the berries down the damp slanting surface to which the leaves clung. She was incredulous when Alta confessed to not having a ptarmigan wing among her kitchen implements. The berry-cleaning lesson, punctuated by choice words from Fanny's extensive vocabulary, came to an abrupt halt.

Life on the Creeks during the short summer was relatively simple; winter life in town was more complex. Alta shopped, cooked, kept house, and resumed social events she had enjoyed while single—dances, evening card parties, skating, and skiing. She also took on a new social requirement, attending "at home afternoons."

Later in life she described these dutiful entertainments to me with considerable humor. It was customary for senior matrons, often wives of mining-company officers, to have a specific afternoon when they were "at home" to receive women who wished to pay a visit. Guests arrived with calling cards ("engraved" with their names by the local printer), which they placed on a silver salver on a table near the front entryway. The hostess, carefully coiffed and wearing an afternoon dress of subdued color and expensive cut, would serve tea in decorated china cups that had been individually acquired as wedding or Christmas gifts. In addition to dispensing tea and tiny homemade cookies crafted to fit on a saucer, the hostess frequently offered helpful advice to young wives on pastry making, garden planning, and home remedies.

My mother would walk from her modest cottage to these at-homes wearing an afternoon dress (appropriately less glamorous than that of the hostess), high heels, and white gloves under her heavy coat, galoshes, and mittens. In truly cold weather, she carried her shoes so that she could wear mukluks and long wool stockings over her silk-clad legs. Some women even wore cloches from which, moments before making their entrance, they removed a loosely wound wool scarf. The polite thirty-minute visit required a five-minute clothing change coming and going, but the guests did not mind. The young women, freed from aprons and stoking a heating stove in a small house, enjoyed the half hour of respite in a spacious home warmed by steam heat or an "automatic" coal furnace and decorated with oriental rugs, framed oil paintings, and crocheted doilies pinned to stuffed furniture. The hostess offered approval and support to young helpmeets; the grand, Company-owned residence offered hope for more comfort in the future. Perhaps the matrons passed on personal opinions to their husbands about whether the attendees were creating a stable family life from which an engineer could work without undue distraction. Maybe they felt gratified to offer helpful advice to younger women, providing a sense of community that deepened, although probably narrowed, social ties. Maybe at-homes were a painful and unavoidable duty. The hostesses' opinions are unpublished.

For my parents the honeymoon was over. They were a settled couple busy establishing a home and a life in the community. In the world around them, the Great Depression was worsening.

Audrey Loftus, Lola Cremeans (Tilly), and Alta Crawford. Richardson Highway, 1931.
Author's collection.

{4}

HUNKERING DOWN IN THE DEPRESSION

WHEN WORK AT THE FE COMPANY slackened in the winter of 1931, Alta and Jim took a vacation, reboarding the train and the steamship for a trip Outside to meet in-laws. My father also wanted to apply for mining work in the States, where the climate was temperate and the housing was middle-class. He believed that two years in the Fairbanks goldfields had given him the experience he needed to get an interview and perhaps a job with one of the companies that had rejected him as a new graduate. My parents and their Fairbanks relatives still assumed that their stay in Alaska was temporary. The four young couples often talked about where they would settle in the States. They failed to understand the severity of the Great Depression because the Territory was shielded from unemployment by its principal product—gold. During the early part of the Depression, even though the White House was occupied by the Republican mining engineer Herbert Hoover, the price of gold was held at its mid-nineteenth-century value—$20.67 per troy ounce. The FE Company had used this price to calculate its mining costs and was able to continue operating with only minor cutbacks. Then in 1933–34, as part of an effort to halt the Depression, President Franklin Roosevelt, a Democrat with no ties to the mining industry, devalued the dollar by increasing the price of gold to $35 per ounce. In response the Company hired more men and patented more claims (which eventually totaled some thirty thousand acres). The pages of legal advertisements for patents helped to sustain the *Fairbanks Daily News-Miner* through the remainder of the Depression.

Jim and Alta's trip south was informative. The recently weds were cordially received by their new in-laws. In Missouri, Pearle approved of Alta's precise English and natural good manners. Alta, in turn, was awed and slightly scandalized by what appeared to be a Southern custom. Each morning her father-in-law—always referred to as "Crawford" by his wife—made up a breakfast tray with a linen cloth and fine china that held toast, tea, and jam. He left this offering at Pearle's bedside before he went to work so that she could comfortably awaken, eat, and read until 11 am before emerging from her room to begin a day of social activity. Laundry and heavy housekeeping were managed by a sturdy black woman who came to the house for several hours every morning, freeing Pearle to introduce her daughter-in-law to friends at a series of afternoon tea parties.

In Oregon, Jim astounded his mother-in-law, Lillian, and Alta's friends by arriving with a Southern treat for them, one he had often dreamed about in Fairbanks—extra-large frog legs frozen on dry ice. The local butcher agreed to keep these delicacies—the size of small chicken legs—frozen until a dinner party could be assembled, provided he could display them in his window to astonish customers. In Eugene, with Jim's approbation, Alta used some savings to purchase a "silver marten" fur coat at an excellent price. (The coat, with its shawl collar and light-colored pelts meeting in a chevron pattern down the back, proved a good investment. My mother was still wearing it in 1950.) However Lillian may have felt about the frog legs, she was reassured that, in the midst of the Depression, her daughter was married to a good provider.

The truth was that neither Jim nor Alta fully understood the extent of the Depression until they arrived in Eugene, where they received replies to the letters of inquiry Jim had sent to various mines in the States. There were no employment offers; indeed, two letters were answered by managers soon to be out of work themselves and eager to find out about jobs in Alaska. Even Lillian, recently unemployed, planned to travel to Anchorage to look for work. My mother's married sister, Frances, was also starting to dream of going to Alaska. At the time she was living in a converted chicken house on an Idaho ranch leased by in-laws so desperate that they were angry at her for not having an abortion to save the cost of a second child. It was clear that no state was being spared economic hard times the way that the Territory was.

My parents ate the frog legs with guests and returned to Fairbanks with the marten coat, grateful for my father's secure employment. They ignored the lack of plumbing in their rented house and settled in for a longer tenure, sending money from time to time to family members back in the States. The three Loftus families did the same. Only Florence and Tommy Thompson left Alaska, off to distant adventures with the U.S. Foreign Service in 1933.

Committed to Fairbanks, Jim and Alta set about making themselves comfortable on my father's salary. In 1931, according to his meticulous account book, he made $2,687.50 less $32.66 income tax. Their first "settling-in" family purchase was one that they anticipated would save money in coming years—a used treadle Singer sewing machine. My mother, already a competent seamstress, took sewing lessons from the Cooperative Extension Service to increase her skill. Alta and Jim's reasoning about the economics of homemade clothes was correct; however, technology was advancing so quickly that the treadle machine was replaced within a few years by a new $25 electric model.

They also bought a Model A Ford with a starter and dual windshield wipers from Sampson's Hardware, which—thanks to its farseeing owner, James Barrack—doubled as the Ford dealership. The black Model A cost over $500, but Alta's substitute-teaching salary paid the bill. Like many Fairbanks cars, it rested in an unheated garage, shiny and undisturbed during the six months of winter, but a summer photo shows it in the sun, its nether portions coated with mud and dust from the dirt roads that led to fishing spots, berry patches, and the Crawfords' summer living quarters on the Creeks.

In the summer of 1931 married but still childfree, my mother, her cousin Audrey, and their friend Lola Cremeans (subsequently Lola Tilly) decided that the Model A could provide them with needed adventure. Alta's and Audrey's husbands were working long hours, barely coming home. Jim and Ted could eat at the FE Company mess house for a few days while the women made a round-trip on Alaska's longest road, the 371-mile Richardson Highway, which crossed the Alaska Range and Chugach Mountains to connect Fairbanks to Valdez on the Gulf of Alaska.

Lola had been a passenger on this "military highway" the previous summer. After her first year teaching home economics at the Alaska Agricultural College and School of Mines, she returned to Illinois for a visit. Lola was vivacious, willowy, and adventurous; she had already made a solo visit to Cuba. She chose a round-about, seldom-used route to travel from Fairbanks to Seattle. She rode the Alaska Railroad to Nenana, where she boarded a riverboat to churn down the Tanana and up the Yukon to Dawson. A Canadian paddle wheeler carried her south, upriver past Five Finger Rapids to Whitehorse. After an overnight, she and her small suitcase left Canada on the twisting, narrow-gauge White Pass and Yukon Railway to

Skagway, where she caught the steamship for Seattle. On her return from Illinois she bypassed Skagway, disembarked at Valdez, and rode the Valdez Stage (a seven-passenger 1929 Cadillac) over the Richardson Highway to Fairbanks. She was the sole passenger on the two-day road trip, and the driver was cooperative in stopping whenever Lola spied grouse. Somewhere she had learned a low croaking call that often brought the chicken-sized birds into the open. Her father's parting gift to her in Illinois had been a brand-new Sears and Roebuck .22 rifle. She arrived in Fairbanks with three freshly bagged birds and fond memories of the trip.

The Richardson Highway, ten years old, was an upgrade of a dogsled and wagon route, the Valdez Trail. Still a summer-only auto road, it was considered a highway because its graveled surface was sixteen feet wide, broad enough for two lanes of cars. Most of the stream and river crossings had been bridged over. The exceptions were the Tanana River, which was crossed at Big Delta by cable ferry, and a number of small creeks that were simply forded by the early cars with their high undercarriages. In periods of high water, the Alaska Road Commission stationed heavy equipment at the worst crossings to help winch travelers across.

Mother told me about their dusty four-day round-trip. There were no gas stations. The friends bought gasoline, food, and lodging at roadhouses along the route. These inns, originally spaced one day apart for horse and dog teams, had long (twenty-to-thirty-mile) stretches of uninhabited road between them. The three adventurers carried a Model A tool kit, a tire pump, a spare inner tube, a rubber patching kit, extra gasoline, water for the radiator, matches, emergency blankets, and a couple of rifles. A Brownie snapshot shows them snappily dressed in jodhpur-style pants tucked inside high-laced boots, cloches on heads, and rifles in hand in front of a log cabin. Based on their dashing appearance, it seems likely that had their car broken down, some gallant traveler would have stopped to offer aid.

Audrey wrote fondly about the luxurious features of some of the roadhouses where travelers ate $2 meals at long tables and paid $2 a night for a bed or cot with cotton sheets and a Hudson Bay blanket. Many of the inns still had gold scales for the occasional prospector headed for town to turn his gold dust into silver dollars. Munson's Roadhouse, forty-seven miles from Fairbanks, had hot and cold running water. The thirty-bed Richardson Roadhouse, eighty miles from Fairbanks, fed people from an extensive garden and fed horses from a large grain field. Meier Roadhouse, just beyond the halfway point to Valdez, had "all spring beds." The Rapids Roadhouse, 147 miles from Fairbanks, provided a unique long-distance telephone service. The proprietor could receive a call from

Fairbanks on one line, telephone Valdez on a separate line, and relay important conversations by holding a receiver to each ear. Copper Center Roadhouse, 260 miles from Fairbanks, advertised that it was near "Mt. Wrangell, a smoking volcano." Others touted good hunting or scenic views appealing to photographers. Alta, Audrey, and Lola used Brownie cameras to take never-labeled photos of sunlit peaks, distant glaciers, and streaming falls.

During their single day in Valdez, population 450, the women walked a rocky beach surrounded by mountains and watched Pacific breakers roll in. They returned to Fairbanks triumphantly, the Model A intact.

Alta was not the only one in the family attracted by new geography. In 1932 Jim was promoted to head the FE Company's two-man mineral exploration department. He was particularly happy with this advancement because it raised his yearly salary by $700 and meant that he would have a chance to travel. For the next two summers, he and his colleague investigated mining claims for sale in distant mining districts with evocative names—Chulitna, Juneau, Circle, Kantishna, Fortymile, Seventymile, Kuskokwim, and Goodnews Bay. They bumped over rutted roads in pickups, crossed swollen streams on horseback, ran out of gas in riverboats, surprised bears while hiking, and wrote reports. Years later he was pleased to point out to me that some of our adult paths in Alaska crossed. Near my cabin in Kantishna, he once had to spend forty-five minutes searching for his glasses in a willow patch after he was knocked aside by a frightened moose. Near my house in Juneau he investigated the Ebner Mine, which was for sale, visited the Mendenhall Glacier, which extended one and a half miles farther down the valley than it does today, and dined with Governor George Parks and the crew of the *Karlsruhe*, a German military cruiser welcome in Alaskan waters during the two-decade hiatus between the world wars. His stories and photos from these trips show his joy at being outdoors. But even when he was young, Jim never hiked into the woods just to commune with nature. Boy and man, he entered wilderness with a purpose—fishing, trapping muskrats, or exploring mine prospects. Being employed in the mineral exploration department, paid to travel in the backcountry, was a rare mix of pleasure and duty. Most of the claims Jim investigated between 1932 and 1934 came to naught; only those in the Fortymile eventually reaped dredging profits.

As Jim advanced in the Company's professional staff, he gained a privilege that must have been comforting during the Depression. He and his family were invited to watch gold, the solid product of his labor, being formed into bars at the "Gold Room," a small freestanding smelter built of the same textured concrete blocks as the office behind which it stood.

FE employee pouring molten gold into mold. Previous brick cooling on table.
Author's collection.

The dredges captured gold in riffles lined with mercury, which amalgamates with the gold to form a crumbly gray mass. Every few weeks, a dredgemaster would shut down the bucketline on his boat to clean the gold-mercury amalgam out of the riffles, replacing it with fresh mercury. Two Company employees transported the heavy amalgam, locked in a strongbox, to the office vault. The next day, the amalgam was carted to the Gold Room and loaded into a retort, which heated it until the vaporized mercury was driven off and condensed back to a liquid state for reuse. (Visiting children especially liked the droplets of escaped mercury that could be rolled across the floor and be made to run together.) Once the mercury had been driven off and only pumice-like lumps of "sponge gold" remained, the retort was heated further to some 2,000 degrees Fahrenheit to liquefy its contents. Then in a dramatic moment, men wearing asbestos gloves and using tongs would open the door at the top, tilt the retort, and pour the glowing, molten gold into brick-shaped molds. Despite the stifling temperature in the room, the bars quickly solidified. The retort men turned them out onto a board and chipped off a thin crust of black slag to reveal the shining fruit of the men's labor.

Although as an engineer my father would have been fascinated by the problems of mining copper or lead, the ingots on the Gold Room floor during the Depression produced a thrill that copper or lead could not match. The mining engineers must have had a moment of sympathy for old-time stampeders—men with rumors for news, who rushed arduously from one creek to another, eager to be among those arriving in time to stake claims from which gold washed from dirt could be immediately spent or deposited in a bank. (Banks of early boom-towns had their own gold-melting retorts, miniature versions of the one in the Gold Room, in which they transformed deposits from dust into bars.)

In addition to Gold Room privileges, my father's job in the mineral exploration department meant that he was no longer stationed at one of the mining camps during the summer. My parents became year-round downtown residents. Jim's raise in 1932 enabled them to buy a small house on the corner of Sixth and Cowles streets. They hoped that by choosing a house a full six blocks from the riverbank, they would avoid being swamped by the frequent spring floods. The frame house had five rooms, one of which was a proper bathroom with tub, sink, and toilet. The back "extra" bedroom was unheated, and the coal furnace was tricky, requiring careful stoking and frequent removal of clinkers; but in buying the house Jim and Alta declared themselves satisfied to be settled in Fairbanks.

All that the house lacked, from my mother's point of view, was a child. Audrey had one child, Florence had two, and Dorothy had three by 1933. Even Frances, still in Idaho in an increasingly troubled marriage, had given birth to her second child. Alta consulted doctors who diagnosed her as infertile but could find no cause for her condition; neither could they suggest any treatment. Doctors, folk healers, and patients all regarded infertility as a female problem. My father did not consult a doctor, nor did my mother's experts suggest he be examined. Alta accepted the medical verdict and may have even blamed herself, but Jim did not blame her. Immersed in work and with no particular ambition to establish a dynasty, he brushed aside the concerns she developed during her days at home. His contribution to enlarging the family and offering my mother distraction was to bring home a cocker spaniel puppy. The Depression and my father's disposition did not allow him to sanction frivolous pets. According to him this curly black dog, the first of a series, would earn its living in the family by retrieving ducks during fall hunts. (The dog did learn to retrieve dead birds—including, on one embarrassing occasion, a fully cooked turkey left untended by a neighbor.)

The dog did not satisfy Alta's yearnings. However, there was nothing to be done about her situation. She had beliefs about how to respond to adversity. One did not linger over regrets or chew over insoluble problems; one went on with life. Letters to her friends and her mother remained chatty and cheerful. There was no mention of disappointment, doctors, frozen pipes, or mosquitoes. In the winter Alta found a minor outlet for her maternal instincts by substitute teaching. In the summer she took Girl Scout troopers camping.

Girls in the 1930s did not play organized athletics or go to book clubs at the library, but they did become scouts. A week of scout camp at Harding Lake, fifty miles from Fairbanks, was a high point of summer. Girl Scouting had been strong in Fairbanks since the mid-1920s, thanks to the energy of its local founder, Jessie Bloom, a well-educated Irish immigrant known for her liberal views on suffrage and the education of women. In the summers of 1934 and 1935, before the Junior Chamber of Commerce built a community campground at Harding Lake, three landowners lent cabins and tent sites so that Girl Scouts could learn to swim, paddle canoes, and build campfires. Among the childless volunteers who camped with the girls were my mother and her friend Lola Cremeans.

Harding Lake covered five square miles and was surrounded by low hills that were largely free of permafrost; birches and aspen grew down to its rocky shores. The lake was part of the Salcha River drainage and at that time had both an inlet and an outlet that kept the clear water circulating. In 1921, when Judge Cecil Clegg homesteaded the first lot and cut a two-mile trail from the new Richardson Highway to the shore, this body of water still retained its Athabascan name: Salcha Lake. But after President Warren Harding made his ill-fated trip to Alaska in 1923 to inaugurate the Alaska Railroad, visit Fairbanks, and eat tainted crab in Cordova that some blamed for his death two weeks later in San Francisco, the lake was renamed in his honor. Harding's own honor was impugned a few months later when the bribery scandals of his administration reached the newspapers. But by that time Salcha Lake had already become Harding Lake.

Even before Judge Clegg built his waterfront house, the lake had been a destination for trappers, prospectors, and fishermen. In the 1920s the *Fairbanks Daily News-Miner* regularly alerted hunters when the fall migration of ducks appeared at the lake. By the early 1930s the newspaper was also reporting Harding Lake arrivals and departures of pontoon planes traveling from Juneau to Fairbanks and beyond. Weeks Field, the town's sports field *cum* airstrip, had been accommodating small planes since Ben Eielson took off in a Curtiss Jenny in 1923, but it did not have sufficient length for multi-engine commercial airplanes. Similarly, the Chena River that wound through Fairbanks could accommodate only small or lightly loaded floatplanes. The pontoon Clipper planes of Pacific Alaska Airways (a subsidiary of Pan American Airways that eventually assumed the parent company's name) needed the long surface of Harding Lake to take off fully loaded with fuel, passengers, and mail for the six-hour flight to Juneau.

By the 1930s airmen and hunters on Harding Lake found themselves competing with owners of cabins and recreational boats. As soon as a one-mile road along the shore was connected to the Richardson Highway in 1928, locals began "squatting" on lots. They staked land and, to meet the customary requirement for title in Alaska, erected permanent dwellings within two years of staking. Soon the west shore was dotted with weekend cabins. Several motorboats, two sailing kayaks, and an eighteen-foot home-constructed sailboat joined the fleet of canoes and rowboats crisscrossing the lake.

Lola and Alta enjoyed their summer days with the Girl Scouts. The women daydreamed aloud of owning cabins themselves. But these were still Depression years. Alta's substitute-teaching checks were down to about $100 per year; the only real money in the family was what Jim earned. Lola was working full-time as the head of the home economics department at the recently renamed University of Alaska (previously the Alaska Agricultural College and School of Mines), but her salary was modest, and it was due to end. The university required female professors to be single, and Lola was engaged to Gray Tilly. Gray, a nonprofessional employee of the FE Company, earned more than Lola did, but not much more. Moreover, he had recently spent most of his savings to build a stucco house on Kellum Street for his bride. Although gold production had partially sheltered Alaska from the Depression, all FE employees had taken a 10 percent pay cut in 1933, almost halving my father's $700 raise of the prior year. By 1935 the cuts had been restored, but the mood of employees remained cautious. Alta and Lola were not deterred by their finances. They conceived a plan that would allow them to become lot owners. The only property still available to squatters was on the south side, beyond the end of the road. Building a one-room cabin in that location would require labor from more than just one man and his wife, and it would require more money than either couple had individually. The women decided to combine their family funds and their men's building skills to construct a single communal cabin.

My sister and I never understood how my father came to agree to this plan. He was certainly attracted to the idea of a summer retreat on the water, and he had visited cabins owned by upper-echelon men in the Company. He also understood precisely how small his savings account was. On the other hand, he had been brought up by people of reserve and dignity who valued their privacy. Jim considered the Tillys close friends. He had first met Gray in 1928 at Kennecott; he and Alta would be the witnesses who signed their marriage certificate. But even good friends may not be soul mates, and should perhaps not be cabinmates. Lola was energetic, self-assured, and intent on her profession as a home economist in Alaska. (Her most famous university

Gray and Lola Tilly, Alta Crawford, and Marie Mackey, ca. 1933.
Author's collection.

course was Camp Cookery, which included training in making biscuits by opening a sack of flour, making a hollow in its contents, and pouring in baking powder, salt, fat, dry milk, and water. These were kneaded into a lump of dough, which was rolled around a clean stick to bake over the fire.) She was a popular teacher, sympathetic toward her students, especially those on scholarships, and she took the "economics" part of her profession seriously. The meals she served were exemplary in this regard, but tended toward spartan. Her recipes omitted expensive spices, and portions were never larger than the recommended size. In private my father complained that her scrupulous truth-in-serving was downright unappetizing. "Would you like a glass of reconstituted, dried, skimmed milk?" he would mimic.

Gray was handsome, good-natured, and more than loquacious—in a crowd he seemed to chatter without pause, playing the entertaining blatherskite. It was years before I chanced upon the fact that when he and Lola were alone together, they worked and read in companionable silence. In his youth Gray was not only entertaining, but strong and capable of hard work. In his middle years he managed, despite careful nutrition at home, to grow heavy, and he spent a good deal of his free time reading or napping on the couch. The idea of living communally with these friends in a one-room cabin with bunk-bed privacy provided by only a burlap curtain must have alarmed my father. But the fall of 1936 found the two couples

View from Harding Lake cabin. *Author's collection.*

in a borrowed riverboat, hauling lumber across the lake to a site a mile and a half from the end of the road, getting ready for the next summer's building season.

The sixteen-by-twenty-foot cabin and its outhouse were completed the following summer. The couples' friendship survived construction and three subsequent decades of cohabitation. The compact lake retreat had four large windows and a porch that overlooked the shore. The interior was furnished with chaise longue (Gray's special province), a table and chairs, a Yukon stove for heat, kerosene lamps for light, and a Kerogas cookstove. The long daylight of summer meant that the kerosene lamps were rarely used. The kerosene cookstove was used even less because the odor of the kerosene burners overpowered the aroma of dinner. Fortunately, the Yukon stove had a flat surface that could heat a griddle or a couple of pans. Buckets of lake water supplied a sink that drained into a slop bucket. The windowless west wall of the cabin was covered by two sets of three-tier bunks. Floor-to-ceiling burlap curtains concealed these beds from the rest of the living space, and a thin wall of Celotex (compacted cane fiber also used for insulation) provided a modicum of privacy and quiet between sleeping Crawfords and sleeping Tillys. The four builders were wise to build triple rather than double bunks because both these couples, now in their mid-to-late thirties, were about to have a grade-schooler join their families. My parents were the first to be surprised in the fall of 1937.

Main School class photo, ca. 1940. Jane Crawford in front, fourth from left.
Courtesy of Jane Crawford Tallman.

{5}

ADOPTION AND WAR JITTERS

Alta's family responded to the Depression by going on the move. Her mother, Lillian, aged fifty-seven, found a job cooking for an Alaska Road Commission crew headquartered in Talkeetna. She returned to the States long enough to gather her belongings in Eugene and to take two gifts to her daughter Frances in Idaho. The gifts were her most prized and least portable possessions—a cast-iron cookstove and a Model A Ford. Frances was grateful: she was strapped with bitter in-laws, scant money, two children, and a husband stricken at the impending loss of his leased sheep ranch.

A few months after returning to Talkeetna, Lillian wrote some big news to her daughters and her sister. She was not only cooking for the road crew, but she had married the foreman, James Van Winkle, known as "Van" to his friends. Decades later when Van died, there was trouble with survivor's social security benefits; only then did the family realize that Grandmother's happy announcement had been slightly exaggerated. Although a stable couple (his calmness balancing her fire), they had omitted to buy a marriage license or partake in a wedding ceremony. But in 1934 Lillian enthusiastically described her new husband and her new hometown Talkeetna, population one hundred. The majority of Talkeetna's citizens were Athabascan Indians, although the town had originated not as an Indian village but as a railroad construction camp on the Susitna River. It continued to exist because it supplied the gold mines at Cache Creek thirty miles to the northeast on the opposite side of the river.

Frances Tanner Weatherell at home in Talkeetna.
Courtesy of Gale Weatherell.

Talkeetna was a frontier town with a post office, two stores, two schools, and two roadhouses. The latter provided rooms, simple meals, and—now that the Twenty-first Amendment had canceled Prohibition—liquor. Lillian's hardworking neighbors were cordial and willing to lend a hand. Local hunters shared their moose meat; no one had to lock their doors. My grandmother encouraged Frances and her husband, Glenn Thompson, to leave Idaho and move to Alaska. Van would give Glenn a job on the Cache Creek road crew, which was working on the other side of the river.

Frances and Glenn sold what they could—some sheep, one horse, and a few pieces of furniture. The Model A Ford fetched $150. The cash paid for rail and steamship tickets and for the freight charge on Grandmother's cast-iron stove, which Lillian had warned Frances she would need in Talkeetna. The family, including four-year-old Jane and one-year-old Gale, took the Northern Pacific to Seattle, an Alaska Steamship to Seward, and the Alaska Railroad to Talkeetna. Frances was energetic, curious, and attractive, with curly auburn hair that she described as red. She loved outback Alaska from the moment she arrived. She enjoyed the camaraderie of the sparse populace and admired the wild country. Like her sister, she was a good shot and impressed locals early on by killing a bothersome bear. A hard worker, she broke ranks with her mother and other Talkeetna women by regularly wearing pants instead of cotton print dresses. Not only did she prefer more masculine clothing, she also adopted the local male custom of swearing her way through a conversation. An attentive observer of wildlife, she often wrote about what she saw. In the late 1940s, when I was an avid child reader, she would include in letters to my mother a story about a weasel or a squirrel written for me. But Frances's husband was not attracted by the wildlife, the dense forest, the surrounding mountains (which included Denali), or the swarms of mosquitoes. He pined for the open range and sheep. The marriage dissolved by degrees as Glenn moved from Talkeetna to Anchorage to Idaho and Frances moved from Talkeetna to Anchorage to Talkeetna, working long hours and trying to keep an eye on her children.

In 1936, when Frances moved to Anchorage to run a boarding hotel for men, she took Gale with her but left Jane in Talkeetna with Lillian and Van. Van was a slim, erect man. His face was a topography of smile wrinkles, and we step-grandchildren loved him. When Van was not working, he always seemed to have more time than did our blood relatives to hold a child on his lap and tell true stories of ventures and misadventures in the Klondike—perhaps how he was conned by Soapy Smith in a shell game. Van had rushed to Skagway with a partner in June 1898, packed over the Chilkoot Pass, and boated to Dawson. Although most of the rich creeks surrounding Dawson had already been staked in 1897 by the original prospectors and by miners who had hurried upriver from gold camps at Circle and the Fortymile, he and his partner acquired one claim in 1898. When Dawson emptied out in the rush to Nome in 1899, the partners stayed in the Yukon and bought two more claims. By 1903 they had made $100,000—the equivalent of $2 million in 2001 dollars. Van thought they should invest in a new motor-car company, but his partner felt the investment was too risky. So instead of buying Ford Motor stock, they sank their money into a fourth mining claim that absorbed their entire bank account and gave no appreciable gold in return. Years later in Talkeetna, Van still suffered intermittently from gold fever. He was eventually cured by taking a summer off from the Road Commission to work a prospect with paltry paydirt near Talkeetna. But during the winter that Frances went to Anchorage and Jane stayed in Talkeetna, he enjoyed entertaining his step-granddaughter during the dark evenings, reminiscing about the gold dust of the past and speculating about nuggets of the future.

On school days Jane attended first grade. Lillian enrolled her in Talkeetna's downtown, one-room school that served a dozen white and mixed-blood pupils.

Full-blooded Indian children, most of whom spoke fluent Athabascan and little English, attended a school on the outskirts of town. Jane's teacher was a remarkably ineffectual man who had difficulty teaching many of his pupils, even the older ones, to read. Jane, smart and artistic, completed her first school year as illiterate as she began.

Troubled by Jane's lack of academic progress and not prepared to raise a granddaughter, Lillian took Jane to Anchorage and left her with Frances, who was already overwhelmed with work and caring for Gale. Anchorage, established by the Alaska Railroad, was a booming city of 2,500 with a large percentage of transient men. Frances, short of money and barely able to mind her son, suddenly had two children to worry about. She was concerned not only about Jane's education, but about her safety; Frances was working too hard to keep a close eye on her shy six-year-old daughter.

As fall approached, Jim and Alta decided to travel to Anchorage to visit Frances. The trip may have been suggested to them by Lillian. Alta delighted in her sturdy nephew, but she was distressed to find her quiet little niece with the curly auburn hair being minded haphazardly by Frances and the men of the hotel. Alta and Jim offered to take Jane to Fairbanks to stay with them. She could live in a house rather than a shared hotel room; she would have not only her own bed but her own bedroom. And she could reattempt first grade under a teacher more proficient than the one in Talkeetna. Frances was frankly relieved. When Jim and Alta returned to Fairbanks, Jane rode north on the train with them.

Jane was welcomed to Fairbanks by aunts and uncles—Audrey and Ted Loftus and Dorothy and Art Loftus—and by their children, cousins close to her in age. The Loftus households were unlike any she had known in Talkeetna. Dorothy's was filled with music and books. Play rehearsals, practice for piano recitals, and read-alouds took precedence over organized meals. Audrey's house was orderly and her meals well balanced, but she was easily drawn outdoors into informal baseball games or spontaneous berry-picking trips. When Jane arrived in Fairbanks, each of these families and some of the neighbors presented her with gifts. Nearly all the wrapped packages contained dolls, mainly stiff little manikins clothed in pretty foreign costumes. One box contained a soft blue bear, her beloved Blueberry. Several years later she passed Blueberry on to Gale, who also nurtured him.

Alta and Jim fixed up the unheated back bedroom on Sixth and Cowles. Jane finally had a bed of her own. She was not a maternal child, but she had never before owned any toys, and she felt obligated to bring not only Blueberry but all the dollies to bed with her to keep them warm. The single bed was so crowded and the manikins so spiky that she couldn't sleep. By morning dollies were scattered on the floor, and Jane and Blueberry had the bed to themselves. When winter came, the lack of heat in the back bedroom required fortitude and morning speed to dress and dash to the warm kitchen. Life in Talkeetna had also contained cold moments, but it had not held intense pressure to mind the clock regardless of weather. Jane was urged to be "on time" at home, at school, and at ballet lessons (financed by Alta in the hope that dance would cause her niece to become less awkward around the delicate furniture and bric-a-brac that decorated some Fairbanks homes). According to Jane, the ballet lessons represented misguided hope, but with the aid of Blueberry and the family cocker spaniel that slept next to her bed, she succeeded in making other adjustments. In the end she did more than simply adapt to the demands of the clock, the teachers, and her relatives; she prospered. In the integrated Fairbanks Public School with well-trained teachers, she easily learned to read and calculate. She completed two grades in one year and slowly learned to overcome her shyness. Alta fell in love with her. Jim was also drawn to her, but he was critical of her rudimentary table manners and harsh in his rush to train her in social customs. Alta began her career as intermediary between Jim and the girls he raised.

As the school year drew to a close, Alta and Jim began to dread Jane's return to Anchorage. They felt a duty to care for her properly, and for once love and duty coincided. Although Frances seemed willing to have Jane stay in Fairbanks indefinitely, my father did not trust his sister-in-law's changeable moods or marriages. There was something versatile and daring in her personality; it was not hard to imagine Jane suddenly snatched out of Fairbanks and out of their lives. Furthermore, Jim felt that the fact that he was supporting Jane gave him some rights. He wrote to insist on formal adoption. Frances was initially reluctant, but she had no allies. Jane's distant biologic father expressed only transient objections. Even Lillian felt Jane was better off permanently in her elder daughter's home. Frances reminded herself that she could visit Jane at any time and finally consented to sign the papers—but she required Jim and Alta to agree to one condition. Frances smoked, drank alcohol and caffeine, and did not attend church; but she read the Bible and she studied *Science and Health* by Mary Baker Eddy. She considered herself a Christian Scientist. Five denominations had churches in Fairbanks when my family arrived: Roman Catholic, Lutheran, Episcopal, Presbyterian, and Christian Science. Jane was to be raised a Christian Scientist like Frances and not an Episcopalian like Alta. The papers were signed and the agreement was honored. It was an agreement that gained Jane the support of kind and powerful Christian Science women—including Rosamund Weller, a popular teacher and principal, and Mary Earling, the wife of Jim's boss. At the end of a successful first-grade year in Fairbanks, Jane Thompson became Jane Crawford, the newest member of the James Crawford family and the newest member of the Christian Science Church on Front Street.

The following year Frances returned to Talkeetna with Gale. In 1939 she married Talkeetna resident George Weatherell, whose affectionate nickname for his new wife was "Butch." Rough and ready for work or drink, George was better suited as a stepfather for a boy than for a girl. Although his idea of child-rearing included regular use of belt and switch, he was fond of Gale. Frances's son became Gale Weatherell without the folderol of formal adoption papers—to the mild distress of Gale's Idaho father, and many years later to the frank disapproval of the U.S. passport office.

Four years after Jane moved to Fairbanks, my parents took her to Missouri to visit her St. Louis grandparents. When they returned to Seattle on their way home, they picked up Gray Wangelin, Gray Tilly's nephew, born the same month and year as Jane. Young Gray's father was seriously ill, his family was in disarray, and he was being sent to Fairbanks for the next school year. When my parents delivered him to his new home, his antic uncle promptly inverted his nephew's name to Yarg to relieve the confusion of having two Grays in one family. Yarg settled well into Fairbanks. Like his uncle who had intended to simply visit when he came to Alaska on a weeklong cruise seventeen years earlier, Yarg stayed. And like my parents, Lola and Gray were delighted with their expanded family. Even Claire and Jule Loftus, living in distant Juneau, had dealt with their lack of biologic children by adopting a boy and a girl.

The bunks of the Harding Lake cabin were full. Its painted floor was wet from the dripping suits of blue-lipped children who periodically rushed up from the lakeshore to warm themselves by the Yukon stove while they tried to learn to swim in the chilly lake, which froze in September and melted in May. The adults, who had memories of warmer lakes, rarely swam. When they did, Jim excited admiration by diving unhesitatingly into the breathtaking water and popping to the surface, spouting a stream of water like a red-skinned porpoise. By contrast Lola entered inch by inch, the skirt of her wooly swimsuit floating around her like a navy-blue water lily. The adults actually had little free time for swimming. My father built a dock that, with Gray's help, was taken out every fall before the lake froze and replaced every spring. He regularly added shims to the front corner posts of the house to counter its tendency to sag down the hill. He built an eighteen-foot centerboard sailboat, using the same plans that his admired boss, Roy Earling, had used the year before. Then he built a boathouse to winter the canoe, rowboat, and sailboat. The women prepared meals, kept the fire going, hauled water, enforced the no-swimming-for-one-hour-after-eating myth, and sprayed the children with DDT at bedtime to prevent mosquitoes from keeping them awake.

The families were growing and the Depression was lifting. When Jim visited his parents in the winter of 1936, he brought a gift to his mother, Pearle: a braided gold chain from which was suspended a one-inch nugget with a tiny gold miner's spade soldered across its surface. Pearle wore this pendant, surely unique in St. Louis, and enjoyed explaining its origin. Jim's brother Gus had begun working for periods up to a year in South America for an East Coast engineering firm. As a result, Jim's Alaska residence had begun to seem to his mother less distant and quixotic. While Jim was in Missouri on this trip, he bought a new Ford sedan to replace the Model A. In St. Louis a reporter considered this newsworthy both because of the destination of the car—which was to be driven to Seattle and shipped to Fairbanks—and because the purchase was concrete evidence that the economy was improving. The *St. Louis Post-Dispatch* published a captioned photo of the Missouri immigrant to Alaska, poised with one foot on the sedan's running board.

Purchases of new cars by working men were no longer newsworthy in Fairbanks. The *Fairbanks Daily News-Miner*'s enthusiasms were road extensions and new landing fields designed to replace impromptu airstrips on gravel river bars and beaches. These and other improvements were coming to Fairbanks via Roosevelt's anti-Depression agencies.

Alaskans habitually complained about the federal government, particularly the Interior Department's Division of Territories and Island Possessions. But Alaskans' disdain did not extend to smaller agencies such as the Alaska Engineering Commission (which ran the Alaska Railroad), the Civil Aeronautics Authority (which built airstrips), the Signal Corps (which provided telegraph and long-distance radio-telephone service), the Army Corps of Engineers (which built dams), or the Public Works Administration (PWA) and Civilian Conservation Corps (CCC). In Fairbanks PWA money built an addition onto the public school, extended the sewer system, replaced downtown boardwalks with cement, and paved a half-dozen of the main streets. And the "conservation" mission of the CCC was stretched to include widening and lengthening the dirt runway at Weeks Field from 1,200 feet to 5,200 feet.

In response to this runway improvement, Pacific Alaska Airways (PAA) purchased ten-passenger Lockheed Electras for the Fairbanks route. In 1940 these unpressurized planes began daily nonstop, eight-hour flights to Seattle. The Electras were faster, although not cheaper, than the PAA Clippers, which spent twelve and a half hours in the air traveling from Seattle to Juneau (where they stopped overnight) to Whitehorse to Harding Lake. Despite the pricey tickets, the Electras proved popular. Soon the *Fairbanks Daily News-Miner* was able to brag that forty-two passengers, traveling in five airplanes, had reached Seattle in a single day. The pontoon Clippers were retired and stopped landing on Harding Lake.

Another federal contribution to Fairbanks was the Army Corps of Engineers' Moose Creek Butte dike, eight feet high and three miles long. The dike was designed to prevent Tanana River water from entering the Chena River via the Chena Slough. Because the Chena River was narrower and deeper than the Tanana, high water during spring ice jams and fall rainstorms flowed from the Tanana through the slough into the Chena and right through the center of town. A few months after the Corps of Engineer project was finally completed in 1940, a small notice appeared in the newspaper. Readers were urged to get their nets to catch the salmon that were schooled up trying to find an opening in the new dike. That last year of the upper Chena salmon run was a good one for our family and for others who liked fish. The dike was a calamity for the hapless salmon, but it did decrease Fairbanks floods for a quarter century until the disastrous flood of August 1967.

However, in 1938 Fairbanksans were not worried about the impact of the dike project on the seemingly inexhaustible run of salmon from the Bering Sea up the Tanana River. They were busy enjoying their town's progress toward modernity. In May PAA began carrying airmail letters once a week between Fairbanks, Whitehorse, and Juneau. Mail to the Alaskan bush had been carried by air for more than a decade, but letters from Juneau and from outside the Territory had continued to arrive by boat and train. Even though the six-cent airmail stamp was double the normal postage, and the flights were only once a week, Fairbanks celebrated the arrival of the first 418 pounds of airmail with newspaper headlines and a welcoming committee of dignitaries and the high school band. My mother's letters in graceful Palmer penmanship began to be written on thin, almost transparent, stationary and mailed in envelopes preprinted with red-and-blue edging denoting airmail.

The town also cheered for progress in October 1939 when the community's first radio station, KFAR ("Key for Alaska's Riches") began broadcasting locally produced programs—classical and swing music, news, weather forecasts, aviation reports, and hints for homemakers. Established by Austin E. "Cap" Lathrop, Interior Alaska's premier entrepreneur, the station had a modern one-thousand-watt transmitter that could reach well beyond Fairbanks to isolated mines, trappers' cabins, and river villages. One program designed for this audience turned out to have lasting popularity and regional value. Every night at 9:30 Al Bramstedt, the announcer at *Tundra Topics*, would read messages that had been delivered to the station for out-of-town listeners. All over bush Interior, listeners tuned in to find out when the charter pilot would be flying out to deliver a Caterpillar part or what day a mother and newborn were leaving St. Joseph's Hospital to return home. The program created a community among its listeners. Maury Smith, an early KFAR employee, relates an anecdote:

> Nels Jackson, a miner on the Totatlanika, up against the north slope of the Alaska Range, had not been heard from for some thirty days after his leaving Fairbanks. KFAR broadcast a message asking him to place a signal on the ground. A plane, the message read, would fly over the next day. Bush pilot Bill Lavery flew over Jackson's camp and found a large OK stamped in the snow.

On the following night, listeners were glad to hear Al Bramstedt tell Jackson that his "OK" message had been received.

KFAR also brought Fairbanksans closer to the rest of the nation by adding network "transcription programs," like *Grand Ole Opry* and *Quiz Kids*, which arrived by mail on newly pressed 78 records with carefully timed silences in appropriate places for local advertisements. National news transmitted to the station's shortwave radio in Morse code was transcribed to be read on the air, and KFAR became an NBC shortwave affiliate.

Before the new station began broadcasting in 1939, many Fairbanksans owned shortwave radios and tuned them carefully to listen to radio from distant cities—at least, they listened when reception was good and there was little static from "disturbances in the ionosphere" (the term used by the science-minded) or from "the invisible aurora" (used by the more poetic). Although KFAR was popular, my family and others continued to use shortwave sets to listen to sophisticated stations in Seattle, in San Francisco, or from overseas.

With the 1933–34 increase in gold prices, the mood of the FE Company and its parent, USSR&M, also became expansive. In 1938 they ventured beyond placer mining in the Fairbanks area to lease an underground mine where a narrow, rich vein of gold coursed through rock near their placer property northeast of town. By 1940 they had expanded the McCarty Mine by almost a mile of new tunnels and shafts and started milling ore at the site.

The Company also expanded into a new geographic area, taking options on the Chicken property Jim had recommended after his mineral exploration trip to the Fortymile district in 1933. In 1934 Jim advanced to chief of the FE engineering department. In his new position he took charge of prospect drilling, mapping, and developing dredging plans not only for the Fairbanks properties, but for Chicken.

Small claimants had mined at Chicken since 1896, but the paydirt had not been exhausted. Drilling showed good value remained. The biggest impediment to working the ground was the lack of a road into the Fortymile. A Fairbanks dredge would have to be dismantled, trucked down the Richardson Highway, and dragged sixty miles over a Company-constructed winter trail to Chicken. The cost of building a trail of that length and freighting a dredge was prohibitive. The Company decided to solve the equipment problem by purchasing a small steam-driven dredge already in the Fortymile, planning to convert it to electric power.

Then in 1939 Jim was sent to evaluate an even more remote site. He and Andy Johnson (FE drill foreman) met Jim Huntington Sr. at the mouth of the Hogatza River where it entered the Koyukuk River. They traveled up the Hogatza with Huntington and his sons Sidney and Jimmy, first motoring in the Huntingtons' tunnel-hulled boat, then poling when the river became shallow. Jim Huntington Sr., a longtime trapper and canny prospector from this region, had staked valuable claims on several creeks flowing into the river. The ground was free of significant overburden or permafrost, but Huntington had trouble mining because the high water table caused repeated flooding as he approached paydirt. Based on what he saw, Jim wrote a report that convinced the Company to option the property and to begin exploration drilling.

The drill cores from Hogatza proved even richer than those from Chicken, but Hogatza was formidably remote. Chicken had partial road access; Hogatza had none. A dredge would have to be barged northwest from Fairbanks some 750 twisting river miles. Moreover, the dredge could not be a familiar electric-powered Company machine; the site could not be supplied with enough coal to run a power plant. Jim began to research diesel dredges, studying professional journals and books in the evening at home.

With Jim's promotion to chief of the engineering department came a benefit Alta had hoped for—subsidized Company housing on Garden Island close to the main office. The apartment offered was fully furnished, included a detached garage, and was heated with surplus steam from the power plant. Steam radiators often dripped water from their valves and produced spectacular banging noises blamed on "air locks," but steam was clean—no clinkers, no coal dust—and my

Jim Crawford, pilot Bob Lyle, and FE drill foreman Andy Johnson, perhaps headed for Hogatza. *Author's collection.*

mother was delighted. Alta was not discouraged by the fact that the housing offered was the Company minimum—the upper two stories of FE Residence No. 4, the once-grand house built by Fred Noyes when he owned the sawmill. The Company referred to it as the Staff House because it housed two staff families. The main floor, which still contained the original owners' oriental rugs and stained glass, was occupied by the family of the Company steward (expediter), C. E. "Cap" Osborne. The Crawford quarters were less grand and reached by an outside stairway, but they included a heated bedroom for Jane, and Jim would no longer have to stoke a coal furnace.

My parents promptly sold the Sixth and Cowles house and did not buy another home until after Jim retired some thirty years later. However, they officially became half owners of the cabin and lot at Harding Lake when they purchased a share of the title in 1938. The government sale of lots at Harding Lake was attended by a brouhaha that generated eleven articles in the *Fairbanks Daily News-Miner* in a period of nineteen days. The excitement was typical of misunderstandings between Alaskans and the federal government. The federal land office abruptly announced that it would auction off all Harding Lake lots, regardless of improvements—to the highest bidders. Cabin owners who had believed that, for the cost of the survey, they would gain title to land they had

The FE Staff House a decade before the Crawfords moved into the third story. Visible up
Illinois Street are the FE compound houses, where the family lived after World War II.
Courtesy of Nancy Earling Allen.

staked and improved were unpleasantly surprised. The land office cited a 1927
presidential proclamation, which had ordered a survey and an auction. At the
time, the survey had been completed but the auction forgotten. In 1937 George
Parks (previously the Governor of Alaska) was hired by the land office to do a
second cadastral survey, making adjustments for lot lines staked by amateurs.
He identified seventy-three cabins and seventy staked lots without permanent
buildings. This comprised most of the property the land office was putting up
for auction to the general public. In consternation, cabin builders threatened to
go beyond the federal land office and seek title through an act of Congress. The
land office gave in. Improved lots were sold to their squatters for the price of the
survey. Staked lots without improvements were sold to their stakers at assessed
values from $7 to $47. The remaining lots were auctioned. Audrey and Ted Loftus obtained a lot close to my parents' and also built a frame cabin. Dorothy and
Art often joined them at the lake. Six more cousins learned to boat and swim in
cold lake water.

As the economic worries of the Depression waned, new concerns began to
occupy Americans. Newspapers were suddenly full of stories about Germany's
expansion into neighboring countries. World War I (still called the World War)
had ended only two decades earlier. American distrust of Germany had not had
time to fade. Descendents of German immigrants, like my grandfather Frederick Tanner, again began to describe their ancestry as German-Swiss. Alaskans
were concerned about the events in Europe. But they were even more anxious

about an expansionist Axis nation closer to home—Japan had already taken over Manchuria and occupied eastern China.

Although Japan was closer to the Territory than to the States, Alaska was not alone in its prewar jitters about the nation across the Pacific. Military planners understood that in modern warfare, airpower was as important as ground or naval forces. Polar air routes meant that Alaska was close to both Asia and Europe.

In 1939 Alaska's only military post was Chilkoot Barracks in Haines. The post, which housed four hundred men, was accessed by ship, a fifty-two-year-old harbor tug, the *Fornance*. Governor Ernest Gruening described his 1939 inspection trip to the barracks during which the tug was stopped for three days by thirty-knot headwinds and required a coast guard rescue. His summary: "Chilkoot Barracks had about as much relevance to modern warfare as one of those frontier Indian-fighting posts from the days of Custer and Sitting Bull." Congress recognized the gaping hole in its West Coast defenses and appropriated money, not only to arm Pearl Harbor in Hawaii, but to build and garrison a series of military air bases in Alaska. By June 1940, five thousand troops had been transferred to Alaska. The population of Fairbanks was abruptly increased by men in uniform and by civilian contractors building a "cold-weather experimental air station." The purpose of this facility was clarified when, even before it was completed, it was renamed Ladd Field and designated as an army air base. In 1941 the Civil Aeronautics Authority and its contractors built eleven new long rural airstrips—several in bush communities supplied by Fairbanks. Despite the title "Civil" Aeronautics, these airstrips were designed to be used by military as well as civilian pilots. With all the defense construction, it seemed that no one in Fairbanks was unemployed, and housing suddenly was difficult to find.

However, preparing for possible war and finding oneself at war are quite different experiences. Alaskans were as shocked as the rest of the nation when Japan attacked Pearl Harbor on December 7, 1941. Within a few days Germany also declared war on the United States. Suddenly the U.S. government, which had remained neutral even during the blitz of London, was at war on two fronts. In December 1941 the U.S. military had only 22,500 troops, eighteen airplanes, and six ships dispersed in the 590,000-square-mile Territory of Alaska. Fairbanks began to brace for a possible attack by Japan. And Alta, infertile and approaching forty, learned from the doctor that what she thought was early menopause was instead not-so-early pregnancy.

Sally and Jane Crawford, 1942. *Author's collection.*

{6}

WAR, BIRTH, AND EXILE

M Y FAMILY GREETED THE NEWS of my impending birth as if they had longed for an unexpected infant in wartime. Jane, age twelve and rather embarrassed by Alta's condition, nevertheless proclaimed that she couldn't wait to play with the new baby. Jim tried to hide his pride, secretly hoping for a son. His brother and male cousins had fathered only girls; perhaps this child would be the next James in the Crawford line. Alta was frankly delighted to find herself pregnant. Some of her friends who offered their congratulations could not resist adding wry comments about an infant's idea of nightlife, but my inexperienced middle-aged mother brushed aside the commentary. Jim, of course, was not concerned about women's issues such as midnight feedings and diaper changes. He was worried about his continued employment with the FE Company. During the war would the federal government cease to purchase gold, a nonstrategic metal? How safe would Fairbanks be if Japan attacked the West Coast or Alaska? Wives and children of military men in Alaska had been ordered to depart for the States. Some civilian women and children were also packing up and purchasing tickets. But Jim agreed with Alta that she and Jane should stay put; the family would stay together. The baby would be born in Fairbanks.

The town was organizing for possible attack. Women knitted socks and hats for soldiers, practiced first aid at Red Cross classes, and sewed white canvas parkas for civil defense volunteers. The volunteers, organized by the American Legion and the Civil Defense Committee, stood shifts guarding against sabotage at KFAR, Weeks Field, Standard Oil's storage tanks, the coal bunkers near the railroad, the

Federal Building, the Alaska Communications System telegraph office, and the power plants operated by the FE Company and the NC Company.

The Civil Defense Committee appointed air-raid wardens for each part of town, and blackout drills began. Jim was one of the wardens. He had been too young to fight in World War I and was now beyond draft age. When the NC Company's steam siren signaled an air-raid drill, Jim put on his overcoat and went from street to street on Garden Island knocking on the door of any house where a slit of light escaped between the curtains. He even remonstrated with homeowners who stirred their fires, sending telltale sparks shooting out the chimney. He was diligent in the face of brave dogs protecting not-quite-blacked-out households. He made his rounds regardless of temperature and regardless of a fact that everyone knew: when the moon was full, the darkened town silhouetted against the bright snow was unmistakable from the air.

In case of actual attack Jim's duties multiplied: air-raid wardens were to report damage, direct people on the streets to shelter, prevent the formation of crowds, administer first aid, and put out incendiary bombs. These firebombs contained magnesium and could not be extinguished with water. Households were ordered to keep a bucket of sand handy for putting out flames. Jim was also ready to fight. Like most Alaskan men, he owned a hunting rifle and a shotgun. Jane discovered that he also had hidden in the closet a saber in a sheath, perhaps a family heirloom from the Civil War, perhaps part of some decorative Masonic regalia. She was puzzled about what her father was supposed to do with the bucket of sand in the front hall, but she imagined him, as perhaps did he, bravely drawing his sword or aiming his Winchester .30-06 at invaders.

In 1941 pioneer ingenuity, previously directed at circumventing the harsh climate, was redirected at defense. Whenever local planes were not landing or taking off, workers at Weeks Field parked cars in the middle of the runway to stymie alien airmen. When summer came, Fourth of July fireworks were banned because "under cover of the noise of exploding firecrackers, sabotage would be facilitated."

The Fairbanks Civil Defense Committee also issued automotive directives. No one was to drive during a blackout except doctors and emergency workers. Those permitted to drive were to place a half-inch strip of adhesive tape across each headlight, paint the headlights black, and remove the tape. The resulting slit of clear glass provided slight illumination of the road ahead and a faint warning to oncoming vehicles. This may have reduced accidents during a blackout, but it must have increased the risk of night driving when no alert had been called. In the event of actual enemy attack, all drivers were to remove the distributor caps from their cars, incapacitating them for enemy use. (It was unclear how this maneuver fit with the order to stay off the streets during raids.)

Civilians were also advised to assemble survival gear and two weeks' supply of food in case they needed to escape to the hills by car or on foot. The Civil Defense Committee outlined a plan for emergency evacuation of women and children to outlying mining camps, "the only flaw being the probable objection of some women to being evacuated. But if they are docile, the plan calls for removing 100 an hour from the town."

Any plan predicated on Fairbanks women being docile was probably flawed, but the most impractical plan was promulgated not by the Civil Defense Committee but by the Army Signal Corps. The corps brought "a censored number of pigeons" to Ladd Field in December 1941 with the intent of releasing them from an army bomber to carry messages. Apparently no one had questioned why the poorly insulated pigeon was not indigenous to the North. In a fine misunderstanding of the physiology of warm-blooded animals, the pigeons' army handlers reasoned that the "winged troopers should be able to stand the cold better than men, since their body temperature is as high as 107 degrees."

In a more pragmatic vein, Fairbanksans shuffled tasks in response to the war: older men took over quasi-military work, freeing younger men to enlist; women and high school students took up jobs normally done by men who were now occupied elsewhere. Gray Tilly, a forty-six-year-old World War I veteran who had always stated he would re-enlist if war broke out, now did so. While he was absent in this good cause, the University of Alaska revised its policy on married female professors, and Lola returned to work. Lola commented to Alta that finally men and women were being treated equally with regard to hire; now she was looking forward to the day when they would be treated equally with regard to pay. (Lola, who served under the first four presidents of the University of Alaska and retired in 1963, ended her career without seeing that day. Salaries did not approach equality until the university was finally sued under the Equal Pay for Women Act in the mid-1970s.)

But despite the urgent preparations to defend the town, and despite the relentless advance of the Japanese in the South Pacific, the mood in Fairbanks was not predominantly one of anxiety or alarm. A Japanese attack on Alaska would have to be launched from aircraft carriers. Towns on the coast 350 miles away would be struck first; Fairbanks would have warning. In the meantime "cost plus" government contracts at Ladd Field meant that everyone was employed, and wages were cheeringly high. Newsreels and censored news reports were optimistic about the long-term outcome of the war against the Emperor and the Führer. Of course, many people did fear daily for husbands, sons, and brothers fighting in undisclosed locations. Dorothy Loftus fretted about her sister, Florence Thompson, whose husband was in the foreign service. Florence had fled Singapore with her two little boys shortly before the city fell to the Japanese. Four months passed without news while Florence and the children made their way through the beleaguered Dutch East Indies to Australia, where she was reunited with her husband, who had escaped by another route. Florence and the children returned to the United States on a troop ship while Tommy spent the war years in India.

Fairbanksans, worried about relatives in danger and worried about an attack on Alaska, were strongly patriotic, but patriotism did not prevent them from criticizing the military command in Alaska. The military's power to order civilian affairs often rankled. Four days after Pearl Harbor, the War Department declared the Territory of Alaska a war zone. General Simon Bolivar Buckner, head of the Alaska Defense Command, was to act as governor for issues of military importance; Governor Ernest Gruening would continue to govern civilian affairs in the Territory. In wartime almost everything seemed to assume military importance.

One of Buckner's first actions in December 1941 was to order all military dependents and dependents of civilians working on military bases to return to the States. Fairbanksans accepted with equanimity the first half of this order, the portion concerning the evacuation of military dependents. My father's niece, Susan Campbell, was one of these dependents. Susan, daughter of my father's sister Anthony ("Toni"), had inherited grandmother Pearle's beauty. Her parents divorced while she was still in grade school. Susan and her mother, tainted by the scandal of divorce, had lived with our Crawford grandparents in the Webster Groves house. After Susan graduated from high school in 1934, she traveled north to attend the University of Alaska and to live with Jim and Alta. Soon after enrolling she met Tom Campbell, a handsome, pipe-smoking engineering professor and ROTC instructor. He and she were quickly and equally smitten. At the end of her freshman year she dropped her studies to become a faculty wife. Tom's ROTC work teaching military drill and coaching the university's rifle team was part of his army reserve duty; he was subject to General Buckner's orders. No one in the family considered protesting when Susan, eight months pregnant, was evacuated to Seattle. Tom remained in Fairbanks to complete the semester before traveling south for a brief reunion with his wife and new son Tommy (the next in a family line of Tom Campbells) before reporting for active duty in the Pacific.

Fairbanks 1939. FOREGROUND: Garden Island with hospital, Catholic church, and rail station.
ACROSS BRIDGE: Cushman Street with Federal Building (block 3) and Main School (block 8).
DISTANT RIGHT: Weeks Field. WATERFRONT RIGHT: NC Company store and power plant.
Author's collection.

The other half of Buckner's order, however, regarding the evacuation of
dependents of civilian base workers, stirred the ire of Fairbanksans. What about
wives and children who were long-term Alaska residents? Local men working
on base threatened to quit rather than send their wives away. In a January 1942
editorial in his weekly paper, Ernie Jessen pronounced, "Forced evacuation
of people from their homes is a Nazi practice." When it was clarified that the
general's order did not include women who were "habitual residents" of Alaska,
local protests subsided.

A broader issue, one that united all of Alaska in protest, was censorship, which
was imposed in the Territory the day after the attack on Pearl Harbor. Military censors read telegrams before they were sent; business cryptography (such as the code
used by the FE Company) was banned. Ham-radio operators were ordered off the
air and did not return until November 1945. Weather reports—other than current
temperature—were classified information. For the first time airlines declined to

tell callers what time the next mail plane was leaving or whether Uncle Ralph was listed on the manifest for the flight from Seattle this afternoon. Alaskans found these measures annoying but reasonable. It was the actions of the civilian Office of Censorship in Seattle that provoked widely circulated jokes and bitter complaints to Governor Gruening and Anthony J. "Tony" Dimond, the nonvoting territorial delegate to Congress.

Steamship passengers leaving or entering the Territory had to carry military travel permits. In addition, censors searched their baggage for illegal materials describing Alaska's rivers, mountains, or shorelines. One passenger's copy of Robert Service's *The Spell of the Yukon* was reportedly confiscated; the government snoop had recognized in the title a major river. Robert Atwood of the *Anchorage Times* wrote an editorial poking fun at this practice; censors cut it before publication. Mail to and from the States was opened; sometimes it arrived at its destination with portions blacked out. Worse yet, if censors found a letter to a spouse complaining about some action by the Department of the Interior or other agency, they forwarded the letter to the agency in question. Magazines and newspapers mailed to individuals in the Territory had articles snipped out, even though the same magazines were sold unaltered in Seattle and sometimes reached Alaska retail stores intact when shipped as bundled freight. Alaskans sent samples of mutilated mail to Governor Gruening and to Delegate Dimond, pointing out that a letter or newspaper could be sent from New York to Los Angeles without similar interference.

The matter reached the U.S. Senate Judiciary Committee, which held a hearing. J. Edgar Hoover, director of the FBI, asserted that the censorship had benefited the nation but cited only one example in support of his position. He testified that by examining the mail, censors had discovered the arrival in Alaska of a Japanese woman disguised as an Indian (whether the woman was a Japanese American from Alaska or a Japanese national spy was unstated). In contrast, Gruening and Dimond supplied evidence of repeated abuses. The committee was especially disturbed to discover that some of the letters intercepted by censors and sent to other agencies had been letters of complaint mailed to U.S. senators. Censorship of mail and of periodicals between the States and the Territory summarily ended.

Another unsettling military order related to Japanese Americans. Mistrust of newcomers and foreigners was not typical in Fairbanks. The town had been founded by a trader from Ohio because a prospector from Italy had discovered gold nearby. The townsite had never been an Indian village or even a fish camp. The citizens of Fairbanks—whether Athabascans from Interior villages; Eskimos from the coast; miners from Finland, Scandinavia, and the Balkans; or businessmen from Russia, Germany, and the States—had all started as newcomers to the town. Most of the foreign immigrants were quickly assimilated and naturalized. Thus wartime enforcement of the Alien Enemy Act, which allowed detention of German, Italian, and Japanese citizens "considered dangerous to the nation," created little more than concerned rumors in Fairbanks. Whether anyone in Alaska was being detained under this law was unknown; the FBI declined to release an official statement. The *Fairbanks Daily News-Miner* responded to gossip by reprinting an editorial from the *Juneau Empire*:

> Some of the rumors as to the number of aliens already interned in Alaska indicate a healthy imagination on the part of the persons telling the stories.... It is probable that few will be temporarily detained for the duration of the war because they are considered dangerous to the country.... We are not condemning wholesale our alien residents.... Such a move would stamp us on a par with the tyranny of Hitler.

But fair-minded editorials did not sway the federal government. In February 1942, President Roosevelt signed Executive Order 9066 permitting the secretary of war and designated military commanders to prescribe areas from which specific individuals or groups could be expelled. On April 2, 1942, General Buckner decreed that all persons over sixteen years of age, whether U.S. citizens or foreign nationals, who were half or more Japanese by race would be excluded from the Territory of Alaska. The evacuation from Alaska to internment camps in Washington and Idaho was scheduled for April 20. The only exception to this wholesale order was for women married to white men other than enemy aliens. The order specifically did not exempt Japanese American women married to Eskimos, Indians, or Filipinos. Who locally would be evacuated and interned did not require speculation; there were only five Japanese Americans in Fairbanks, all fairly well known. Flora Mikami, a graduate of the University of Alaska who worked at the Cooperative Extension Service, immediately married her boyfriend, Simon Newcomb, a white Canadian graduate student. The wedding was held in the home of a well-known businessman and attended by members of prominent families. The four remaining internees were two couples who had been born and raised in Seattle. The husbands, Frank Migawa and Robert Terao, worked at the Model Café. The previous February they had been cited as a case in point when the Fairbanks

Chamber of Commerce unanimously passed a resolution introduced by Ralph Rivers, the local U.S. Attorney, opposing witch hunts by

> certain persons...of misdirected patriotism and prejudice [who] have agitated for discharging...citizens of alien parentage from their jobs.... Our country needs the skills of all able-bodied and loyal persons—citizens and aliens alike.... The defense of our country will be hurt, not helped, by any persecution....

Three days after the internment order, Migawa and Terao were quoted on the front page of the *Fairbanks Daily News-Miner* under the title "Regret to Leave." The article noted their loyalty to the land of their birth, their patriotism in obeying the army order, and their sorrow at leaving Fairbanks. Many Fairbanksans were uneasy about evacuation, but no one staged a public protest. Governor Gruening, who privately disapproved of internment, visited the Puyallup, Washington, camp ten days after the Alaskan contingent arrived. Territorial newspapers reported that the governor was satisfied that internees were being treated well. In December 1942 the *Fairbanks Daily News-Miner* printed a photo and an article about Michael Hagiwara, a University of Alaska scholarship student from Ketchikan. Michael had been a business major and basketball star until he was interned at Camp Minidoka, Idaho. The article consisted largely of a reassuring letter from Michael to his university friends. Then during 1943 and 1944 the evacuation and internments seemed to be forgotten. There were no further articles in the *Daily News-Miner* until 1945, when return of individual evacuees generated brief mentions. Perhaps protests would have been louder had there been more Japanese Americans in Fairbanks. Some townspeople, like Dorothy Loftus, an outspoken Democratic candidate for territorial legislature in 1940, probably did later regret not making a fuss. Dorothy's future beloved daughter-in-law, Mitzi Asai, spent the war years in California and Wyoming camps.

The executive power of government to exclude people from the Territory also affected certain white American men described by the *Fairbanks Daily News-Miner* as "drunkards, ex-convicts...undesirables...parasites of the community." The federal War Manpower Commission and the Fairbanks Police Department combined forces to identify these unwelcome binge drinkers without roots in Alaska. They offered about a hundred men in 1943 and another twenty-five in 1944 a choice between working somewhere in Alaska where no alcohol was available or being "evacuated" at their own expense to Seattle. A spokesman explained that the War Manpower Commission had received "complaints from contracting companies that construction men were working for a few weeks then disappearing when they had enough money to go on an extended drunk. Their vacancies were irreplaceable during the current manpower shortage and defense projects suffered." Moreover, the spokesman complained, "they took up precious housing space." The newspaper reported that "so far the evacuees have taken their orders to clear out without objection."

In more trivial ways the war also upset the lives of upstanding residents. Despite the partial exodus of women from Fairbanks, the city population was increasing steadily. Construction workers and soldiers seemed to arrive daily. Demand for necessities sometimes outstripped supply. One fall month Murray Smith's Ice Service, and consequently the entire town, ran out of ice for iceboxes and drinks. In January 1942 there was a gasoline shortage. For a couple of weeks taxicabs disappeared from the streets, and grocery stores limited home deliveries to three days a week. Property crime increased; some residents began to lock their doors. Respectable families forbade their high school daughters to date worldly eighteen-year-old soldiers.

A crisis flared at Weeks Field. The Civil Aeronautics Authority threatened to close the airport unless new security regulations were implemented. Owners of commercial air services rushed to the city council to complain. Spokesman Frank Pollack's plea is reminiscent of Alaskan protests during our current century:

> Unless we put into effect by Monday regulations that require a staff of airport managers, police officers and guards totaling about 15 persons at a cost of many thousand dollars, all commercial planes will be closed down.... The regulations require clearance officers to check all passengers at both ends. This is impossible in Alaska where planes stop at remote spots to pick up individuals. We feel the CAA is trying to...apply here with no deviation, rules [written for] the States. Here people are dependent upon planes for food and transportation.

The council sent a telegram of protest, and the airport stayed open.

The conflict over hunting took longer to resolve. Almost from the beginning of the war, local subsistence hunters had worried about competition from young men with military rifles hunting for trophies. The residents' concern was only partially allayed by the fact that the Territory did not consider soldiers posted in Alaska to be permanent residents and refused to issue them $1 resident hunting licenses, instead charging $50 for nonresident licenses. For a soldier making GI wages, the $50 fee (the equivalent of about $540 today) presented a significant barrier. But in spite of the price of nonresident licenses, the number of hunters increased, doubling in the first year of the war. In 1942 the Alaska Game Commission responded by closing the season on mountain sheep and decreasing bag limits and season lengths for other species. Tension between military and civilians over hunting continued to build. In 1943, when there were 144,000 military and only 81,000 civilians in the Territory, General Buckner announced that he had convinced the Alaska Game Commission to open hunting in Mount McKinley Park for military personnel. The park had been given over to the army as a rest and recreation site to be administered by Buckner as army commander. To the relief of civilians, a federal judge ruled that neither the army, claiming wartime emergency, nor the Alaska Game Commission had the power to institute this type of recreation in a national park.

In Fairbanks, as the war progressed, both the number of men in uniform and the variety of uniforms increased. Hundreds of Russian military pilots and support personnel rotated through Ladd Field picking up Lend-Lease airplanes flown by American pilots from Great Falls, Montana, to Fairbanks. The program to transfer fighters, bombers, and transport planes was a response to Stalin's request for aid after Germany attacked Russia in the summer of 1941. The United States declined to enter the war on the side of Britain and the Soviet Union, but it did offer war matériel. By the time the program was under way and the first planes were delivered in September 1942, the United States and the Soviet Union were allies in the war against Germany. At Ladd Field Russian mechanics carefully inspected each airplane before accepting it. Then after a few days of training, Russian pilots flew the planes to Nome, Siberia, and hence to their western front. Almost eight thousand planes and their crews passed through Fairbanks. Russian airmen, some on welcome leave from combat, found time to shop downtown for consumer goods—shoes, cosmetics, jewelry, and watches—which were even scarcer in the Soviet Union than in wartime Fairbanks. Enterprising local merchants signed up for Russian-language classes at the university.

In 1942 work began on the Alcan (the Alaska-Canada Military Highway) to provide a land route between Alaska, Canada, and the States. Such a road had been proposed and the route selected by an International Highway Commission in 1938. At the time the Japanese government asked the British government to intervene, protesting strongly that it considered construction of a highway to Alaska "inimical to Japanese interests." The 1,500-mile gravel road wound through mountains, bridged rivers, and crossed bogs of mud on a roadbed of rock fill. Despite the challenges of constructing this all-weather highway, U.S.

Army troops, inspired by the fervor of war, completed the initial haul road, passable when frozen, in just nine months.

In March of that same year (1942) and after a gestation of similar length, I was delivered at St. Joseph's Hospital in Fairbanks by a mother who later marveled at her naïveté. The nun who was Alta's nurse had to inform her, with some exasperation, that it was necessary to push to deliver a baby. Mother followed this advice, and I was born soon thereafter. It was ten years to the day after Alta's cousin Audrey Loftus had delivered her first child at St. Joseph's. (Later I perceived this coincidence as a special bond to my cheerful, teasing cousin Nancy, whom I greatly admired.) When Alta was wheeled out of the delivery room to greet Jim, Jane, and Lillian (who had come from Talkeetna to care for Jane), my mother's celebratory announcement was a typical understatement: "I didn't enjoy that one bit."

Because I was a girl, the chosen name—James Frederick, after the grandfathers—was discarded in favor of Sarah Anthony. This combination of my maternal great-grandmother's first name and my paternal grandmother's maiden name accommodated my mother's distaste for "Pearle" and my father's for "Lillian." But in the 1940s Sarah was an old-fashioned, rarely used name. As soon as the birth certificate was signed, my parents gave me a modern nickname, "Sally," by which everyone—including the school district and the doctor's office—knew me.

Alta intended to nurse, but when her milk had not come in by the second day, her doctor explained that "white women north of the sixtieth parallel are unable to nurse." Alta accepted his dictum, and the nuns worked diligently to train me and other unruly babies to take bottles of canned milk and Karo Syrup on schedule every four hours. My mother remained in bed in her hospital room, receiving visitors and playing with her baby, for the requisite ten days believed necessary to prevent prolapse of a new mother's pelvic organs. She returned to the apartment in the FE Staff House weak from lying in bed but in good humor.

The family had eleven weeks to adjust to being four persons instead of three before the Japanese attacked Dutch Harbor in the Aleutians. The U.S. military force in Alaska was still small—about twenty-five ships and a hundred airplanes. The Japanese easily established strongholds on Attu and Kiska islands. The fears of Alaskans had been realized. Anxiety and battle rumors spread, exacerbated by the military rules that restricted communication and censored the press. In Fairbanks, more than a thousand miles from the Aleutians, the Alaska Command felt it necessary to publish a notice in the *Fairbanks Daily News-Miner* that "persons who spread rumors, disregard censorship regulations, or in any way hamper the defense of this area will be excluded from the Territory of Alaska." War jitters led to the bombing of a whale believed to be a submarine near Sitka. The United Press reporter who released this story without consent of the censors was deported from the Territory.

The battle for the Aleutians continued for another year, until the Japanese left their final battle stations on Kiska Island under cover of fog, signaling that the attack on Alaska had been a feint designed to distract the Americans from more serious Japanese operations in the South Pacific. Among the noncombatant victims of the Aleutian War were some eight hundred Aleuts, who were evacuated by the U.S. military from the islands and transferred to deplorable "duration camps" in abandoned mines and canneries in Southeast Alaska. Although the Japanese left the Aleutians in 1943, the Aleuts remained paternalistically interned in crowded, unsanitary camps until 1945. One-tenth of these American civilians, mainly children and elders, succumbed to diseases associated with crowding and malnutrition. The death rate of interned Aleuts exceeded the 7 percent death rate of Americans serving overseas during World War II.

On October 8, 1942, with the Aleutians still occupied, the War Production Board issued the executive order that the FE Company had been dreading: L-208 closed all but the smallest "mom-and-pop gold mines of Alaska and the nation. The last date of legal mining was October 15. Companies were given an additional two months to shut down to minimum maintenance level. The goal of the closure was to deflect miners and equipment into the production of strategic metals such as copper, tungsten, and antimony. In Fairbanks, the army promptly rented bulldozers, a dragline, and other heavy equipment from the FE Company. The military also bought dynamite, lumber, and electric wire from Company supplies and rented or bought several buildings. Russian flyers were housed in the FE Staff House as soon as the Crawfords and Osbornes moved out. Jim joked that dredge shutdown was added to his portfolio before dredge start-up was.

Jim was permanently grateful to the Company that he and fifteen other Fairbanks employees were transferred to USSR&M mines in the States. Jim became assistant geologist at the copper, lead, and zinc mines headquartered in Salt Lake City. The salaries of the transferred employees and the cost of moving their families were paid by the FE Company. The Fairbanks subsidiary wanted assurance that a professional workforce would be available to return to Fairbanks as soon as L-208 was revoked. Ted Loftus declined a USSR&M transfer. During the winter of 1942–43 he worked on the Alcan, daily testing the ice of the Johnson and Robertson rivers and marking routes across them with willow wands so that truck convoys could safely cross while permanent bridges were being constructed. For the remaining war years he managed Livengood Placers, located about eighty road miles north of Fairbanks. This mining company maintained a dredge, ditches, and a partly completed 1,600-foot dam on Hess Creek, although it could not mine gold during the war. During the summers Ted and his family lived at Livengood; during the winters they rented a house in town from Art and Dorothy Loftus, who also stayed in Fairbanks through the war years.

South of Fairbanks in Talkeetna, my Aunt Frances and her husband, George Weatherell, stopped hauling freight when L-208 idled the Cache Creek gold mines. They took young Gale and spent the years between 1943 and 1945 gypsying to Oregon, New York, Florida, and back. Van and Grandmother Lillian left the Territory and retired to an Oregon orchard. Jule Loftus, supervisor of the University of Alaska's experimental fox farm in Petersburg, moved his family to Oregon in 1941 for reasons that had nothing to do with L-208. When the Petersburg Fox Farm was established in 1938, fur prices had recovered from the Depression. There were 273 fox, mink, marten, and other fur farms in Alaska competing with trappers. But with the onset of war, the fur market crashed. Ships could no longer carry exports to Europe, and fashions in the United States changed. No-nonsense, broad-shouldered wool greatcoats were in; mink was out. Even Eleanor Roosevelt took to wearing a fabric coat. By 1947, there were only sixty-two fur farms left in Alaska. Jule Loftus stayed in Oregon after the war, devoting the rest of his veterinary career to conventional farm animals.

In order to travel to Salt Lake City in 1943, my parents needed military exit permits with their photos and fingerprints. Alta's paperwork was complicated because she had no certificate of her birth in the Montana ranch house with only an aunt, now deceased, in attendance. Her father had ridden to town in a snowstorm to fetch the doctor, but on the way back to the ranch the doctor's carriage got stuck in a drift. By the time the weather cleared, his assistance was no longer needed. Despite a shortage of witnesses to her birth, Alta finally obtained a Certificate of Delayed Birth Registration from the State of Montana on January 15, 1943. This precious document was based on a baptismal certificate, a 1925 life insurance policy, an affidavit from her mother, and a letter from the vice president of the First National Bank of Hinsdale. Our family was finally free to leave the Territory.

We traveled south in April, not by steamship but by airplane. It was a two-day journey with an overnight in Whitehorse, a town so crowded that to Jim's indignation he had to bribe a war-profiteering hotel clerk to retain our reserved room. By May, three Fairbanks Exploration expatriate families—the Boswells with three children, the Crawfords with two, and the Ashurkoffs with one—had settled into rented houses in the capital of Utah. The transplanted children of these families discovered a new world in which there were fireflies, sidewalks for roller-skating, and summer nights that were dark and hot simultaneously.

Salt Lake City was on wartime footing. Food and gasoline were rationed. In Alaska, food rationing had never been imposed, although citizens had been encouraged to conserve the same way they had during World War I, by observing "meat-free Wednesdays." The government's request that Alaskans omit animal meat from their meals on Wednesdays was probably heeded less than similar Friday restrictions imposed on Catholics by the Pope. During the war, meat in Alaskan butcher shops was already painfully expensive due to a 47 percent increase in freight charges, an increase blamed by steamship companies on the cost of insuring ships traveling in a war zone. The voluntary closure of butcher shops on Wednesdays was irrelevant for the many Alaskans who couldn't afford beef any day of the week and who subsisted on game. In a patriotic response to the wartime meat crisis, the FE Company in Fairbanks had even made a special offer to hunters: free space in the Goldstream cold-storage plant for skinned moose, caribou, and sheep from the beginning of the fall hunting season until freeze-up, when hunters could hang the meat outside their homes.

At the grocery stores in Salt Lake, Alta had to present ration books not only for meat but for other commodities. She also had to settle for wartime food substitutes. Instead of coffee she purchased Postum; instead of butter she bought white margarine, which came with a color packet that had to be massaged into this butter substitute to create an appetizing shade of yellow. Mother planted a victory garden as her patriotic contribution to the national food supply; it also provided us with affordable fresh vegetables.

During the war, manufacture of new cars was banned, and used cars were not shipped to Alaska because of freight costs. My parents had had no difficulty selling the 1936 Ford sedan before leaving Fairbanks. In Utah they switched their automotive allegiance and purchased our first Studebaker, a 1941 pea-soup-green model. They drove this sleek, low-slung vehicle sparingly because of gas rationing. My father had a generous C-ration gasoline card for a Ford assigned to him by USSR&M, but he was too upright to bring the card (much less the Company car) home, so we were limited to short excursions in the Studebaker, fueled by our three-gallon-a-week A-ration family card.

My sister's life was changed by Utah's war preparedness. The Salt Lake school system eliminated eighth grade in order to save money and allow earlier graduation for young men headed for the armed forces. As a consequence, Jane jumped a year ahead of her classmates in Fairbanks. The high school she attended was experimental, set up on campus by the University of Utah's education department to test new teaching methods. To her surprise, she got credit for a rock collection she had assembled while accompanying Jim on his Saturday geology work. And to her delight, she was allotted one period each day to study a subject of her choice. Jane, whose family had never comprehended or responded to her desire for art lessons, spent all of her elective time in the art room.

Alta, Jim, and Jane adjusted to Utah's school schedule, summer heat, and ration books; but they were by now thorough Alaskans, sojourners in wartime exile. Jim was just biding his time until he could return to the FE Company; he no longer sought a permanent job in the States. We felt separate from our Salt Lake neighbors, both because of our northern roots and because we were not Mormon. Jane intermittently traveled to the Christian Science Church, a bus and trolley ride away. My parents temporarily defected from the Episcopal Church to the Unitarians. (My father felt that this denomination, which had no branch in Fairbanks, was sympathetic to his skepticism about certain miracles and the virgin birth; in the Episcopal Church he always recited the Nicene Creed with critical little gaps of silence.) Although some of my mother's distant cousins were Mormon, no one in the immediate family was attracted to the Latter Day revelations treasured by our Salt Lake neighbors. Jane recalls the family's shock and indignation when the elderly gentleman across the street was identified in the newspaper as a religious bigamist.

In 1945 Jim's niece Susan Campbell and her son Tommy joined us in the Salt Lake house. Soon after young Tommy's birth in Seattle, Tom Campbell had left Buckner's command and the University of Alaska for army intelligence in the Pacific. He remained there for the duration of the war, eventually returning to teach in the engineering department at the University of Washington. Young Tommy, also destined to become an engineer, was congenitally eager to investigate mechanical devices. In Salt Lake, rendered incautious by curiosity, he caught his hand in the crank wringer of the washing machine. He was freed, howling and intact, but was cited by Alta for many years thereafter whenever she gave me safety lectures.

Every night the Campbells and Crawfords gathered in the living room in front of the tall wood-and-fabric case of our RCA radio to listen to the evening news. We felt united by patriotism to the announcer and the rest of the nation. When the momentous announcement of victory in Europe came, we children were thrilled. The adults were more somber, aware that the war Tommy's father was fighting in the Pacific was not yet over, despite recent victories against Japan.

However, the end of the European war did mark the end of our Salt Lake City exile. The restrictions of L-208 were eased in the spring of 1945, and then revoked completely at the end of June, well before the atomic bomb was dropped on Hiroshima. My father flew nonstop from Seattle to Fairbanks in March. My mother, my sister, and I followed in June. Our family had left our steamship and train days behind. Alaska transportation was changing quickly. Commercial airplane flights were becoming faster and safer, and within a few years the Alcan Highway would be opened to the public. The Studebaker, built for paved roads and warm weather, was shipped north filled with bedding and kitchen utensils. We returned to Fairbanks cheerfully with this rather unsuitable car, and moved into a furnished single-family Company house. My father had been promoted to a new and challenging FE Company job.

POSTWAR ON
GARDEN ISLAND

Dredge No. 2 at Goldstream, digging toward left side of photo. The rafts in the pond support power cables. *Author's collection.*

{7}

DREDGE SUPERINTENDENT

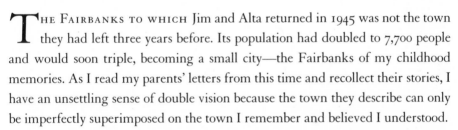

THE FAIRBANKS TO WHICH Jim and Alta returned in 1945 was not the town they had left three years before. Its population had doubled to 7,700 people and would soon triple, becoming a small city—the Fairbanks of my childhood memories. As I read my parents' letters from this time and recollect their stories, I have an unsettling sense of double vision because the town they describe can only be imperfectly superimposed on the town I remember and believed I understood.

For example, there is my father's work. The position to which Jim Crawford returned was dredge superintendent. It was a challenging job that made an intense and ambitious man excited and irritable. In the mornings, just before the eight o'clock whistle, he would stride off to the corniced office building where he worked at his desk or picked up a Company car for a trip to the dredges. He usually returned home at noon for lunch and again in the evening, not with the five o'clock whistle, but with the six o'clock whistle. At noon he would still be agreeable, but by dinner his arrival was often marked by a slammed door and mutters about the day's outrage. Sometimes he overstayed the last whistle to finish a task; then he was grumpy about the overcooked or cooling potatoes. Alta, who had a mind for diplomacy, observed that sending a child to walk him home from the office both distracted and calmed him. Moreover, it guaranteed that he would arrive on time and that she could cook in childfree peace. As soon as I was old enough to safely cross busy Illinois Street, I was regularly dispatched on this mission. Consequently, in contrast to some of my friends who did not know where their fathers disappeared to during the working day, I knew where my father went, and I believed that I understood his work.

On workdays my father would dress in a tan shirt, brown wool tie, and the Filson whipcord jacket and pants preferred by most of the FE Company engineers. (Wits from the States called the greenish-brown Filson suits "Alaskan tuxedos.") I would watch him check his notebook inside the brass-snapped breast pocket and make sure that his pencils and fountain pen were secure in their special sewn cylinders. In winter he would add galoshes, a sheepskin coat, wool gloves, and a beaver-fur hat for the three-minute walk.

In the evening when sent to fetch my father, I would follow his route down the boardwalk of our house, across the graveled street to the concrete sidewalk that led to the wide imitation-granite steps of the office. Inside, most of the workers had already left, and the dark composition-tile floors creaked impressively to even my light step. In those days, which predated handicapped access, the building's two floors were connected by a wide staircase with a handsome railing and newel posts made at the FE sawmill on the bank of Noyes Slough. Both the stairwell and the roomy offices had screened windows that could be opened during the warm days of summer. But for most of the year the steam-heated building had little ventilation. It retained a distinctive odor compounded from damp wool, boot leather, cigar smoke, "snoose" accumulating in the brass cuspidors, and a Pleistocene essence emanating from glass cases of local minerals and extinct animal bones. It was a male realm in which two or three female office workers (headed by tiny, formidably efficient Hertha Baker, secretary to a series of general managers) were treated with careful courtesy.

When I reached my father's corner office, I might find him standing, balding head bent, inspecting large blueprints or elevation surveys unrolled on the broad surface of his oak desk. The elevation drawings showed the depth of various layers of frozen earth comprising the "overburden" between the surface and the rich prehistoric river bottoms. These representations of the three-dimensional world usually put my father in a good mood, and he would stand me on his wheeled desk chair and point out what interested him. I would gaze inattentively, thrilled with my queenly position, wishing someone of consequence, the third-grade bully perhaps, would walk through the door and see me. My lack of aptitude for interpreting drawings did not disappoint my father; he did not expect spatial talent in a girl. I know of only one professional woman hired by the FE Company in a permanent position—Genevieve Parker. Born into a family that mined on Fairbanks Creek, Genevieve was handsome, intelligent, and a winning dog

Removing ice from dredge pond in March. *Author's collection.*

musher. In 1929 she became the first woman to graduate from the Alaska Agricultural College and School of Mines in mining engineering, making her one of the first ten women to receive mining engineering degrees in the nation. She was hired by the FE Company in Fairbanks, but after a short tenure she transferred to the Boston office where, four years later, she confirmed Jim Crawford's notion of the proper role of women by marrying John Metcalfe, a second-generation USSR&M engineer-manager destined for the Company's high echelons.

If my father was not looking at drawings when I arrived to fetch him, he was probably seated, leaning intently forward and frowning at columns of numbers. These made him curt and crabby. Although Jim never chewed tobacco and had long ago given up cigarettes, on a few occasions I caught him taking thoughtful solace in a pipe. On these evenings I felt like the child at the tavern in the melodramatic ditty sung by my mother: "Father, dear father, come home with me now, the bell in the tower strikes ten" (or in my case, "the blast of the whistle marks six").

What I believed about my father's work in the office was this: blueprints fascinated him, mistakes galled him, and financial sheets made him snappish. I also thought I understood his work on the Creeks. Both the responsibility of his position and Jim's own inclinations drew him to the dredge ponds on Saturday mornings during the mining season. The season began in March when five-thousand-pound blocks of ice were cut with steam, hoisted out of the dredge ponds, and sent crashing onto shore. This dramatic industrial sign of spring often drew spectators. Had Murray Smith, the ice man, been alive and present, he would have envied the technology. Dredging continued until late October, when the ponds refroze. During the summer, as a Saturday-morning treat, my father would take me with him to the Creeks in his black Company Ford.

When Jim dressed for the Creeks, he still wore a tie with his Filson suit, but he replaced his oxfords with shoepacs, lacing the leather uppers shin-high over his pant legs. In the summer, the dredges ran twenty-four hours a day, seven days a week, except for two-hour closures twice a month to clean the gold-mercury amalgam from the riffles. The Company used these two-hour shutdowns to do hurried maintenance and minor repairs. Occasionally, of course, something major would fail and bring the digging to an abrupt halt. Regardless of time—day or night—whenever my father received the call that a dredge had broken down, he and the master electrician or the master mechanic drove to the site to begin immediate repairs. During an average mining season the FE Company dredges were shut down only 10 percent of the time.

On the Saturday mornings when I got to ride along, the two of us would jounce north or west over gravel roads to Cripple Creek, Goldstream, Pedro, Cleary, Ester, Little Eldorado, or Fish Creek to inspect one or two dredges and their week's progress. My father, in good humor, would sing a snatch of "Going up Cripple Creek/Going at a run/Going up Cripple Creek/Gonna have some fun," substituting the name of the creek that was our destination. Had I been a son, rather than a daughter, these rides would likely have been more pressured, full of quizzes on geology or instruction in mechanics. It was probably fortunate for both of us that we sang silly songs instead.

As we drove down a temporary dirt road toward a dredge pond, we could hear the boat's machinery banging and groaning before its great gray sides appeared through the windshield. Waste tailings clattered from the stacker at the back. Cables tethering the boat to shore squealed as the winchman took them up or played them out, shifting the hull and its huge digging ladder—around which the endless chain of buckets revolved—into a new position. The empty buckets swung down the bucketline, splashed as they hit the water, and clanked as they bit into the thawed gravel before rising, full and dripping, to be dumped into the sorting equipment on the upper deck of the dredge. My father and I would walk to the edge of the muddy pond, a deckhand would lower the gangplank, and we would climb aboard into the racket.

I had strict instructions to stay close to my father, well away from the cranking exposed machinery, which was tended through each shift by two oilers. We would stop on the lower deck to watch the panner take a scoop of gravel and sand from the bucketline and pan for gold in a tub of water set on deck. His samples showed whether the buckets were reaching paydirt. Then I would follow my father and the dredgemaster up a series of steep narrow stairs to the control room, where the winch operator stood in front of floor-to-ceiling windows intently watching the bank of the pond in front of him as he cut it away. A dredge pond is a traveling body of water; it creeps slowly along a valley bottom as dumped tailings fill in the pond behind and the bucketline claws away rich ground in front. The winch operator controlled the boat's movements and the ladder's digging depth by adjusting ten to fifteen upright winch handles, setting and resetting them like stops on an organ. As the dredge swung slowly back and forth, chewing away the front bank, it pivoted on its central digging spud, a pointed steel column that pinned the dredge to the bottom of the pond. As soon as the front bank was cleared away as far as the dredge could reach, the winchman would briefly raise the buckets clear of the bank and swivel the boat forward using a second spud, the stepping spud, to gain a new anchorage for the digging spud. A skilled winchman left only a few buckets empty when he "stepped" the dredge forward. Efficient winching was an art, and skilled winchmen were highly valued by the Company. While my father and the dredgemaster conferred, I would gaze down from the five-story height at the omnivorous buckets and the bead of narrow rafts stretching from shore to bear the electric cables that powered the dredge.

The men would push back their fedoras and discuss the drilling samples being taken a few hundred yards ahead of the dredge, voices loud in competition with the machinery. My short, energetic father spoke and moved quickly. He admired and trusted men who knew their trades—engineers, miners, electricians, mechanics, pattern and die makers, blacksmiths, dredgemasters, and carpenters—but he was not a hail-fellow-well-met. His relations with the men on the dredges were purposeful and respectful. I never saw his temper explode on these trips the way it did at home, although I suspected work explosions were not unknown. Certainly no one slapped him jovially on the back; he was "Mr. Crawford" to most and "Jim" to only a few. He also had a less complimentary sobriquet, as my sister learned from overhearing a parental argument. Alta did not utter the nickname but cited it sharply to show that his behavior was open to caricature. Marital loyalty, however, was strong in both my parents; my mother would never tell my sister what this hinted-at name was. (We did learn that some workers called my father's boss "Little Napoleon." It was a half-admiring nickname based on Roy Earling's height and leadership style.) In any case, men on the dredge deferred to Jim and treated me kindly—perhaps because I was a boss's daughter or perhaps because having a child on the dredge was a welcome diversion.

There was one dredge that my father refused to take me on. Dredge No. 10, with its 167-foot hull, was the largest in the Company fleet. When my father went aboard her, he would leave me on the shore to catch grasshoppers or to stamp dried puffballs into clouds of brown spores. Dredges are ships, and dredgemen are prone to watery superstitions: no women or girls were allowed to board this huge dredge lest ill luck come to it. The mystique of No. 10 was enhanced by the parade of famous male visitors who boarded her—including General Dwight Eisenhower, not yet president but everyone's hero in 1947. Several years later, when Ralph Strom, a dredgemaster with a skeptical mind, invited me and my friend Judie Tweiten aboard Dredge No. 10, I was a little disappointed to find it no different from other dredges except for its size and some extra separating equipment (vibrating jigs) in front of the riffles. When our fathers heard about our escapade, Jim Crawford was outraged, and Oscar Tweiten was amused both at our adventure and at my father's anger. Confident in my teenage reliance on a scientific view of the world, I shrugged the episode off. The following April at Fairbanks Creek, a deckhand on Dredge No. 2 tried to clear an ice jam in the rock chute near the boat's stern by using a stick of dynamite instead of a pike pole. The blast blew a twelve-inch hole in her hull, and the dredge sank to the bottom in less than an hour. Suddenly I understood the vulnerability of boats and felt a shiver of guilt at having trespassed on a superstition designed to keep one afloat. The early evening news of this disaster reached Jim at home. It was the only time he ever swore in my presence. The accident caused substantial mining loss. Although no one was injured and insurance paid for patching the hull and refloating the boat, the dredge missed twenty cleanups that year.

But as I learned later from my father's diaries and records, it was not the occasional dredge disaster or the columns of numbers that made him tense and curt in those years, it was employment. In the spring of 1945 Jim's assignment was to get the FE Company's eight Fairbanks dredges running again. From an engineering point of view restarting the great machines was not difficult. During the war, a skeleton FE staff, under the direction of Robert "Bert" Ogburn, had kept the power plant running and had performed regular maintenance on dredges and other equipment. The Company had both a moderate inventory of parts on hand and extensive shops for making and repairing machinery. The problem Jim faced was that the Company's workforce had disappeared. Skilled miners and seasonal laborers alike had scattered into military service and high-paid civilian contract work. The crowded Fairbanks to which Jim returned was filled with strangers—men without mining experience or skills, men who had come north to make big money in construction, not modest wages in mining.

At first Jim rationalized that men were just beginning to be demobilized and that restrictions had just been lifted on travel to Alaska. He hoped that war spending would soon end, and the old employees would trickle back. But by the end of 1945, the victors on the east and west shores of the Bering Strait were already turning to face each other in a cold war founded in atomic fear. Defense appropriations continued to flow to the Territory after the armistice. In Fairbanks a second military post was built—Eielson Air Force Base, with a 14,500-foot runway. And Eielson was only the beginning of a construction boom that included new roads, radar installations, communication sites, airfields, and schools. In town a burst of apartment buildings, offices, and stores appeared with each postwar construction season. Jim soon realized that assembling crews to run the dredges would continue to be his number-one problem.

Before the war each dredge had a crew of fourteen men—a dredgemaster (who functioned as captain) and three shifts of deckhands, oilers, and winchmen. Dredgemasters and winchmen were skilled employees whose jobs could not be mastered in a few days or a few weeks. My father asked the Company's employment department not only to advertise for dredgemasters and winchmen, but to personally contact each man who had held one of these positions before the war. Management was offering an across-the-board wage increase of 15 percent. Jim hoped it would be sufficient inducement to bring skilled workers back.

The Company also began aggressive recruiting for unskilled workers who could be trained as oilers and deckhands. Oilers simply followed a set maintenance routine and alerted the dredgemaster to any trouble. The work of deckhands was more varied: they raised and lowered the gangplank, did tasks on shore, and acted as general handymen. One deckhand task did require special skill—panning. The designated panner scooped earth from rising buckets, panned it for gold, and carefully recorded the results so that the dredgemaster would know whether the winchman was reaching paydirt and how rich that paydirt was. Panning requires talent and experience. Jim noted that the best panners were old-timers who were not apt at pencil pushing, while the new trainees were better at record keeping than at panning. One of his postwar frustrations was that his panners could sift out gold or produce meticulous records, but not both.

In 1945 and subsequent years the Company set up temporary hiring offices in Seattle and Portland. In Seattle, Company agents tracked down regular seasonal employees who had spent the winter in cheap hotels and watering holes to offer them good pay in dry camps. Some employees even grew to expect the Company to come find them when it was time to return to work. On the East Coast agents recruited university students, particularly those attending school near the Company's main office in Boston. Students were not the most desirable workers—some showed poor aptitude for manual labor and all exited in a body when school began in September before the mining season was over—but the Company needed every willing worker. In Alaska hiring agents traveled to Indian and Eskimo villages, recruiting strong young men who would stick out a summer of paid labor. Native subsistence priorities were troublesome mysteries in the business of mining. The question "How could a good worker, making good money, quit abruptly to go to fish camp?" remained unanswerable to my wage-oriented father.

But it was not Eskimos going to fish camp or college boys returning to school that made it impossible for the new dredge superintendent to get more than two dredges running in 1945 and more than four running in 1946. Even after the Company decreased its workforce by installing mechanical point-driving machines and trimming the dredge crews, the increased pay offered to its remaining workers did not attract enough skilled men. The Company, which had thrived on $35 per troy ounce of gold during the Depression, was now trapped by this fixed price. Jim's mining journals optimistically forecast that the government would soon raise the price to $41. The Depression was over; the war was won. Without the drain of military spending the economy should boom. These enthusiasts were correct about the economy but wrong about the price of gold; it remained pegged at $35 an ounce for another two decades.

The FE Company's postwar reputation and weak position in the local economy is summarized in an anecdote by geologist Charles "Riz" Bigelow, who arrived in Fairbanks in 1952 as a young man with no skills and in need of an immediate job. He asked a bartender for advice. The barman directed him to the FE Company; he was sure to get work there "since they paid bottom dollar."

Considering the situation, Jim was pleased to get the dredges at Cripple Creek and Fox running in 1945. Restarting the Cripple Creek dredge near Ester was especially pressing because the Company had invested heavily in preparing the ground just before the war. Drilling had shown that the claims on Cripple Creek were exceptionally rich. Getting to this paydirt, however, was exceptionally challenging. Even after the frozen muck was stripped off by hydraulic giants, there still remained sixty feet of barren gravel overlying the paydirt. To remove this gravel, in 1938 the Company purchased and assembled an enormous Bucyrus-Monighan "walking" dragline, said to be the largest in North America. It gouged out twelve cubic yards of gravel in its Volkswagen-sized bucket and dumped it onto a chain of conveyor belts. The conveyors rolled the waste rock away, eventually creating a quarter-mile-long rock plateau. As a child I was thrilled to watch this behemoth take an occasional ponderous step with the "duck feet" attached to the sides of its broad base. The elongated feet would rise slowly above the ground, slide forward through the air, and drop down to replant in a solid new position. Then slowly the base of the dragline would, in the same lumbering fashion, rise up, shift forward, and sit back down between the feet. From its new position the great machine would resume slinging bucket loads rhythmically from excavation to conveyor belt.

I asked my father many questions about this thrilling and powerful piece of equipment. But I never asked about the rock plateau it left behind. Neither did most grown-ups. The land seemed vast. No one pondered or cared about how long it would take for the dragline's rock dump or the dredge tailings to revegetate. The only environmental question locals asked concerned game fish. When muck overburden was washed into streams and rivers, did it kill salmon and grayling? Miners sturdily proclaimed that the mud they added to the runoff was not noticeable in the midst of nature's mud. Perhaps they were correct; the Tanana River had its own muck-stripping operation on the outer banks of its meandering course, and many of its silty tributaries came from active glaciers. The expense of postwar wages may have threatened Company profits, but the price of environmental protection did not. In the end, Jim's five-year tenure as dredge superintendent proved satisfying. He managed to get most of the Fairbanks fleet back into full-time operation (although it was not until 1957 that the Company had as many dredges running in the Territory as it had in 1941). And there were moments of engineering triumph each time a thousand-ton dredge was successfully moved overland from a creek exhausted of gold to a fresh one.

A few of these dredge transfers were easy and even took place during the summer; Dredge No. 6 was floated a mile and a half from Ester to Gold Hill through a specially dug canal. But most of the Company's nine dredge moves were challenging. Winter was moving time. Temporary winter roads bear more weight than temporary summer roads, and dredges need to be digging, not traveling, during the summer mining season. A dredge dismantled in the fall could, during the winter, be moved and reconstructed in the dry excavation for its new pond. When spring thaw floated the boat, its bucketline could begin gathering paydirt. The weight of the dredges made these moves daunting. Even after the stacker, bucketline, spuds, and waste-separator screens were removed, a hull often weighed almost seven hundred tons. Chains of Caterpillar tractors were needed to drag huge sleds of boat pieces over a roughed-out trail.

I don't remember the three-and-a-half-mile move of Dredge No. 5 from Cleary to Little Eldorado Creek in the winter of 1947–48, but its importance to my father can be seen in the drawings, detailed reports, and photos he saved in his personal files. It was the first move he superintended. The dredge's hull could not be moved in one piece by the equipment of that day, so in the fall it was cut into five sections. Then, during a thirty-day period in January, the pieces were sledded over the 18 percent grade by three Caterpillar tractors. Reassembly took four months. Total cost: $162,500 (about $1.3 million today).

I and a lot of other people remember the seven-mile move of Dredge No. 6 from Gold Hill to Sheep Creek in 1958. It was public entertainment, with newspaper coverage and an audience of more than a hundred "trailside superintendents." A dredge on dry land looms larger than a dredge floating in a pond, and for the first time the Company was attempting to drag an entire 680-ton hull as a single piece down a winter trail. Boris Ashurkoff, the mechanical engineer, designed an ingenious set of four steerable box-sled runners. Inside each runner was a line of propane heaters to prevent the runners from freezing to the trail during long stops. In the fall, workers stripped Dredge No. 6 down, floated her over a supportive pillar of cribbing, and drained her pond. They bolted the runners to the bottom of the hull, welded a tongue with a ball hitch to the bow, and bulldozed a ramp up the bank. On March 19, to the sound of cheers, eighteen Caterpillar and Allis-Chalmers tractors, hitched together in four long strings, began to pull the load. The arrangement of the tractors meant that if a tractor not in the lead quit, the driver could shift into neutral and be hauled by the others without having to stop the dredge's movement. Three D9 Caterpillar tractors at the stern provided pushing power and could also serve as brakes by digging their rear rippers into the earth.

Jack Boswell wrote a detailed description of what happened next. The D9 Caterpillars in the back had excellent traction and moved too rapidly. Before the dredge had traveled two hundred feet, it overran the tractor hitched to the ball, jackknifed the sled, and bent the tongue of the hitch. Men scrambled

Dredge No. 6 being dragged over winter trail, 1958. *Richard F. Ludwig, "Sled Transportation: Heavy Single Loads in Interior Alaska," unpublished report, ca. 1958, n.p.*

to repair the damage in 18-degree weather. They finished in three hours, but after three attempts they could not budge the sled. The runners had frozen down and daylight was disappearing. They quit for the night. The *Fairbanks Daily News-Miner* headline read "They Huffed and Puffed But Dredge Bogged Down."

On the morning of March 20 an early crew started the propane burners inside the runners, and, again to encouraging shouts from observers, the rig started and traveled smoothly two thousand feet before one of the lead tractors quit running—water in the gas. By the time the drivers had unhitched the offender and dragged it off the side of the trail, the runners had again frozen down. The dredge must have been partway up a rise because this time the runners not only had to be heated but the men needed to lay a bed of corduroy poles under each runner to get started. To lay the corduroy, they had to jack up the load, the 680-ton hull. By the time this task was completed, it was again time to quit for the day. Distance accomplished in two days: 2,200 feet. The *Fairbanks Daily News-Miner*'s article for the day was titled "Operation Continues."

On March 21 the tractors were ready to move at 10 AM, but the crew from the power company, who needed to lower the Ester power line, was an hour late. Finally, a smaller and more subdued audience saw them off. The tractors paused only briefly for lunch and to maneuver across Goldstream. The dredge arrived at the Sheep Creek dredge pond pit at 4:45 PM. Actual travel time during the three-day, seven-mile trip was four hours and twenty-eight minutes. The *Fairbanks Daily News-Miner* was finally able to report "Tractors and Men Finish Dredge Moving Project."

There were celebrations in several Company houses that night, including ours. I was awed by the ability of men to move such a large, familiar, and relatively immobile object. For once I may have grasped the correct reason for my father's mood changes. The previous week at home he had been preoccupied and prone to flares of anger. The successful arrival of Dredge No. 6 at Sheep Creek transformed his mood into playfulness, restrained pride, and partially suppressed exultation. But that was March 1958, Jim was already general manager instead of dredge superintendent, and I was sixteen years old. In the immediate postwar years, when I was still in primary school and believed that columns of numbers determined my father's mood, I let his humors simply blow around the periphery of my real life, a life at home centered on my mother and the children of the FE Company compound.

{8}

ALTA'S DOMAIN

WHEN ALTA BROUGHT her daughters back to Fairbanks in June 1945, she found her husband immersed in working the long hours of miner's summer. She took over the task of settling into our new home. As dredge superintendent earning $6,000 a year, my father was entitled to rent (for $80 a month including utilities) FE Residence No. 10, one of the four cream-colored frame "cottages" inside the rectangular fence of the housing compound across the street from the office.

The similar, although not identical, one-story furnished bungalows with green corrugated-iron hip roofs had been built in 1928 as modern housing for families of midlevel employees. In summer FE maintenance men painted the houses and installed window screens; in winter they replaced the screens with storm windows and plowed the driveway bisecting the compound. The cottages had niceties not found in many Fairbanks homes—a large screened front porch, a utility room with indoor clotheslines, and a fireplace in the living room. Each yard had flower beds lining the wooden sidewalk to the front door, a vegetable garden behind the house, and a greenhouse heated by steam from March through September. Just beyond the communal fence a long building was divided into six heated garages. In the compound's other three houses lived Audrey and Ted Loftus with my cousins Nancy and Jule; Jewel and Jack Boswell with John, Marion, and Robby; and L. E. "Jack" and Alaska Linck with son Jimmy Moody. South of the compound was a baseball lot (or skating rink as the season dictated) bounded by the FE Staff House where Cap and Margaret Osborne lived with their two younger children, David and Eddie. To the north, beyond a grassy field, in another Company cottage lived Boris and Tanya Ashurkoff and son Peter. My sister and I considered the neighborhood to have a quite satisfying number of children, and my mother delighted in the garden, the comfortable house, and the daytime company of her cousin and the other wives.

I was the youngest child in the compound by four years and second youngest by seven years. My sister and most of the other kids were in, or almost in, high school before I started kindergarten. As a result I spent a lot of time playing alone or trailing after Mother. As with my father, I thought I understood Alta's life. She tended her husband, supervised her children, laundered, sewed, cooked, picked berries and mushrooms, and gardened. The latter two activities are especially vivid in my memory because they were summer tasks that included the children of the compound.

For us, "gardening" meant raising vegetables in the greenhouse and in the plot of annually rototilled ground in the backyard. In front of the cottage Mother grew a string of pansies along the wooden sidewalk and some perennial delphinium and lilies of the valley against the house, but the important part of the garden, the part that yielded produce, was in the rear.

Gardening began indoors in February when Alta started seedlings in flats, shallow wood boxes set on tables inside our sunniest windows. Some were transplanted to the greenhouse in March when the steam pipes under the elevated beds were turned on; others were moved to the garden in late May when nighttime frosts ceased. Once the plants began their rapid growth in the long hours of sunlight, mothers of the compound not only worked in their gardens and yards but assigned and supervised tasks for their children. Boys mowed lawns and rotated the lawn sprinklers (through which we children ran during occasional 80-degree "heat waves"). Girls weeded and watered. Daughters, easily recruited to stand in a redolent greenhouse soaking plants with a hose, had to be pressed into tasks like squatting in the dirt to pull chickweed out of the onions. But Alta and the other mothers needed our help; moreover, it was a parental principle that early work training built character. We kids, of course, had no interest in improving our characters, but we were bribable. In direct contravention of the no-eating-between-meals rule, we were allowed to nibble little sweet carrots, juicy tomatoes, and plump peas while weeding or watering.

Each greenhouse provided more tomatoes, cucumbers, and peppers than a single family could eat. Alta had the pleasure of giving away hothouse vegetables in a town where store produce could be in transit for weeks. Excess outdoor crops—potatoes, onions, lettuce, rhubarb, zucchini, chard, cabbage, broccoli,

Two FE compound houses visible within fence. *Courtesy of Nancy Earling Allen.*

cauliflower, beets, and strawberries—were harder to dispense because many people had gardens that thrived in the long daylight of summer. The oversupply of rhubarb, zucchini, and end-of-the-season green tomatoes led to imaginative local recipes. *Favorite Recipes,* produced by St. Matthew's Church Guild in 1944, lists six recipes for green tomato pickles, seven for rhubarb jam, and one each for Swiss chard pickles, carrot ketchup, and gingered beet preserves. Of course, not all plants were happy imports to northern gardens. Despite Alta's talent and hard work, spinach bolted, corn produced tiny kernels, and our single pumpkin was bested by the grocery store's worst import.

Perhaps because gardening was so successful, two families in the compound branched out to raising farm animals. Our communal fence kept unauthorized dogs and other marauders away from these husbandry projects. For several summers the Boswells raised chickens, and one notable year the Loftus family raised a pig. The chickens lived in a small fenced area with a chicken house. They never acquired names, and their annual fall beheading, attended by the children, was an exciting mixture of the gruesome and comic: blood spurting and bodies moving without heads. The cleaning and plucking that followed was women's work, presided over by Jewell.

The pig Chester, my cousin Jule's 4-H project, was a different matter. The Loftuses acquired him as a piglet early one summer while they were staying in an FE cabin at Chatanika. In August they moved back to their house in the compound and penned Chester in the backyard. In theory young Jule was in charge of cleaning the pen and feeding Chester. However, overseeing this commitment required considerable energy from Audrey. Fortunately Chester's personality made his care less onerous. Pigs can be clever and friendly, and Chester was both. Moreover, he was healthy and gained weight at an astonishing rate, becoming the fattest pig at the Tanana Valley Fair in the fall. Unfortunately, after fall comes winter, when no pig can survive in a backyard pen. Chester had been nurtured as a winter meat investment and it was time, so to speak, to bring home the bacon. The slaughter was Ted's duty, and he feared a children's crisis when the pig met its destiny. The children of the compound understood where meat came from. We were used to creels of grayling, bags of grouse, and hanging moose haunches. But the pig had petlike qualities that neither chickens nor moose possessed. Ted and his assistants—Art Loftus, Jim Crawford, and Jack Boswell—decided that Chester would meet his fate out of town near the cabin at Chatanika. Jule was the only child invited to attend; none of the rest of us witnessed Chester's slaughter. Cousin Jule was not talkative when he returned, and the grown-ups shook their heads and spoke together privately. Those of us excluded eavesdropped as best we could while pretending to be napping or deep in games. Later we compared notes. The butchering had not gone well. The pig's death had not been immediate. Moreover a plan to scald the carcass to simplify removal of the bristles before tanning the hide had run into mechanical difficulties embarrassing to the engineers. The men devised a tripod over a fifty-five-gallon drum of water brought to a boil over a campfire. They intended first to scald the hindquarters, and then to turn the carcass around to scald the forequarters, but the initial dip displaced so much water that the barrel overflowed and extinguished the fire. Despite the awkwardness of Chester's end, the Loftuses, and the rest of us who received a share, enjoyed eating pork as an alternative to moose that winter. However, there were no more 4-H projects in the compound involving farm mammals.

In our family's lore, homegrown pork and garden vegetables were free foods, never discounted by the price of seeds, feed, or fertilizer (any more than fishing rods, ammunition, or boat gasoline were charged against grayling, grouse, or moose meat). But our cheapest free food was picked not from a garden, but from wild plants, especially berry plants. The picking season began in July with raspberries, then progressed through blueberries, highbush cranberries, and currants to end with lowbush cranberries (lingonberries) in September. On a rainless day, Alta and a few friends would gather to drive to a favored site (revealed only to trusted confidantes) to harvest the pick of the week. The women packed sandwiches, cookies, and a thermos of tea. Then they assembled their buckets, their offspring, and 6-12 mosquito dope to set off for the afternoon. Early in life we children were coached to pick cleanly and to leave more berries in our bucket than we ate.

Berries are appreciated not only by humans but by voles, jays, and other omnivores. When the fecund blueberries ripened in July, animal scats turned purple; seeds and fertilizer were spread at great distances from the mother plants. But of our berry-patch competitors, we really cared about only one: bears. We tried to avoid them, and we believed they would try to avoid us as long as they knew where we were. As we picked, we talked together in clear voices. Or if we found ourselves separated from the group, we sang our favorite bear solos, songs with many verses. I solemnly memorized the instructions of Laura Anderson, an Athabascan master picker, who told me that if a bear threatened me and refused to run away that I should pull up my shirt and say in a calm voice, "Bear, I am not here to hurt you. I am just a woman picking berries." I was not sure that my skinny chest would convince a bear of my womanliness and decided that, if I could find my voice, I should describe myself respectfully as a harmless child.

Despite possible bears and certain mosquitoes, berry outings were popular with kids. They were a chance to poke around in the woods, fool a younger child into tasting a bitter soapberry, or squirt your cousin with red-staining highbush cranberry juice fired by pinching the berry just so. But mainly we liked berry picking because of its delicious natural consequences. Alta and the other mothers made blueberry pies, cranberry muffins, hand-cranked raspberry ice cream, currant jelly, and a year's supply of jam, including imaginative flavors like cranberry-banana and blueberry-rhubarb.

There was another free wild food that my mother and a few other women picked—mushrooms. Alta owned a comprehensive mushroom book printed in Czechoslovakia with 120 full-page colored drawings. She learned terminology and made spore prints; friends consulted her as a self-taught lay expert. As the only family member who shared her enthusiasm, I often went along on mushroom expeditions. I thrilled to the hunt even when it meant plucking a meadow mushroom out of a dried cow pie in the field at Bentley's Dairy. She showed me how to find the right habitat—mossy open spots for *Lactarius* species, dry disturbed gravel for *Coprinus*—and then spy (or, in the case of boletus, smell out) young, worm-free mushrooms half hidden in moss or soil. With time I learned to identify a half-dozen edible species and to avoid their inedible cousins, like the *Lactarius* pepper pot, which resembles the orange delicious in appearance but not in taste. Alta also taught me to recognize and to avoid poisonous species, like the two *Amanitas*—the red-and-white fly agaric that adorns fairy-tale illustrations, and the pale, dangerously nondescript deadly angel.

As a child, I learned another lesson from Alta's mushrooms. I was scrawny and a picky eater, born too late for Depression food shortages when home-canned tomatoes with sugar was a festive dessert. Jim and Alta at first failed to realize that although you can put a plate before a stubborn child, you cannot force her to eat. They ruled that I must stay at the dinner table until bedtime or until I had eaten three bites of sauerkraut, moose liver, mashed turnips, or whatever I was balking at. Every other night we faced an impasse. There may be something genetic about stubbornness. Finally an under-the-table solution satisfactory to everyone's pride was reached. When my parents left me alone with three bites of caribou heart or a spear of canned asparagus, they left the cocker spaniel in the kitchen. Our cocker would eat almost anything that was liberally smeared with ketchup from the bottle that sat on our table.

By contrast, my sister was an exemplary eater, often held up as a model to me. But Jane had a weak point: she disliked eating mushrooms: puffballs, shaggy manes, inky caps, meadow mushrooms, boletus, morels, and even orange delicious. Mushrooms presented a seductive opportunity; I could best my older sister. Sibling rivalry forced me to eat with apparent enthusiasm second helpings of the sautéed treat of the week. To my surprise, I found that what Alta claimed about rejected foods was true: familiarity bred enjoyment. Although I never generalized this lesson to brussels sprouts, kidneys, or canned okra, my mother taught me to relish, as well as to collect, Fairbanks mushrooms.

But the perpetual food task in Alta's life was not growing, gathering, or preserving food. It was cooking three daily meals. She was not a regional kitchen artiste, the kind of cooking mother or aunt glorified in food memoirs garnished with recipes. Instead, to use language of Lake Wobegon, she was a "pretty good cook," a woman who had emerged from the Depression conservative with food and limited by the raw materials and kitchen implements available in Fairbanks.

Aside from Alta's taste for wild mushrooms and Jim's for frog legs and chopped kidneys on toast, we were—like many in Fairbanks—a meat-and-potatoes family. Sometimes Alta served spaghetti or rice, but potatoes—easy to grow and cheap to purchase—were our common starch. In Fairbanks homegrown potatoes lasted through the winter stored in underground food cellars entered by a trapdoor from the kitchen or utility room. These miniature versions of the farmer's root cellar took advantage of the insulating quality of thawed soil beneath a heated house: potatoes, carrots, beets, turnips, and cabbage remained cool but unfrozen.

Alta boiled, baked, or mashed potatoes only for dinner, but she prepared meat for every meal. Breakfast meats (bacon and sausage) and lunch meats (canned tuna and Spam) were similar to those eaten in the States, but our main dinner meat was moose. Each fall, often thanks to the hunting ability of my mother, we would put in a supply of moose meat. Butchered, packaged, and stored in the green steel locker we rented at Fairbanks Cold Storage, the moose supplied us nightly with steaks, roasts, and meat loaves for the next eleven months. Occasionally the locker held caribou or gifts of mountain sheep from friends who hunted in the Alaska Range. This is not to say that we never ate store-bought chicken, turkey, lamb, pork, or beef; but they were expensive, and particularly the latter seemed tasteless and fatty compared to moose.

Wild fish or fowl also qualified as dinner meats. In the summer Mother pan-fried grayling, easily caught even by children, or baked salmon bought from Athabascans running a downriver fish wheel. Fresh and canned salmon, and especially dried smoked salmon strips, were welcomed even by a picky child like me. However, grayling required such patient effort to separate the fine bones from the white flesh that it was associated in my mind with what I understood to be a Catholic penance, eating fish on Fridays. In the fall Jim and our cocker spaniel brought home mallards, pintails, and Canada geese. Plucking the birds and removing the lead shot involved so much work that Alta claimed that by the time she was ready to roast the birds, she had lost interest. Perhaps that's why, no matter how she cooked them, they tended to be tough and strong-flavored. My parents also hunted grouse and ptarmigan with .22s. With the exception of spruce hens, which tasted of spruce resin, we preferred eating land birds to waterfowl.

In addition to meat and potatoes, our summer dinners included fresh vegetables, salads, and berries. In winter we bought and appreciated canned vegetables and fruits. In the 1940s, Fairbanks stores also had a small quantity of uncanned fruit for sale. Each autumn there were fresh, although not always crisp, apples, which had been in transit at ambient temperature for about ten days. In December we received fresh California oranges (and after memories of World War II subsided, Japanese mandarin oranges) for our Christmas stockings. However, the Alaskan use of the word "fresh," as in this paragraph and in the Northern Commercial Company's advertisements ("We receive fresh fruit, vegetables, eggs and butter weekly") had an extended meaning that would have been scorned in California.

In the compound cottage, Alta's equipment for preparing meals was utilitarian. Her two large appliances were the electric stove and refrigerator. Dishes were hand-washed. Her small equipment consisted of a pressure cooker for canning, an electric Mixmaster, and a meat and vegetable grinder that clamped onto the table and was operated by hand. In this she was typical of the women she knew, although my Aunt Audrey possessed an additional unforgettable kitchen gadget—a machine that could be pumped to force a mixture of melted butter and evaporated milk through a pinhole-sized orifice to produce whipping cream. This was a useful utensil on the Creeks where no fresh milk or cream was available. In Fairbanks two dairies delivered bottled, unhomogenized milk to the doorstep. (In winter, those lax in retrieving their milk bottles from the doorstep found a column of frozen cream topped by a round cardboard lid rising dramatically from the bottle neck.)

Alta's cooking was also utilitarian. Meats were fried, broiled, or roasted. Vegetables, except for sautéed zucchini or baked squash, were boiled. Spices consisted of salt, pepper, garlic salt, celery salt, cinnamon, and nutmeg. She prepared proper portions for each meal, cooking one-half chicken for three people. Our refrigerator and cupboards held few prepared foods or leftovers. She offered one welcome daily snack after school: a glass of milk and two homemade chocolate-chip or peanut-butter cookies. Her approach to feeding a family was typical; my class pictures show groups of skinny, or at least thin, children. Classes rarely had more than one chubby pupil.

However, we children were not bereft of sweets. For holidays Alta made fudge, divinity, peanut brittle, and messy pulled taffy. On other special occasions, by closely following instructions in cookbooks or on three-by-five handwritten recipe cards contributed by friends, she constructed a variety of filled layer cakes. (Applesauce-spice, crimson velvet, and coconut were among her favorites.) Baking from scratch could be suspenseful. Her recipe files contain cautionary notes to herself: "A heavy cake or one which falls may be due to too slow an oven, too much flour, too hot an oven, too coarsely granulated sugar, too much shortening, insufficient creaming of shortening or insufficient beating of batter before egg whites are folded in."

My mother had one dessert specialty that did not require a recipe—snow ice cream. This was not "outdoor ice cream," a mixture of sugar, flavoring, and cream stirred in a bowl and buried to freeze slowly in a snowbank, where the temperature was a steady 25 degrees. Instead, snow was one of the ingredients in Alta's ice cream, and the concoction contained no cream at all. It was made instead with evaporated milk, which (often still in a can opened with two small punch holes) was served as "cream" for coffee in Fairbanks homes and restaurants. Evaporated milk, when chilled, can be whipped with a hand or electric beater to form soft peaks. Mother would add vanilla and sugar or a package of fruit Jell-O to the whipped milk, then walk outside to stir fresh snow into the mixture until it stiffened into a soft ice cream. We ate it as soon as she returned, before it had a chance to melt, and laughingly subscribed to the superstition that a stray spruce needle in your bowl was a sign of coming good luck (in the same manner that stray mosquitoes caught in hot grease when grayling are pan-fried over a campfire were dignified as "extra protein").

In fairness to Jim, I should note that he too had a cooking specialty: sourdough pancakes. It was not merely his specialty; it was the only cooking he did in those days of rigid household roles. Sourdough-pancake recipes did not appear in cook-books; they were an oral tradition. Old-timers carried this treasured wild yeast as a stiff moist ball inside their flour sack in summer and under their shirts in winter. Jim kept his thick liquid starter in a glazed pottery canister, using a portion of it every Sunday for pancakes served with syrup homemade from sugar, water, and Mapleine flavoring. He rejuvenated the remaining starter with flour and water in preparation for the next Sunday's use. Like many starters it had a story and a pedigree, which I can no longer reconstruct, as the sourdough that my husband now uses came not from Jim but from Earl Pilgrim in the Kantishna Hills. Jim's sourdough starter accompanied him to Harding Lake on weekends but was dried to prevent stagnant spoilage if he planned to be out of town for several weeks. Its dry flakes sprang back to life with warm water and flour regardless of whether they had been held at 80 degrees above or 40 degrees below zero.

However, compared to Alta in the kitchen, Jim was a trifler. Before home freezers, dishwashers, and prepared food, cooking was time-consuming. So was laundry without clothes dryers and permanent-press fabrics. At home Alta was always busy; she could not listen to a Saturday-night radio comedy without darn-ing a sock or hemming a skirt. But in the letters she wrote and the stories she later told, her life in the compound did not focus on the quotidian.

Alta enjoyed companionship. She could love her children and her tempera-mental husband, but she could not relax with them into wide-ranging conver-sation over an idle cup of coffee. Deep friendships sustained her. She and Lola Tilly remained close for more than sixty years. And Lola was not her only special friend. Alta, Audrey Loftus, Dorothy Loftus, and a dozen other women joined together to form a local chapter of the PEO Sisterhood. The initials of this orga-nization stood for a secret title and provided a childhood guessing game. Jim claimed it stood for "Papa Eats Out" since the evening meetings interfered with dinner routines. Jane, who noted the group gave scholarships to women, was the

Inaugural meeting of PEO, Chapter B, 1945. STANDING: Mildred Nerland, Lydia Fohn-Hanson, Audrey Loftus, Sylvia Pratt, Esther Hall, Dorothy Loftus, Esther Turnbow. SEATED: Laura Carr, Helen Wilcox, Alta Crawford, Harriet Hess, Clara Woodden, Eva Taylor, Margaret Haggland. *University of Alaska Archives, Harriet Trimmer Hess Family collection.*

only child who hit upon the correct meaning. The women of the PEO chapter referred to themselves as sisters, and their bond was so strong that their husbands took to calling themselves the BILs (brothers-in-law) because they were often thrown together to help the women set up fund-raising activities or to attend PEO picnics or potlucks. The family album contains photographs of the sisters as young matrons and as white-haired elders, still friends.

Alta's sociability benefited not only her companions, but her reticent husband and shy children. My father was swept into the BILs. He also followed his wife's lead in joining, with my aunts and uncles, the Sourdough Dance Club. The thirty-five or so members of the club met to dance on the third Thursday of each month, usually in the Odd Fellows Hall. Older children were infrequently allowed to attend. When we came, we watched carefully, memorizing the steps of the dances while we waited to be invited on to the crowded floor by some patient adult. The band usually consisted of Billy Root or George Rayburn on drums and Charlotte Ames on piano. Once or twice during the evening a caller

Sourdough Dance Club masquerade. STANDING: Walter and Sylvia Pratt, John White, Alta Crawford, four unknown, Ruth Ogburn. SEATED: Elizabeth Crites, unknown, Eva McGown, Peggy Lyle. *Author's collection.*

would sing out arcane directions for a square dance, but most dances were of the defined ballroom variety: the hambo, the varsouvienne, the polka, the schottische, and the broom dance (a waltz with amusing scrambles each time the music stopped and partners changed, leaving one man to dance with the broom).

A high point of the Sourdough Dance Club's year was the annual masquerade. Children, who were considered to have their fun at Halloween, were not invited. Adult outfits for the costume ball involved weeks of planning, searching for accessories, and earnest discussion or secret laughter with friends. In a small community, meeting new characters is always diverting, even if those eccentrics are simply transformations of people you have danced with once a month for the last year. Photos memorialize these occasions. One year my mother is a dance-hall girl with a feathered hat; in another she is a Spanish lady in a black lace mantilla that drapes to her knees. My father is a Pilgrim; then he is a card dealer with a drooping cotton-wool moustache and goatee. My aunt Audrey is almost unrecognizable as a clown, then handsome as a Dutch girl with winged hat and tulips appliquéd on her apron. My uncle Ted first appears to be a Serbian folk dancer, then an Austrian cowherd. Uncle Art wears a black gown and pearls. Cousin Susan Campbell, a beauty in gardening clothes, is dazzling in a suit from the previous century with leg-of-mutton sleeves.

The cleverest costumes my parents made were a matching pair of puppets. My father used a coping saw to cut out headless, jointed plywood bodies. The puppeteer would tie a body around his neck and move the short arms and legs with hidden wire handles. Mother clothed the puppets initially in rube outfits and later in elegant opera clothes. She and Jim dressed all in black except for hats to match the puppet costumes. When they stood in front of a black background with the puppets' feet prancing on a table, there was a credible impression that the midget bodies had human heads and were enacting a witty skit. (The puppets were a durable disguise; fifteen years later Judie Tweiten and I dressed them as cool teenagers complete with cardboard guitar and acted in "Arctic Capers," the high school variety show. Forty years later my daughter gowned one as an Arabian dancer for Halloween.)

Alta saved photographs of the puppet shows, the PEO picnics, and the Sourdough Dances. Her cheerful letters describing these events occasionally included a paragraph about gardening or sewing, but never contained a paragraph about cooking, cleaning, or raising children. These tasks were simply a part of Alta's daily life. She collected a few recipes and occasionally asked friends for advice about her daughters, but she did not read books on cooking or child development. She espoused no theories of nutrition or child-rearing. A house needed to be clean but not immaculate; meals needed to be nourishing and served at regular hours; children needed to learn common sense and spend plenty of time out of doors.

The three-bedroom, furnished houses of the compound probably seemed large when just two adults were at home, but the addition of two or three children made them shrink. Our mothers, most of whom came from rural backgrounds, shooed us outdoors to play—not only to be rid of our mess and noise, but also because they believed that outdoor play was healthier than indoor play. We were glad to obey this maternal instruction; outdoor play was less closely observed than indoor play. Even summer mosquitoes—too numerous and aggressive to be referred to by the casual diminutive "skeeter"—did not discourage us. In Fairbanks, where military planes swept overhead spraying DDT as a community service, the swarms were thinner than on the Creeks, where pools of water, suspended on top of permafrost, nurtured eggs and larvae. At the mines, mosquitoes could reach head-net-requiring density and interfere with a man's doing a good day's work. In town during the first few weeks of June, we kids scratched until we bled at the big scattered welts inflicted by lumbering *Culicidae* mosquitoes. But by July, when multitudinous tiny, swift *Aedes* mosquitoes arrived, we seemed to develop a kind of immunity. We used less and less citronella and 6-12 mosquito repellent, and wore shorts and sleeveless blouses on hot days. Alta taught us to value our anti-mosquito allies—the iridescent dragonflies and clever spiders. She called the dragonfly (whose Athabascan name means "mosquito hawk") our "double defender." As a nymph it preyed on mosquito larvae in ponds; as an adult it scooped the flying pests out of the air. The spiders, trappers rather than hunters, were less handsome but equally effective. Spiders native to Alaska are not poisonous to people; those found in the Crawford cottage were never stomped but tenderly released outdoors to continue their predatory ways.

Not only were children encouraged to play outdoors, but Jim, Alta, and other parents sometimes joined their games. On June and July nights when the big kids' bedtimes were suspended for vacation, I would sometimes fall asleep in my sunny bedroom to the shouts of parents and children playing baseball in the field south of the fence.

Alta not only competed with us, she also gave us a constant and unrehearsed stream of lessons in punctuality, honesty, work ethics, kindness to playmates, and respect for teachers. Punctuality was taught with a police whistle. Each of the mothers in the compound had a code of long and short blasts to bring offspring home. We were allowed to play at each other's houses and beyond the compound fence as long as we stayed within the audible boundary of the whistles. But the child who did not come home promptly after her whistle was blown faced parental disapproval. As when dawdling caused me to miss the morning school bus and I had to shuffle shamefacedly home to ask for a ride, I did not soon repeat my tardy error.

Honesty, an even higher virtue than punctuality, was encouraged vigorously at an early age. The first reproof I recall was in response to a four-year-old's sin of gluttony and false testimony. One 30-below winter day Mother discovered some finger-shaped divots in a container of outdoor ice cream buried in the snow. The scarf over my lower face (which was supposed to keep my lungs from freezing should I manage to run fast enough in my pudgy layers of clothing to breathe deeply) had definite vanilla smudges, yet I blamed our clean-muzzled black cocker spaniel. I received not only punishment of no dessert that evening, but the natural consequence of snickers throughout the compound when Alta advertised my misdemeanor. The wound to my pride pressed her lesson home more effectively than the missed dessert.

Training in work ethics came from paid jobs available to children. For a fee, boys mowed lawns and shoveled walks not their own, but their work was inspected before money exchanged hands. When I was small I could get a penny for every dandelion I dug out of the lawn with an old kitchen fork—but the long central root of each plant had to be attached. The weed was abundant and the work kneeling in the struggling grass, listening to bees, and watching for lucky four-leaf clovers was pleasant. But after Mother discarded plants without roots, my pile of shining copper and dull war-minted zinc pennies was smaller than I expected; I learned to be more thorough.

Alta also taught Jane (and me as I grew older) to enjoy the thanks that came from unpaid civic duty like watering the roads. The unpaved streets of Fairbanks were laden with tan powdery loess blown from the melting glaciers of the last Ice Age. Every passing vehicle produced a cloud of dust that settled in a fine layer on cars and inside our mothers' clean houses. Hosing down the road aided both housekeepers and drivers. How pleasant it was to have a neighbor praise me for an act that I could perform while daydreaming or even reading a book, needing only to glance up periodically to continue a spray pattern or to avoid open-windowed cars.

Kindness was taught not only by direct instruction and discreet suggestion, but by example. Alta pushed me to invite certain children over to play after school: a pair of unkempt sisters whose mother seemed more interested in her pedigreed dogs than in her children, the unfortunate son of alcoholic parents, and a desperately shy little girl learning English as her second language. Unforced, I wouldn't have invited them, but to my surprise I often had fun while they got a good meal and some motherly attention.

Alta's approach to children—her own and others—was firm, rarely angry, never distant, and sometimes delightful. She retained enough naïve excitement in the immediate moment to set aside her tasks so that she could sweep us into making baskets of May Day flowers to hang on people's doorknobs, or into blowing soap bubbles that at 40 below became stiff and "permanent," or into running quickly outdoors at 10 below to see mote-like ice flakes in a sunbeam drift down from an apparently cloudless sky.

Alta's standards of child-rearing were reflected in other houses in the compound. While we children played in the semipublic yards and semiprivate houses, we were observed and prodded. Mothers, unashamed collaborators, did not hesitate to reprimand an unrelated child or call a parent to report egregious misdemeanors like playing on the far side of Illinois Street or being seen with matches. Despite the potentially suffocating situation of finding ourselves surrounded by adults of probity, we children were fortunate. Alta and others pressured us to conform to certain norms—to be polite (especially to adults), to be reasonably clean once a day, and to work out differences with others while avoiding serious verbal or physical injury. But we were not asked to achieve high-status goals: to be smarter, prettier, or more athletic than our classmates. Our parents did not press vicarious ambitions on us, and we gave little thought to the longings of our parents. Our attention, or at least mine, was centered on our communal life as compound kids.

Top: David and Eddie Osborne; Jane Crawford; Jim Moody, Johnny Boswell.
Bottom: Marian Boswell; Nancy Loftus; Peter Ashurkoff; Robby Boswell; Jule Loftus.
Courtesy of Barbara Hale.

{9}

KIDS AT PLAY IN THE COMPOUND

THE OUTER BOUNDARY of the children's play area surrounding the compound was audible. Our mothers' "come home" whistles could be heard beyond the fence north to the grassy field and Peter Ashurkoff's house, and south to the baseball field and the Staff House where the Osborne boys lived. The whistles' shrill warbles also easily penetrated the willow thicket to the east. To us it was a big area that allowed us to play big games.

My favorite big summer game was one I imagined was unique to the compound. Only recently did I learn that it was also played in Fort Yukon and in Kennecott under variations of the name we used: Annie Annie I Over. Full of rushing and excitement, the game was played by opposing teams stationed on opposite sides of the garage that housed the family cars of the compound and Staff House. This long, narrow building had a corrugated-metal roof that sloped north and south from a central ridgepole. Team members on one side in a strict rotation would throw a tennis ball blindly over the roof with the warning call "Annie, Annie, I over." If the ball were caught by the opposing team before it touched the ground, the catching team would respond with "We're coming over" and rush in a body around the east end of the garage. An opposing player tagged by the onrushing team before she could escape by running around the west end of the garage to take up the opposite playing position would be captured. The excitement of the game came in the suspense of not knowing until the last moment if the ball had been caught and the opposing team would shout the warning and burst around the side of the building ready to tag, or whether the ball would come immediately winging back with another "Annie, Annie, I over." As the ball cleared the ridgepole and hit the corrugated roof on the opposite side, it careened off with an unpredictable trajectory toward the catching team. Annie Annie I Over required strict honesty from the teams, and like most young people we were scrupulous about fairness and adhering to the rules of our games.

The visible boundary of the compound provided another outdoor game: Walking the Fence. The four-foot fence that enclosed the houses and blended lawns was made from upright posts and wire fencing topped with two-by-fours, creating a long balance beam. The challenge consisted not merely of walking the beam, but of passing hazards without falling off. One hazard was of a pair of fifteen-foot stretches of barbed wire rising eighteen inches above the two-by-fours. These had been placed to protect two vegetable gardens just inside the fence next to the willow thicket. We children theorized that they were to keep moose out, but later I was told they were to protect the gardens from the craning necks of wandering packhorses. By the time I was growing up packhorses had disappeared from Fairbanks, and moose were the more familiar ungulates.

A bigger challenge than edging along the barbed wire without catching clothes or bare legs was crossing the gates. There were six of them. The four "front gates" for the houses were only three feet wide, and their iron pipe tops were fairly easy to wobble over in a single step. The two large driveway gates were another matter. Only the boldest kids attempted the ten-foot-wide crossing. Not only was this feat difficult, it was forbidden by parents as harmful to the hinges and dangerous to children. Since both gates were in full view of all four houses, the risk that an adult might spy an attempted crossing and pick up the party-line phone to call a primary discipliner was great.

Beyond the fence, children, at least older children, played more standard games. Since my sister was usually required to mind me, her pesky tail of a sister, special playing rules were often designed based on size. In baseball, I got to stay at bat until I finally hit something or the pitcher finally managed to hit my bat. My outfielder's post was the most distant imaginable, allowing me to study ladybugs and look for four-leaf clovers since no ball was likely to reach me. Kick the can and hide and seek required little modification, although sometimes when the big kids grew tired of me, they would encourage me to hide, then fail to find me for long periods. I was excluded outright from some wild games like Beating the Yellow Jackets in which the object was to run so fast across a stretch of boardwalk with a wasp nest under it that defending insects did not have time to swarm out and sting you. I was too slow and the copious tears that followed my attempts occasioned a maternal no-play rule, although the big kids who had to mind me in the midst of their play may have felt the little copycat deserved a few consequences.

Not all our games required speed or daring. In the flat dirt of the driveway, we drew circles and played marbles "for keeps"—although when playing with me the big kids adopted a type of catch and release, keeping me in suspense until we were called home for dinner about whether my marbles in the winners' leather pouches would be returned. Other days we would spend in the willow thicket to the east of the fence. Our secret paths crisscrossed the lot to hideouts under saplings naturally bent by winters of snow and reinforced with willow withes. By the time we were well into grade school, we all owned jackknives, and we crouched in our hideouts making useful objects like whistles. We would carefully work an intact cylinder of bark off a short length of willow and carve a flat fipple and notch for air escape before reinstalling the bark. The results were variable. A satisfactory whistle often involved many discards, and because the bark dried in a few days, even the best whistles failed after brief use. Their transience meant we became practiced at making them.

In the winter, outdoor neighborhood time was curtailed by school and intermittent cold spells when ice fog formed and the thermometer dropped to 50 degrees below zero. On those afternoons we crowded into one of the houses and resorted to card or board games or Static Electricity, a game that took advantage of dark days and low humidity when it was easy to generate a human charge by sliding our leather shoes across the carpet. We would turn out the light, scuff our feet and advance blindly, arms outstretched, until a spark leapt from our fingertips to a nearby victim, who would respond to the miniscule tactile crackle with a satisfying yelp.

But if the temperature was above minus 10 degrees, even when darkness foreshortened the afternoons, we found ways to play outside. On cold days we sometimes broke off our activities to dash into the steam-heated community garage to warm up. After a little discussion about what to do next, the boys would tell a few jokes that I didn't understand but that scandalized the girls, and we would all rush outdoors again. The Fred Noyes house, in which the Osbornes lived, had been a showpiece when the neighborhood was still pastoral, but like many houses of its time it was poorly insulated. Its eaves produced huge icicles for sword fights and for sucking. Our fathers transformed our erstwhile baseball field into a skating rink with garden hoses so that adults and children alike could enjoy crack-the-whip and pickup hockey games. We were often short of pucks and sticks and made do with a tin can and brooms. The downtown schoolyard had an even larger playground rink flooded from a fire hydrant, and most of us were competent skaters by second grade.

At the beginning of winter, around Halloween, the temperatures were still warm enough and the snow still moist enough that we could make forts, snowmen, and snowballs. As winter closed in, the snow became crystalline and granular as it deliquesced in the dry cold. Accordingly, we made the most we could of wet snowfalls. We played fox and geese in the formerly grassy field north of the compound. Part of the fun was stamping out a huge circular rim with spokes leading to the hub of the fox's den; the preparation for this game took almost as long as the tag within its confines. When the first deep snow fell, we also built snowmen, women, and babies. They were garnished with imaginative accessories, rediscovered when yards were cleaned the next spring. Even more transient than snowmen were snow angels and other figures traced by our bodies in the newest unbroken snow. Fort building was not very satisfactory because when the snow was wet it was not deep, and when it was deep it was not sticky. Eddie Osborne, who intended to be an architect, was the only one who had the patience to dig a fort in the high, hard-packed snow berm left by the plows. But forts or no forts, we had snowball fights. These were considered acceptable play by both parents and teachers. Some of them involved enough children to become snowball wars. The most memorable compound battle was the one involving the police car. It started because the school bus was late.

Each school-day morning the pupils from the compound waited for the bus to Main School at the edge of the road in front of the Boswells' gate. On very cold days we arrived at the bus stop at the last possible moment to avoid a long wait. Mother would have bundled me into snowsuit and boots over the dress and oxfords girls were expected, or maybe required, to wear in class. Older girls, partially free from maternal authority on attire, felt too adult for snowsuits. They would appear in coats or parkas, stadium boots, mittens, and homemade corduroy balaclavas lined with satin. Then they would squat on their heels so that their swinging, calf-length skirts made tents for bare bobby-soxed legs, which were vulnerable to chilblains and worse. The boys in caps with earflaps, heavy jackets, hand-knit mittens, and gabardine pants jumped around and shoved each other to stay warm. To motorists we must have presented an odd group emerging out of the ice fog. But on warmer days, especially before Thanksgiving, when the snow was fresh and inviting, we arrived at the bus stop earlier. With mobility intact in lighter clothes, we proceeded to amuse ourselves. One morning the boys positioned themselves on the snowplow berm across Illinois Street to lob snowballs at the girls waiting in front of the gate. Books were stacked on the flat two-by-four of the fence top and the battle was engaged. As minutes passed and no bus appeared, we had time not only to pelt each other but also a few cars passing down the road between us. In the mutability of children's games that progress imperceptibly from fun to trouble, cars soon became the primary target. Unfortunately, none of us recognized the black-and-white police car until a snowball flattened onto its front windshield. As the car eased over to the shoulder, we ran in all directions. I hid alone behind the painted brick chimney that jutted out from the Lincks' house. By the time I dared come out, the school bus had come and gone. I don't remember how many of the kids came out of hiding in time to catch the bus, but I know that I didn't walk the two miles to school alone that day. Even the horror of having a tardy marked on my report card was not sufficient to send me home to explain why the bus had left without me. We waited, but no policemen knocked on our parents' doors that evening. And at the end of the school year, my parents paid no attention to the attendance column of my report card. Thus from the miscreant's point of view, my first brush with the law came to a happy conclusion, and I continued to play in undiscredited innocence within the sphere of my mother's whistle.

In those years Alta's days were permeated with split-level parenting. In 1947, just as I was completing kindergarten, Jane was graduating from high school and beginning to pay attention to whistles from beyond the compound. Alta worried, but I watched and admired this sophisticated, almost-adult sister.

Jane with rifle and stylish saddle oxfords.
Courtesy of Jane Crawford Tallman.

{10}

SISTER JANE

J ANE GRADUATED FROM Fairbanks High School in 1947. She was sixteen years old and the youngest in a class of nineteen students that included returning GIs. For a time she worried that her grades were too good. Shy about speaking in public, she was relieved when her grade-point average placed her third in her class; she would not have to stand behind a podium to give a valedictory or salutatory speech. My parents wanted to send her to college—but not too far away. That fall she moved into the women's dormitory at the University of Alaska. Thanks to the GI Bill, which paid tuition for veterans, more than half her classmates on the Fairbanks campus that year had already served in the military. Jane's grades were passable, but the unbalanced male-to-female ratio provided a social life too active for much serious study.

The following year Jim and Alta sent Jane to the University of Oregon at Eugene, the college that Alta had attended until the Farm Depression of 1921. Eager for more independence in the warm world to the south, Jane was happy to transfer. In case of homesickness, she had family nearby. Grandmother Lillian and husband Van owned a small orchard on the outskirts of Eugene. Van received all step-grandchildren warmly, and Jane had been a favorite of acerbic Lillian since Talkeetna days. My parents believed that at this new campus Jane would have more time for study. They were right. Her dormitory housemother was a kindly Christian Scientist, her roommate was studious, and the male-to-female ratio was nearly equal.

Jane's main student difficulty was selecting a major that met with her father's approval. Father and daughter agreed that a university degree should have practical value. But they did not agree about what was practical for a woman. As a freshman Jane proposed to major in art. Jim, who was paying her tuition, responded, "Art! Men artists can barely support themselves. Art is a woman's hobby." As a sophomore she proposed geology. The response: "Women aren't strong enough to be geologists; no one would hire them." As an increasingly determined junior with summer earnings in the bank, she proposed anthropology. Jim caved in without comment; perhaps her developing ardor for a woman's right to enter the profession of her choice reminded him of his unstoppable aunt Katharine Anthony. Jane became an anthropology major, successful but restive. Her last summer in Alaska was 1950, the year she left her teens and the compound cottage behind.

In 1945, we had returned from Salt Lake and Jane had entered Fairbanks High School as a junior, Alta and Jim must have realized that they had only a few years to prepare her for adulthood. Jim was engrossed in work, so it was Alta who made sure that Jane knew how to build a wood fire, shoot a rifle, drive a car, behave on a date, and use proper etiquette in formal situations. Alta's worries about Jane as an incipient adult had no meaning to me. To me Jane seemed already grown-up, perhaps less exacting than parent adults but a colluder with them instead of with me and my kindergarten friends. She was a lofty personage, a teenage authority of great capability. She maintained a canvas sailing kayak in which she crossed, by herself, Harding Lake. She attended a church I had seen only from the outside. She had boyfriends. She had a summer office job and a bank account in which to deposit her paychecks. She resigned from a popular Masonic organization for girls when she discovered that racism had excluded an Indian friend. She drove the Studebaker, and once she scooped me up and canoed us both to safety when a black bear almost trapped her in the Harding Lake outhouse. I admired her and I bedeviled her.

I hung around the garage each spring when she painted her green kayak with pungent airplane dope, a viscous waterproof liquid used on fabric-covered airplanes. The kayak, which could be sailed with a centerboard and outriggers, had been one of a pair built in Fairbanks in the 1930s, probably from the same materials as early airplanes. I tried to join the fun and made leaf and twig boats that I hoped to coat with Jane's smelly goo, but I never got the chance. She was too dexterous at defending her clean dope against my twigs and leaves.

In the evenings when Jane rolled her naturally curly auburn hair in rags to create smooth waves for the morning, I would watch attentively even though I knew that—regardless of the blandishments of Toni Home Permanents—nothing Mother or I could do to my fine straight hair would curl it for more than an hour or two. My sister hummed songs that my mother had not taught me. And when Jane played her 78-rpm jitterbug records on our phonograph, her saddle oxfords took a few quick steps, and I sensed that she and her friends danced in a manner not seen on the floor of the Sourdough Dance Club. I never dared try on her lipstick or bracelets, but sometimes when she was not at home, I looked at them.

I learned her boyfriends' names and a trick for exploiting them. When swains came to call, I played directly at their feet until I was finally offered gum or candy on the condition that I go elsewhere to unwrap and enjoy it. These boys were on their own; they could not look to my parents or Jane to rid them of their kinder-gartner audience. My parents considered spinsterhood a sad fate, and they encour-aged Jane to date; but they did not believe in undue privacy for young people. What they did believe in was the economics of having their older daughter babysit their younger one when they had an evening engagement. On one occasion this parental requirement resulted in a desperate young man taking me as well as Jane to an evening movie at the Empress Theater. Afterwards he invited us next door to have a soda at a young people's hot spot, The Upstairs. This glamorous evening was the high point in my relationship with Jane's boyfriends.

Jane enjoyed going to a movie with a boy or sitting at the Co-Op counter drinking a milk shake with her girlfriends. But Alta believed that social life consisted of more than casual dates and drugstore refreshments; she was intent on preparing her elder daughter for formal entertainment. Alta knew how to prioritize. She concentrated on preparing Jane socially in those years; my turn was to come later. The result of her well-organized program was that, as adults-in-training, Jane and I learned independently to attend, and independently to dread, Alta's favored event—the afternoon tea.

Teas are invitation-only women's parties often given to honor a person, such as a young woman newly engaged or an older woman retiring as president of a civic organization. Some teas involve special gifts for the honorees (a "handker-chief tea" for a departee, or a "personal lingerie tea" for the soon-to-be-wed). Jane and I considered them symbolic of Montana, Oregon, and other effete states from which our mother and her friends had emigrated. We, the children of the Territory, lacked nostalgia for refined customs and did our best to rebel. Jane was my model for resistance; unfortunately, where etiquette was concerned, our mother was more powerful than both of us. Alta was an anomaly in her primary family. Her English was more correct, her temper more controlled, her house cleaner, and her manners more gracious than the rest of her family's. She did not indulge in sharp gossip, alcohol, or coarse language. She actually enjoyed teas and wanted her daughters to do the same. An anecdote that Jane tells about one of these attend-or-else events is typical of our mother-daughter skirmishes.

The tea that Jane describes was intended to honor Mrs. Herbert Hoover Jr., a woman eminent by association. She was the daughter-in-law of a former U.S. president and wife of the head of Arctic Contractors, a consortium of stateside companies exploring Naval Petroleum Reserve No. 4 on the North Slope. Mrs. Hoover was due to arrive on a Pan American flight shortly before the event. As it turned out, the plane was delayed, and the tea party was held without its honoree—a fact discovered by the rest of the guests only after they arrived at the home of the hostess.

Jane was a college student, working her second summer for Arctic Contractors. She, my mother, and my Aunt Audrey were invited to the weekday afternoon tea. Jane wished to decline. Mother, trained by at-home afternoons in the social role of women in industry, insisted that Jane had a duty to attend. Jane felt she would be more useful—as well as happier—at work in slacks rather than attending a full-dress tea party. My sister was right, of course. World War II had come and gone, leaving women often underpaid but thoroughly ensconced in the workplace, their role in business more than social. But Mother was a powerful force when she saw a duty, and Jane was swept inexorably to the party.

Jane walked home from work at two o'clock to don garter belt, seamed nylons (less sturdy but better fitting than their silk predecessors), slip (dampened slightly to mitigate static cling), crisply ironed cotton dress with white cuffs and collar, and low (but not comfortable) "high heels." She then carefully applied the modest amount of red lipstick appropriate for a young woman. My mother, a mature woman, used more makeup. She curled her eyelashes with a medieval-looking clamp. She combed out her thick, dark hair, curly thanks to a home permanent. Alta considered hair dyes cheap and deceptive; in her fifties she resisted graying by plucking out invading white hairs. She applied a bit of rouge, a puff of powder, and a touch of fragrant—and to me hilariously named—toilet water behind her earlobes. Neither mother nor daughter used antiperspirant, which had not been invented; women's dress clothes were fitted with washable underarm pads.

Jane recalls riding sulkily in the Studebaker on the way to the tea when it was discovered that she had (perhaps not accidentally) forgotten her white gloves. Maternal crisis ensued; it was too late to turn back. Fortunately, my flexible Aunt Audrey, pointing out that no one actually wore gloves once they entered a party, proposed that Jane carry one of her gloves while she carried the other. Thus both would politely share the handicap imposed on all the guests—balancing a china cup and small crustless sandwich on a dainty saucer held in the left hand (the hand clutching the gloves), so that the right hand was free to use little tongs to pluck a sugar cube from a silver sugar bowl and to pour evaporated milk from a matching creamer into the tea, which was stirred with a decorative spoon.

Their hostess met them at the door with the story of the missing honoree. Jane had a brief hope that the function would be called off and she could return to work. The hope proved vain. With the other women she accepted a cup of tea from a special friend of the hostess who was on duty to pour. The pourer's table, covered with a pale linen tablecloth, held not only the tall silver pots of tea and coffee but plates of tiny decorative snacks. On the occasion of the Hoover tea these treats had been baked by the town's leading caterer, Anna Schiek, who worked out of her small, yeast-scented house on Front Street. Jane had been trained that taking more than one or two of these enticing sweets, like sitting down at the table, would be gauche. Guests were expected to seat themselves in the living room where couches and chairs were arranged in a circle, exposing one's behavior and posture to all (legs crossed or knees together, no slip showing). Not only were guests expected to display balance and dexterity as they ate, they were also expected to smile and converse. Appropriate conversation included weather, recipes, kindly gossip, upcoming social events, and compliments on clothing. Politics, religion, money, and emotional turmoil were reserved for kitchens, coffee mugs, and a few trusted friends. In contrast to her daughters, who remained awkwardly silent while they searched their minds for appropriate trivia, our mother, graceful in handling china and in walking on unreliable high heels, was often able to have brief but real conversations with other guests and at the same time to observe the scene with pleasure and good humor. At this particular tea, she delighted in watching a guest go around the seated circle introducing a new arrival to Fairbanks: "This is my niece Bernice Burness." The woman repeated the tongue twister twenty times without error.

My sister did not consider this verbal tour de force sufficiently amusing to compensate for missing an afternoon at work, but she and Audrey's glove survived the party for the absent Mrs. Hoover without mishap. Jane endured a number of other tea parties, but she set down the burden of attending them when she left home.

Some of the skills Alta taught were more deeply appreciated by Jane—one was driving (on gravel, mud, snow, and ice) and its attendant tasks: changing a

tire, jumping a dead battery, and freeing a stuck car. It was Jane's ability to operate an automobile that made her seem most adult in my eyes. She was still a teenager when she and my mother divided the driving and traveled from Eugene to
Fairbanks on the Alcan Highway, which had just been opened to civilian traffic.
One of Jane's college friends and I were passengers. The vehicle, of course, was
a Studebaker—a brand-new one.

Neither my sister nor I ever knew whether it was the low, sleek outline of these
cars that attracted my parents or simply the fact that they liked Gene Immel, the
amiable, reliable man who ran the Fairbanks dealership and performed all our
repairs. (Jim understood the innards of gold dredges better than those of automobiles.) In any case, when the pea-soup Studebaker began to wear out, my parents
purchased another of these bullet-shaped cars, this one a dignified shade of dark
gray. The mystery of this decision is that aside from the monochrome color that
partially concealed the film of summer dust from unpaved roads, this Studebaker,
like its predecessor, had few Alaskan virtues. Its undersides were perilously close
to the road surface, at risk for scraping the oil pan on deep washboard ruts. The
low, sloped front window seemed to get more than its share of cracks from flying
gravel. Moreover, Studebakers had a poor winter reputation. Like other cars of
their time, they had rear-wheel drive and were prone to skidding on icy surfaces—
most memorably on the several ice roads that were plowed across the river each
winter to supplement the Chena River Bridge. They were also hard to start in cold
weather. Robert Linde, a veteran Fairbanks mechanic, reminisces about this flaw:
"The car that had the most trouble starting in Alaska winters was the Studebaker
V8 or 6. A cloudy day would stop them." Luckily, during their Studebaker period,
my parents lived in a series of FE Company houses with heated garages.

In 1949, when the gray Studebaker, my mother, my sister, and I made our
maiden trip over the Alcan Highway, the highway and I were seven years old. It
was the first year the route was fully open to general traffic, and certain restrictions on motorists still applied: travelers could be turned back by Canadian officials if they did not have car insurance, a designated amount of cash, a spare tire,
and (in winter) extra gas and emergency clothing. Ours was one of 7,300 cars to
pass inspection and traverse the Alcan that year.

Purchase of the Studebaker had been arranged in Fairbanks for pickup in
Seattle. In June 1949 Mother and I, wearing white gloves, hats, and our best
dresses, left my father to the frantic activity of the mining season and joined forty
other passengers, most of whom we knew, for the eight-hour unpressurized—
and for me, airsick-plagued—flight in Pan American's DC-4 to Seattle. There

we changed into more practical slacks and oxfords to take possession of the new automobile, which we drove south to pick up my sister and her friend Shirley Tonseth, in Eugene, where both Fairbanks girls were finishing their sophomore year at the University of Oregon. My mother was cheerful and not intimidated by our proposed trip. After all, eighteen years previously she had driven to Valdez in a flimsier vehicle over a worse road. Moreover, her cousin Audrey Loftus, one of her companions from the Valdez trip, had already driven the Alcan in a Studebaker with a military permit in 1946.

Audrey had traveled with her children, Jule (age eleven) and Nancy (fourteen), her Oregonian sister Norma Dellage (whose son worked for the FE Company), and Ruth Ogburn (a returning college student). Their 1946 Studebaker must have been remarkably full. In an article she wrote about the trip, Audrey speculates that hers may have been the first car carrying only women and children to receive a permit. Both her husband and the army had given her a list of required emergency supplies. Consequently she carried: "an extra fan belt, 2 spare tires, a tow cable, shovel, ax, chains, spark plugs, oil, gasoline, emergency food…blankets, a bucket, jack, tire irons, lug wrench, tire patching, water, a flashlight, and a first aid kit."One emergency item not on either her husband's or the army's list was chewing gum. Fortunately, young Jule had a good supply, which they used to temporarily patch a copper pipe connecting the radiator to the heater. The water in the pipe had frozen and expanded to create a small split during the travelers' final chilly overnight stop in an emergency shelter near mile 1,240.

On our 1949 trip, although Alta and Jane were driving a car with four passengers rather than five and our emergency gear was less extensive, the car was jammed with suitcases of clothing, the college girls' books, two spare tires, extra gasoline, oil, water, and blankets. The Studebaker's trunk had the same stylish downslope as its hood, which not only resulted in jokes about whether the car was coming or going, but also meant that there wasn't much storage space. In those days before seat belts, the plan was for me to sit in the backseat on top of a suitcase padded with a blanket. My mother, Jane, and Shirley would take turns driving and riding in back with me. Within the first hundred miles, while we were still on the paved roads of the States, I proved by throwing up three times that my motion sickness was not limited to airplanes. Despite being dosed with Mothersill's Seasick Remedy ("good for auto trips"), I still became carsick if I sat in the backseat. Soon thereafter, Shirley, who had apparently driven little, disqualified herself as a driver. Once we left the paved roads of civilization she began to have trouble with corners, slewing around the gravel turns at the same speed she drove the straight stretches. For the rest of the eleven-day trip I sat in the front seat, Shirley sat in the back, while Alta and Jane alternated between the backseat and the driver's position. I was not surprised by this change in plan; my sister always seemed to me more competent and skilled than her girlfriends. I could tell no difference between Jane's driving and my mother's.

Despite our cramped seating, Alta chose a route to the official start of the Alcan in Dawson Creek, British Columbia, that was looping and scenic— Oregon to Montana to Calgary to Banff and Jasper national parks to Edmonton to Slave Lake. This circuitous route was partly determined by the Canadian road system: the highway through Prince George (which cuts a thousand miles off the drive from Seattle to Fairbanks) had not yet been built. But our approach was also determined by Mother's desire to show us the wonders of the Alberta national parks—and, in Edmonton, to buy a set of English Wedgwood china at bargain Canadian prices.

The detour east to Edmonton was memorable because of the silent decorum Mother's crumpled passengers were expected to maintain in the china store, which was renowned among Fairbanks women rising in the middle class. Mother spent at least a half hour conferring with the salesman and leaning over the glass cases that formed a long counter I was not to touch. After careful study of the Wedgwood patterns, she selected "Bramble" as her company china. A twelve-place setting was carefully packed and added to our load.

We left Edmonton on a road no longer oiled, a road on which the washboard gradually grew rougher and the lodging wilder. A hotel that seemed quiet when we rented a room at 7 PM erupted in clamorous joy when the bar opened at 9 PM. A dormitory-style room with a bathroom down the hall seemed worse than eccentric when we discovered that to get to the ladies' toilet it was necessary to first walk through the gentlemen's. Some of the rustic auto courts with facilities out back were more appealing.

The Alcan Highway proper began at Dawson Creek (marked by a proud "Milepost 0" in the center of town). We celebrated our arrival by having our wheels realigned and taking an obligatory picture with the Brownie camera. The bible of the Alcan, *The Milepost*, which describes every landmark, roadhouse, and town between mile 0 and mile 1,530 at Fairbanks, was in its first year of printing in 1949. It informed us that Dawson Creek, population 300 in 1942 when Alcan building began, was now 3,500. Not only did *The Milepost* contain useful information, but travelers from the opposite direction offered our gregarious mother helpful advice. We filled our gas tank whenever it was one-third

Sally Crawford on the Alcan at Dawson Creek, 1949.
Author's collection.

empty, since there were often long stretches between roadhouses with gasoline. Alta, meticulous and thrifty, kept records and was pleased to calculate that the new Studebaker got twenty-two miles to the gallon.

Jane, who had learned to drive on Fairbanks mining roads, continued to prove a competent driver as the road deteriorated. She actually preferred the Alcan to the paved roads of the States where some drivers traveled at terrific speeds of fifty or more miles an hour. By contrast, the Alcan presented familiar hazards—dust, mud, and curves. Even in flat areas the early Alcan was not straight. A widely circulated explanation for its sinuous route was that curves had been inserted to prevent the Japanese from using it as a landing field. More likely, early road builders were simply trying to avoid bogs that mired their equipment in man-deep mud. Even on the final route, when rain fell, the dusty surface became a slough of rutted "gumbo." On wet days as the Studebaker churned north, its windshield was repeatedly coated with mud spewed from the high wheels of trucks headed south. Windshield washer sprayers were still a feature of the future; Jane and Alta were dependent on the wipers to smear the brown splatters thin enough to see through.

On dry, warm days the driver enlisted her passengers, even seven-year-olds, into crew duty. Cars of the 1940s had no air-conditioning; we alternated rolling down the windows for air and frantically rolling them back up when approaching vehicles—some traveling at the maximum speed limit of 35 miles per hour—appeared trailing dense clouds of dust. License plates became such a uniform tan that I had to limit my research into the origins of our fellow travelers to cars parked at overnight stops.

Window duty was also complicated by the fact that June was progressing as we drove north; Mother Nature was opening her cornucopia of mosquitoes and other insects. Whenever the car slowed to stop, we rushed to roll up the windows to shut out flying pests. Fortunately, most of the towns along the highway were too small to require the driver to roll down her window to arm-signal a right or left turn. Each time we filled the gas tank, we scraped the windshield clean of six-legged casualties. Some of the better-prepared travelers had installed bug/ rock screens that projected up over the grille to protect the front of the car. By the end of a trip these screens could have provided a day's work for an entomologist who wished to catalog the smashed species and to determine, by study of the layers, the latitude at which specific specimens had been automotively collected.

During our Alcan trip, perhaps stimulated by the struggle with Jim over her college major, Jane expounded her feminist views. Along the Alcan she pointed out strong women, especially those working at "men's" jobs. At Burwash Landing Lodge, run by my father's friends the Jacquot brothers, she noted a woman who served us in the family-style dining room. Short and stocky with bulging forearm muscles, she neatly refilled our glasses by pouring water from a three-gallon bucket that she gripped by the rim with one hand. There was no doubt that she would have been more capable of splitting rock specimens than some of the geologists we knew. Farther down the road we were delayed by a washout caused by a ruptured beaver dam. The boss of the repair crew was a woman built along the lines of the Burwash waitress. Thereafter Jane scanned every construction crew we met. (The Canadian portion of the highway was being straightened, and the Alaskan portion was being prepared for the first blacktop in the Territory.) Unfortunately, we saw no more strong women at work.

We drove into Fairbanks on a Sunday. Jim was at home in the cottage in the FE compound. Aunt Audrey and our other neighbors quickly composed a welcoming potluck dinner. The Studebaker was dust-encased but unblemished except for minor paint chips and rock dents. Drivers Alta and Jane, tired and triumphant, slept proudly in their beds.

The summer after our road adventure, my sister acquired a new boyfriend. He did not own a car, but he did own an airplane. Sid Tallman was a recent graduate of the School of Agriculture at Cornell University in Ithaca, New York. He was a navy veteran who had flown his small plane north for a summer job at Weeks Field before settling down to farm in New York State. He swept Jane off the ground in his airplane, taking her on dates to swim at Circle Hot Springs north of Fairbanks, to circle Mount McKinley, and even to visit Frances, George, and Gale Weatherell in Talkeetna. Frances was enthusiastic and tried to fan the new romance in her own frank (and, to Jane, rather frightening) way, serving the two young people beer and then suggesting she put them up in an empty house together. Jane insisted that Sid purchase himself a hotel room. Alta and Jim were cooler and more cautious, emphasizing to Jane the importance of finishing university. Alta, whose own college career had been involuntarily cut short, was looking forward to the satisfaction of attending Jane's commencement. Jim emphasized the economic value of a degree, remaining silent on the practicality of her anthropology major. (After Jane married, she quit reading anthropology and checked out of her local library every art book she could find. Decades later, free from her father's influence, she completed a degree in art, and her art supported her.)

Sid proposed repeatedly during the summer. When Jane demurred and returned to school in the fall, he flew to Eugene to be at her side. By early December she was persuaded, and they were married by a judge in Eugene. No family members were present; my grandmother declined to attend on the basis that she did not want to encounter the judge, who by coincidence was the official who had divorced her from Charles Tanner. Her scruples about encountering the judge also conveniently distanced her from the event and the reaction of my parents, who were informed by a long-distance telephone call after the ceremony had been safely completed.

Jane was twenty when she flew off to her new home three thousand miles away, proving herself as venturesome as her parents. The three of us who remained in Fairbanks also left the FE compound to move into a large, mildly historic house downtown. The house belonged to the FE Company; Jim Crawford had just been promoted to manager of Fairbanks mining operations.

DOWNTOWN FAIRBANKS AT MIDCENTURY

FE Company staff, 1950, in front of the FE office building.
FRONT ROW: J. R. Weaver, Jim Crawford, Pat O'Neill, Carl Anderson, Roy Earling, Jack Boswell, A. H. Humpheries, L. E. Linck. SECOND ROW: Neva Funk, Louise Parker, Cap Osborne, Hertha Baker, Boris Ashurkoff, Ted Loftus, J.C. Johnston. THIRD ROW: Ralph Norris, M. Dechentsreiter, R. R. Niemi, M.J. Thomson, Mary Chaddon, C. O. Fowler, A. A. Erickson. FOURTH ROW: Ed Hoch, D. F. Eagan, Al Seeliger, A. L. McPherson, K. Rankin. BACK ROW: D. E. Hohenhaus, Donald MacDonald III, R. Saunders.
Author's collection.

{11}

FAIRBANKS OPERATIONS MANAGER

W HEN MY SISTER MARRIED in 1950 and my father became manager of Fairbanks operations, our scaled-down family moved off Garden Island and into the Mary Lee Davis House on the corner of Fifth and Cowles. In 1916 a successful miner had this two-story house built to specifications in a prenuptial agreement with a young and canny bride. However, the miner left her a widow before the interior was finished; she never moved into the house she had designed. In 1923 a local author, Mary Lee Davis, and her husband bought the house, converted the furnace from wood to coal and completed the interior. The residence acquired transient local fame when its photograph and description appeared in a 1931 book by Davis, *We Are Alaskans*. The following year the FE Company purchased the house and its furnishings, described in Davis's book as "many an heirloom from older homes in eastern states." The home had all the necessary features of a Company house—broad screened front porch, fireplace, lawn, garden, greenhouse, and separate heated garage. Its polished oak floors were covered with oriental rugs and substantial furniture. A grandfather clock just inside the front door kept perfect time as long as my father remembered to wind it by shifting the brass weights that hung next to the pendulum. The dark oval dining table and its fourteen matching chairs had legs that ended in carved lion heads. Children hiding in the cavern beneath the table could see the built-in but never-used butler's bell under the table rim. The porcelain bathtub upstairs also had decorative feet and was frighteningly long; a sleepy eight-year-old could drown in it. In summer photographs, the house appears particularly gracious with transplanted birch trees along the edge of the lawn and the aging city tennis court next door.

The only drawback to the Mary Lee Davis House was that it was not connected to the downtown steam heating pipes from the NC Company. During the winter, a coal furnace in the basement ran constantly. Once again, as in the tiny Sixth Avenue house they had owned during the Depression, Jim and Alta found themselves arranging for a coal truck to come once a month and dump a load down the chute that led to our basement coal bin. Inside the house fine black dust settled everywhere. Alta polished, dusted, and vacuumed daily, the cylindrical Electrolux slithering behind her on its runners as she worked to keep the oriental rugs in condition for the kind of entertaining expected of a manager's wife. Once a year she would sweep the wallpaper with a cloth-covered broom, and I would help her in the satisfying task of rubbing the residual dust off with Absorene—a pink, slightly crumbly dough that gradually turned gray as the wallpaper brightened.

Jim's chief household duty was to nurse the "automatic" furnace into steady action. In the morning he removed burned-out clinkers from the firebox with long tongs and dropped them into a bucket to cool. Sometimes a too-large clinker or lump of coal would jam the feed mechanism, and the fire would go out. He would get rid of the offender and relight the coal on a bed of newspapers and kindling. The coal we burned was mined at Healy and brought by railroad to the Healy River Coal Company bunkers near our old house on Garden Island. The bunkers were enormous elevated bins with a sloping train track ascending to their three-story top. A locomotive pushed a coal car up the slope to side-dump a load into one of the bins that dispensed either lump coal for hand-loaded stoves or chestnut coal for furnaces with automatic stokers. Drivers parked delivery trucks or private pickups beneath the proper bin and pulled a knotted rope to open a trapdoor at the bottom of the bin. The coal would fill the truck with a tumbling roar—an amplified version of the clatter in our coal chute when the delivery truck dumped its load. A circle of coal dust surrounded the sloping doors of our coal chute and dusted the ground for many yards around the bunkers, darkening winter snow and filling the summer air with a dusty, pleasing, slightly acrid odor.

During our first year in the Cowles Street house, my father had an assistant with the furnace. My cousin Gale Weatherell moved north from Talkeetna for his freshman year at Fairbanks High School. At that time Talkeetna had no high school. The previous fall Gale had begun ninth grade at home by enrolling in a correspondence course from the Calvert School. Correspondence study did not

Gale Weatherell, age twelve, driving a Caterpillar in Talkeetna.
Courtesy of Jane Crawford Tallman.

engage Gale; he made tortoise progress with the stacks of lessons while the days grew shorter. Just before the winter trapping season opened, Frances learned that a friend was looking for a young man to help him trap marten, fox, and the big-cash fur—beaver, which was selling for $60 per prime pelt (equivalent to about $400 today). Frances went to Gale. Would he be willing to drop school for the year to work on a trapline? Gale eagerly closed his books and put on snowshoes. The trapline was a good choice; during that winter he gained a wilderness education not found in books. But the next year Frances insisted that her son return to regular schooling. Home study at the kitchen table in Talkeetna was prone to distraction, so she sent him north to live with us and attend Fairbanks High.

When Gale arrived in the Cowles Street house, he was fifteen, experienced at hard work, and more capable than most adults at running equipment. However, even today he has not forgotten his struggles with the balky basement furnace. My father was glad to hand over most of the coal tasks to Gale, and I was glad to have his company. The house was livelier than it had been since the departure of my sister, who is also Gale's sister by birth.

Gale was shyer than Jane. Fairbanks High School doubtless handed him a few painful surprises. For example, there was freshman initiation. On a speci-fied Friday ninth-graders were supposed to present themselves at school for hazing wearing a giant diaper, bib, and baby bonnet over their everyday clothes. Alta manufactured the required items with her sewing machine, and Gale was unusually quiet when he left for school wearing them. Whether this humiliating costume caused Gale and eighty other freshmen to establish solidarity with upperclassmen is questionable. Probably the only satisfaction at the end of the day was the seniors' at having discharged the debt of embarrassment from their own freshman year. Gale may have suffered in silence at school, but at home and with our Loftus cousins he was always ready to join the fun. He was a gifted storyteller. He gave first-person accounts of overturned boats, brushes with game wardens, and cabins obscured beneath snowdrifts, speaking with a quiet rhythm that gave listeners time to react. My uncles' stories and punch lines were sometimes obscured in raucous laughter, but I never missed the point of tales that Gale told. Gale left Fairbanks after his freshman year to finish high school closer to home in Palmer. My father resumed charge of the coal furnace, an onerous chore but straightforward in comparison to managing the Fairbanks operations of USSR&M.

Jim's first challenge as manager was not an engineering problem, but an administrative one: miners and trade workers at the FE Company went on strike May 15, 1950. The point-driving machines and hydraulic giants were abandoned; the dredges went silent. Previously busy workmen picketed leisurely, carrying signs and strolling back and forth in front of the main gate to the Company yard. Sometimes they sought shelter from the sun in a canvas-covered hut they had erected near the front door to the office. May was prime mining season. As the days of shutdown turned to weeks, my father's impatient temper rose at home.

In the fifty-year history of the FE Company there were only two strikes. The 1941 strike, which occurred before my time, was settled with a wage increase, camp improvements, and other concessions. However, in 1941, the employees (represented by the International Union of Mine, Mill and Smelter Workers) failed in their goal of unionizing the Company.

In 1950, as in 1941, the chief issue was unionization. The workers were represented this time by the International Brotherhood of Electrical Workers (IBEW), which had an industrial charter and represented not just miners but all trades working for the Company. Strikers wanted a union shop, in which all employees would be required to join the IBEW when they were hired. The Company would be obligated to deduct dues from first paychecks and remit the funds to the union. At home my father was outraged at the notion of requiring employees to pay dues and join an association as the price of getting a job at the FE Company.

On May 21 workers pressed harder: they turned off the FE power plant. This not only cut electricity to the mining camps, it affected the entire city of Fairbanks.

The FE plant had been supplementing the NC Company plant for years. The Company actually supplied two-thirds of the city's power. The newspaper published pleas for conservation: "Do all roasting and baking between midnight and 8 a.m. Cut off refrigerators during the day. Do not operate electric toys. Cut off all neon signs in the business district. Do not use electrical appliances such as toasters, waffle irons, electric razors, vacuum cleaners, or water heaters during the day." Despite the publicity, townspeople found it difficult to break the habit of cooking at peak hours; periodic blackouts became the norm. Caterer Anna Schiek was quoted in a newspaper article as she described consequences: "Lost all my cakes Monday night.... Every time I turned around something came on or went off—lights, then the water pump, then the stove, then the coal stoker." My father waxed indignant about the inconvenience to Mrs. Schiek and the rest of the citizenry.

Jim Crawford was a frugal man who worked for a frugal company. His own salary was not negotiated; it was set by his bosses. For the most part he received a raise only when he was promoted to a new position. He never expressed any criticism of this arrangement. After his death I found a handwritten record of his earnings for each year that he worked for the Company. His longest post was his last one. He was vice president and general manager for fourteen years; his salary during his final ten years remained unchanged at $35,000. His loyalty as well as his duty was to management.

In June 1950, after three weeks of shutdown at the dredges and two weeks of power shortage in town, a federal conciliator stepped in to resolve the strike. The Company managed to avoid a union shop and an increase in base pay. Workers gained new vacation and seniority benefits, and a procedure was put in place to handle worker grievances. The IBEW was to investigate complaints and negotiate solutions with the Company. Niilo Koponen, before he became a school principal and legislator, was an electrician at the Company and was assigned the role of union steward. He remembers that after the strike, negotiating with Al Seeliger, the FE Company business manager, was suddenly no longer difficult. Trickier was the problem of mediating grievances between workers—particularly between the cooks and bakers in the mess houses. He dreaded being called for these "he touched my skillet" disputes between prima donnas. Good chefs had loyal followers in the dining hall; Niilo's efforts to bring peace in the kitchen were closely watched.

Two years after the strike was settled, a second event painful for my father occurred. Eugene Swendsen, a Norwegian who had worked for the Company for about a month, was killed on the job when the hydraulic "giant" he was using to wash away a cliff of frozen muck suddenly swung around and pinned him to the ground. His chest was crushed by the nozzle. He was the seventh employee to die on the job since the Company came to Fairbanks in 1924. Jim considered the FE Company to be a modern, professional, and safety-conscious organization. Caution signs were posted on the dredges and in the shops. The Company had a contract with the Fairbanks Clinic to care for injured workers. The Bureau of Mines was regularly invited to give talks and classes to the workers. The Company's accident rate was about one per thousand work hours, and the majority of accidents were classed as minor. A death, even one that did not involve a safety violation, was serious. It was hard on the morale of workers and bosses alike. Swendsen's brother in Seattle was notified, reports were filed, life insurance was paid, and the funeral attended. But after all was done, the memory, and for Jim a vague sense of discredit, lingered.

Alta supported Jim in his managerial worries. She sympathized, avoided playing the devil's advocate, and made sure his dinner was on time. In her role as family peacemaker, she cautioned me not to pester him with questions until he was relaxing in the living room after dinner—advice I was too impatient to heed. No sooner had he walked in the door than I was asking him to please let me stay up past bedtime to listen to a special radio program. His response was a flash of annoyance; my retort was a sulk that tailed off hours after Jim had forgotten his irritation.

But Alta chose not to be preoccupied with her temperamental family. She was enjoying life on Cowles Street. For the first time, she had a single-party phone line. Callers received a busy signal only when we were actually talking on the telephone, and no stranger was listening impatiently or curiously to our conversations. I am not sure whether our good telephone fortune was related to my father's new job or simply to the fact that we were willing to pay $7.50 a month for the privilege of a single line. Some houses were still on eight-party lines, and the list of newcomers awaiting phones was long (in 1954 it reached eight hundred applicants). Less than a year after our move, a dial system was introduced and our number, Harvard 712, changed to 5514.

Alta delighted in the spacious living-dining room on Cowles Street that made it easy for her to entertain Jim's mining colleagues. She could now also hold large tea parties. Once, she even hosted a wedding for our friends, George and Gina Rayburn. (The late-afternoon vows were famously interrupted by a neighbor who barged in the never-locked back door yodeling the standard Fairbanks greeting: "Yoo-hoo, anyone home?")

Alta also found the location of the Mary Lee Davis house convenient. She could walk to St. Matthew's Church to help with a rummage sale or to the school for a PTA meeting or to the Odd Fellows Hall for a Sourdough Dance. The missed school bus was a problem of the past. Her daughter could walk to school even in the coldest weather, crossing the street to wait inside Christine MacDonald's house while Chris put on snowsuit, boots, hat, double mittens, and a wool scarf tied bandit-style across her nose and mouth. With the cold, dry snow creaking under boots, we two third-graders would walk four blocks to Ruthie Butler's house for another indoor stop. Judie Tweiten's was three blocks farther. By the time Judie had donned her layers and the four of us had trudged the last couple of blocks, our bitter morning trek had taken twice as long as our usual walk on a mild day, but our cumulative cold exposure had been minimal. Alta did not worry even during the dramatic January cold snap of 1951 when temperatures remained between 50 and 60 degrees below zero for thirteen days straight except for a brief rise to 35 below on January 17. Ice fog (called "people fog" in Siberia since it mainly consists of frozen water vapor from car exhaust and furnace smoke) made driving difficult and prevented nearly all planes from landing. A single Pan Am cargo flight landed at Weeks Field on January 17 with mail and fresh food. On the back haul, it took out thirty-two passengers eager to leave the winter behind. But Main School stayed open, and the daily routine of pupils was uninterrupted.

To mitigate winter blues that year, Alta and Jim took up a sport venerable in Fairbanks but new to them: curling. Curling had come to Fairbanks in 1905 from Canada and Scotland; by 1908 it was so popular that Fairbanks Curling Club members combined their labor to build an indoor rink with two sheets of ice. Moving off the river ice and onto an indoor rink meant smooth ice, no shoveling, and good lighting during the long nights. Because the building was heated only during cold snaps, players could still enjoy the sensation of being in the fresh air—important to those members who spent their winters working in stuffy buildings.

Curling was a common recreation in Fairbanks. Not only adults curled; high school coed teams vied for trophies. It was not until curling became a televised Olympic sport that I encountered football and baseball fans who considered curling comical. They laughed that the name evoked a beauty salon, not an ice rink. Others complained that the sport's jargon twisted English in strange ways. Admittedly, curling vocabulary is a little arcane. A rink (team) of four players, including the skip (captain), take turns sliding rocks (forty-two-pound granite stones) down a 15-by-146-foot sheet of ice toward the house (a large bull's-eye visible through the ice). The polished stones are topped by handles that can be turned as the stone is released to create a slow spin that causes the rock's path to curve (curl). The stones are impressive, but the other piece of equipment used in the game is unromantic—a broom. Two members of the rink, following the skip's shouted instructions, sweep the ice in front of the stone to modify its curving path and to make sure it crosses the hog line (short foul line). The brooms used in the 1950s were hard to distinguish from those used on the kitchen floor. Moreover, my parents' rinks lacked today's specialized shoes and natty uniforms. They wore ordinary lightweight boots, wool gloves, wool pants, and heavy cardigans (Alta's was fancied up with a knitted pattern of crossed brooms and curling stones). As a gesture to the old country, some Fairbanks players wore tam-o'-shanters. Others, like Jim and Alta, wore Glengarry hats, which resemble a soldier's folding hat—except that my parents' Glengarries were navy blue with red pom-poms on top and plaid ribbons hanging down the back.

Part of Jim's attraction to curling may have been its origin in the land of Clan Crawford. Although not a devoted genealogist like his DAR mother, Pearle, Jim was interested enough in his forefathers to order a book on the history of minor Scots clans. The book identified the Crawford tartan; he ordered a yard of the plaid so that Alta could sew him a tie and vest to wear to Curling Club parties. Curlers are sociable; neighbors of the club on Second Avenue complained about the evening shortage of parking and the abundance of alcohol. Their complaints had merit. The curlers were modern American players of a five-century-old Scottish game; they honored both Scotland's whiskey and America's automobiles. Cars were driven to the club by convivial spectators as well as players. Whiskey was poured to celebrate the end of a bonspiel (tournament). That some curlers also opened a bottle or two of beer at the end of a simple evening's contest did not seem to bother my parents, who drank little. My father liked the game, enjoyed the camaraderie of the club, and admired the capabilities of its members. In the early 1960s, to the relief of its downtown neighbors, the club moved out toward the end of Second Avenue and erected a new building. Members from various trades combined their skills to do most of the work themselves. The insulated concrete building held six sheets of refrigerated ice and a spectators' gallery.

Alta's attraction to curling was not its Scots origin or its celebratory libations. She was athletic and sociable, and curling was one of the few team sports open to matrons. She also had some natural talent for the game. Scoring in curling is similar to scoring in shuffleboard. The team that wins one of the eight ends (innings) gets one point for each stone that is closer to the center of the house (target) than the opponents' closest stone. Alta had good aim and a feel for the force needed to slide a stone to the spot indicated by the skip standing in the house at the far end of the ice. She was more likely than Jim to be on a winning rink selected to compete in a two-city "international" bonspiel in a Canadian town like Inuvik, Whitehorse, or Dawson City. For several years she was president of the women's branch of the Fairbanks Curling Club, the Rockettes.

A benefit of curling, and of skiing, ice-skating, dogsledding, and Christmas, was that they gave Fairbanksans a reason to look forward to winter. In March, when the hours of darkness no longer overshadowed the hours of light, the city celebrated winter sports and warming weather at the Winter Ice Carnival. The carnival was started in 1934 by Kay Hufman and Clara Murray, a pair of energetic young matrons bent on curing late-winter blues. They were backed by local businessmen with an eye to stimulating commerce, and the carnival quickly became an annual event. Ingenious workmen, forerunners of today's ice sculptors, built back-lit thrones and turreted palaces with blocks of clear ice from the dredge ponds. A beauty queen was elected from a court of princesses, and the Pioneers of Alaska chose a king and queen regent. These temporary royals, representing beauty and wisdom, rode at the head of the ice carnival parade followed by the carnival baby and its family, the high school band, marching military units, glistening jalopies driven by teenage boys, antique cars driven by fathers of teenage boys, decorated business floats, and costumed children with dogs. The evanescent court reigned on chilly thrones long enough to have photos taken and to watch Eskimo dancing and blanket tosses. Athabascans from the Interior regularly won the dogsled races and sometimes the beauty contests, but they lived too close to home to be romanticized. The costumes and culture of seagoing Eskimos were exotic by comparison and captured the imagination of Fairbanksans. Business supporters of the carnival were glad to pay airfare from Barrow or Wainwright for the dance groups or for men who could demonstrate igloo building.

Most of the carnival events were originally held on the ice of the Chena River under the steel bridge, which formed a balcony for spectators. A looping cross-country ski track was set, rinks were cleared for hockey and recreational skating, and a ski jump swooped above the riverbank. With time athletes improved and contests moved to better facilities. Bonspiels were held at the Curling Club. Ski jumping moved to the university campus. Firemen and military volunteers flooded a playing field beside the river to create a smooth outdoor hockey rink with floodlights and bleachers.

But the big attraction of the carnival was not skiing or hockey or snowshoeing. Nor was it the photo contest, the spelling bee, the fireworks, or the coronation ball. The main event was the North American Championship Dog Derby, which started and ended at the Chena River Bridge. The derby was a seventy-mile race, run in three unequal heats over three days. In early days a pari-mutuel booth was erected on the ice to handle bets, but when the authorities insisted on enforcing territorial law, gamblers had to resort to clandestine wagers. The race was covered live on the radio, so fans could follow developments during the hours when the racers were out of sight. Prize money totaling more than $20,000 was divided among the top finishers of each day's heat, with the largest prize reserved for the overall winner, the team with the shortest combined time for the three days.

Our whole family turned out to watch the teams leave the first day and return three days later. I had been cautioned about sled dogs and stayed obediently behind the ropes of the chute. Every other year the newspaper seemed to print a fatal story about malemutes and a child. We pointed out to each other teams that appealed to us, and we admired the superbly conditioned dogs and their drivers, who kept their sleds light by running as much and riding as little as possible. Some teams were not only powerful but beautiful, well-matched offspring of compact Siberian huskies bred by Leonhard Seppala. Other teams were made up of large dogs of indecipherable ancestry. But in racing, size and looks were unimportant. Spectators, especially bettors, watched for strength, endurance, intelligence, and loyalty to the driver. Jim claimed that winning mushers could be seen to use reward more than punishment in training. His experience with dogs was that they were more responsive to love than to the whip.

But no amount of study could guarantee a safe bet: a bitch might go into heat on the trail, throwing a team off; a moose might contest the right of way; weather might suddenly change; or a team might become confused by spectators and roads along the first few miles of trail. Women, men, whites, and Natives competed in the races. For several years the race was dominated by Roland Lombard, a veterinarian from Massachusetts who had been inspired by racing against Leonhard Seppala in New England. During another time period the most frequent winners were Athabascans from river villages—Andy Kokrine Jr., Gareth Wright, Horace "Holy" Smoke, Jimmy Huntington Jr., and George Attla.

About a month after the ice carnival was over, winter officially ended with breakup. The day the ice on the Chena River at Fairbanks and the Tanana River at Nenana gave way, two things happened. First, riverbank towns braced for a possible flood caused by moving chunks of ice jamming together to form a dam.

Fairbanks had major breakup floods in 1930, 1937, and 1948. At least four other breakups during my parents' forty-year tenure in Fairbanks brought moderate flooding. Homeowners near the river moved rugs and furniture upstairs, drove their cars to high ground, and stayed with friends until the water receded.

The second and surer result of breakup was that several lucky people won the two ice pools. In Fairbanks and Nenana, Alaskans bet on the precise minute when a tripod placed in the middle of the river would move a hundred feet downstream on a freed cake of ice or through a newly opened channel. The Nenana Ice Classic was the first and more famous of these two pools. In the spring of 1916 a group of bored engineers, waiting for construction to resume on the Alaska Railroad, built the first tripod, hired a watchman to guard the clock, designed tickets, and sold them at a dollar apiece to create a $600 pot. Joe Mills, Nenana's barber, guessed the exact time: April 30 at 11:30 AM. His winnings were said to have been exhausted in immediate celebration. The ingenious clock-stopping mechanism devised by the engineers was still in use when the *Fairbanks Daily News-Miner* described it in 1949: When the tripod moved, it "jerked the wire which loosed the heavy knife which severed a cord holding the weight which pulled the lever to push a pin into the mechanism" of the onshore clock, causing it to stop and officially record the breakup time.

Territorial law forbade gambling, but authorities chose to overlook this spring outlet for winter blues, and ice pools took their place in territorial tradition unhampered for forty-three years. People like my parents, who did not wager on dog teams or anything else, regularly bought and filled out ice-pool tickets. Some bettors even denied that the ice pools were games of chance. Everyone had an opinion about the weather, the thickness of the ice, and whether snow-melt in the hills would come early or late. Some took a mathematical approach and calculated odds based on historic data. Others relied on intuition, personal superstition, or dreams to give them the day and hour. (Presumably the tickets that arrive in Nenana each year listing the nonexistent date April 31 fall into the dream category.)

The population of the Interior may have been small, but enthusiasm for the $2 breakup gamble was high. The cash value of the pools grew rapidly; Nenana's reached $200,000 by the mid-1950s. People bought tickets together and split the money if they won. Announcers from Fairbanks radio stations moved portable transmitters to the riverbanks, hooked up their microphones, and settled in to wait for the siren in Nenana or the NC Company whistle in Fairbanks to alert them and everyone in town that a tripod was beginning to move. In 1949, the

Ice Carnival dog race, ca. 1930. Leonhard Seppala is in fur parka to the right.
The audience is watching from Chena River Bridge. *Author's collection.*

whistle in Fairbanks sounded at almost the exact time of Alta's guess. I was
thrilled when we learned that she had come within six minutes of winning
$3,836 in the Chena pool. In 1953 a ticket held by my parents' friends Mariette
and Earl Pilgrim and Earl's nephew and wife was one of twelve that named the
exact minute of the Nenana breakup. Years later, when I came to know Earl
better, he told me that he considered himself the recipient of good fortune that
spring, although he never actually received the ice pool check. In a miner's story
typical of the 1950s, his and Mariette's combined win of $8,000 went directly to
the IRS to pay current taxes on the prize money and back taxes on their mine.

My parents also considered themselves to have had good fortune on Cowles
Street. There were no spring floods during the two years we lived in the Mary
Lee Davis House. Jim's career in the Company advanced, Alta's social life
expanded, and their younger daughter overcame her shyness enough to enter
into the town life of Fairbanks.

{12}

THE TOWN THROUGH SCHOOLGIRL EYES

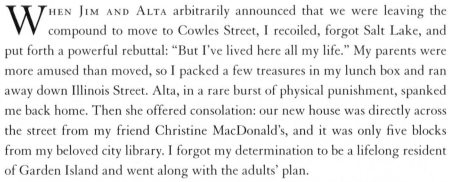

WHEN JIM AND ALTA arbitrarily announced that we were leaving the compound to move to Cowles Street, I recoiled, forgot Salt Lake, and put forth a powerful rebuttal: "But I've lived here all my life." My parents were more amused than moved, so I packed a few treasures in my lunch box and ran away down Illinois Street. Alta, in a rare burst of physical punishment, spanked me back home. Then she offered consolation: our new house was directly across the street from my friend Christine MacDonald's, and it was only five blocks from my beloved city library. I forgot my determination to be a lifelong resident of Garden Island and went along with the adults' plan.

The Mary Lee Davis House was no more than a mile and a half from the compound, but the move to Cowles Street changed Fairbanks for me. Before, I had gone downtown only with my mother. The mile or so to town would have been an easy ride on my pale blue Schwinn bike had it not been for the barrier of the Cushman Street Bridge. The bridge's steel girders formed a vault across the Chena carrying two lanes of automobile traffic on broad tracks of steel plate that protected the wood decking from wear. The lanes may have been spacious in 1917 when the bridge was built, but they were a snug fit for the cars and pickups of the 1950s. Big trucks and wide buses had to straddle the center line, forcing traffic coming up the opposite ramp to back down. The pedestrian walkways, suspended on the outside of the vehicle lanes, were also narrow. Riding a bicycle on the clanking steel plates of the car deck terrified me, but if I walked my heavy bike on the pedestrian catwalk, I was a moving obstruction.

Our relocation to the town side of the bridge meant that my bike and I, no longer trapped on Garden Island, were free to develop business destinations. Alta sent me to Lindy's Grocery Store on Fourth Avenue to charge a loaf of bread and a can of spinach to her account. I browsed in Adler's Book Shop and spent my twenty-five-cent allowance on treats from the Co-Op Soda Fountain or the Red Cross Drug Store. I met townspeople without Alta as intermediary and no longer saw Fairbanks solely through my parents' eyes.

My favorite downtown chore was fetching our mail from Box 1304, halfway up the wall of bronze mailboxes at the post office. Alta often did this task herself for social reasons. In those years postmen did not deliver mail to homes and businesses, so the post office lobby on the main floor of the concrete Federal Building on Cushman Street was a crowded and newsy location. I considered the Federal Building a grand place. Built in Art Deco style in 1934, it had wide marble steps and terrazzo floors with brass trim. A grillwork of stylized eagles surmounted the three main doors. But the building's greatest marvel was its Otis elevator, for many years proclaimed the farthest north lift in the world. Although I was told it "was not a toy," my father once took me for a ride on it to the courtroom on the third floor. I remember nothing about the courtroom, but I do remember the feeling in my stomach as the elevator started and stopped. It was better than bouncing on the swinging pedestrian bridge that crossed Noyes Slough. The second floor of the building housed the federal jail, which also intrigued me. I knew about prisoners from *The Count of Monte Cristo*, and I often gazed at the barred jail windows from the street, although I never glimpsed more than shadows of its mysterious inmates.

As I walked or biked downtown, I encountered grown-ups unlike my parents—grown-ups who did in public things that my father disapproved of: shouting, kissing, eating food on the street, lurching drunkenly in broad daylight. These encounters were usually not frightening; the loud characters and drinkers seemed more a threat to themselves than to a child. I was also surrounded by people who knew my family. As I walked down the sidewalk, I recognized many of the men and women, and probably more recognized me.

But of all the Fairbanks citizens I met, the ones who interested me most were single women who modeled ways to live quite differently than my housewife mother and aunts. Some of these women were teachers, like Martha "Mardy" Hoeckle, a strict, bowlegged veteran of World War II in North Africa. Miss Hoeckle was an uncompromising sixth-grade teacher with a warm heart for students. In her narrow frame house on Second and Hall streets, she housed students needing a temporary place to stay for a day or week at a time. Teacher salaries were modest in the 1950s. Miss Hoeckle planted a large garden each summer and prepared dinners on a chrome-trimmed, wood-burning cookstove. Her living room was a welcome haven with a potbellied coal stove, an upright piano, books, board games, and a cat. At the post office she was famous for her collie, Tam, whom she often sent to pick up her mail. Tam would stand on his hind legs in front of the window, carefully take the bundle in his mouth, and carry it the five blocks home.

Eva McGown was even more well known. In 1914 she was a music teacher nearing spinsterhood when she made a bold move—her first trip away from home. She traveled across the Atlantic by ocean liner, across the United States by transcontinental train, across the Gulf of Alaska by steamship, and across the Valdez Trail by horse-drawn sleigh to Fairbanks, where she married Art McGown the day she arrived. Her groom was part owner of the Model Café and a widower twenty-three years her senior. They had met by mail through the arrangement of friends. In Fairbanks she initially taught school, then gallantly tended her ailing husband until his death in 1930. For a decade she was known only as the choir director at St. Matthew's Church, a colorful widow who lived in a room at the Nordale Hotel and brightened the streets with her broad-brimmed hats, flowing dresses, scarves with a "touch o' green," and stream of unstoppable chatter. Then came World War II, and Eva came into her own. Her generosity and her memories of arriving in strange territory made her a spontaneous arranger of housing and resolver of emergencies for women and families arriving in overcrowded Fairbanks. It was hard for my mother or anyone else to

Eva McGown at her desk in the Nordale Hotel lobby. *Author's collection.*

refuse when Eva called asking for a bed for "a nice little woman from Toledo for just a few days while her husband arranges on-base housing." Recognizing her vocation, the Fairbanks City Council hired her as Official City Hostess.

Eva McGown was a delight for me to meet on the street because she smelled like violets, supplied 90 percent of the conversation (a boon to a shy child), and was an encyclopedia of Irish superstitions: never sing before breakfast; never place shoes on a table, even in a box; never look at the new moon through a window; and perhaps my favorite, stepping in a mud puddle brings good luck.

Old Lady Ford was at the other end of the spectrum of eccentric single women. When I saw her advancing toward me, a small figure in a once-fashionable rusty black gown with an umbrella in one hand and a shopping bag in the other, I crossed the street. She was a figure for childish mockery, but our derision held a frisson of fear and awe. She had once chased my sister with that umbrella when Jane wandered onto her property during a city Easter-egg hunt. Mrs. Ford, as our mothers insisted we call her, walked the streets putting treasures into her shopping bag: screws from a construction site, a cracked dish from café trash, a mushy apple gleaned from behind the grocery store. Into the bag these went, the same bag that held her property titles and valuable papers. No adult in my hearing ever called her "crazy"—perhaps "unusual" or "eccentric," but not "crazy." Not only was Fairbanks a tolerant community, but Hulda Ford was rich, and she was sharp in her business dealings.

She had once been a vivacious dance girl in Montana and perhaps a member of the demimonde in Dawson. She married Sheldon Ford, and the couple opened a hotel in Nome. But when the marriage failed and the hotel closed, she decided on a new start with a new man in a new town. In 1906, while she closed out business in Nome, she sent her lover ahead to Fairbanks with capital to look for a hotel site. She arrived in our town a few months later to discover the lover had squandered their nest egg. From then on she made her own way, founding a general store, buying property, and trusting no one. She even refused to traffic with the IRS men, who wisely decided to settle up after her demise. Longtime businessmen, uneasily fascinated by her inability to profit from her profits, became protective as her personal habits declined and her living quarters on various properties became more substandard. But she kept everyone at a distance, dying in 1957 at St. Joseph's Hospital, obdurately intestate, leaving the two newspapers to publish front-page articles and the IRS and distant relatives to divvy up her half-million-dollar estate.

And there were others: Marie Mackey, a French widow who drove a Model A Ford into the 1940s; Rosamund Weller, school principal and lover of music

Irene Sherman.
Fairbanks Daily News-Miner *file photo*.

who subsidized music lessons for talented children without money; Irene Sherman, property owner and bag lady, profane and gregarious despite a strikingly burn-scarred face. I understood that these women, and other single women less conspicuous but equally independent, were not "old maids"—the ratio of men to women in the Territory precluded that. They remained unmarried by choice. A trip to the post office could be an encouraging experience for the girl who did not dream of husband, children, and pretty house.

Other lessons in diversity came to me in a building even closer to home than the post office: the city library on First and Cowles. This forty-by-forty-foot building of three-sided logs was made beautiful by covered wood porches, flower boxes facing the two streets, and tiny arched attic windows that peeked through its corrugated-iron roof. It had been built in 1909 thanks to the generosity of George C. Thomas of Philadelphia, who sent funds for a building where citizens could "enjoy books and tobacco together."

I had no interest in tobacco, which in any case was no longer being smoked in the building, but I was enchanted by books. I considered my own home to be book-poor. My energetic parents did not read in the evening; my mother's sewing machine hummed, and my father bent over the work reports on his desk. Too many of the thirty-some volumes on our family bookshelves were the sort of book I read only in desperation: collections of "favorite" poems, illustrated mushroom and bird books, a King James Bible without pictures, my Aunt Katharine

George C. Thomas Memorial Library.
University of Alaska Archives, Albert Johnson photograph collection, 1989-0166-265.

Anthony's biographies of famous women, an etiquette book (up-to-date but too upper-class for Fairbanks society), a decorative row of Reader's Digest Condensed Books, a few turn-of-the-century Alaska books I was discouraged from touching, and my father's engineering books. By contrast, the city library was a place of great richness—although penurious with its wealth.

I was already a loyal card-carrying patron of the library when we lived in the compound. Every Saturday my mother would drop me off on her way to shop so that I could return the three books that patrons (at least child patrons) were allowed to check out at a time. I would have an hour or so to pick three more books that would last me a week—one fast exciting read (a Nancy Drew mystery), one long well-illustrated book (a Howard Pyle tale), and one wild card (perhaps something not from the Children's Nook). The only difficulty with the latter was persuading one of the librarians—all whispering, educated, and probably underpaid women—to let me check out an adult book. Mind you, the books I wanted were not *adult* books, they were respectable books written for grown-ups. If a child checked one out, it decreased the supply for adult readers. In a town with two radio stations, two movie theaters, and a limited library budget, demand was high. Sometimes I was allowed to sign my name on the card from the book's pocket and the date stamp was satisfyingly chunked twice, once on the card and once on the tabular sheet inside the cover. Sometimes the librarian shook her head, and I had to select another from the Children's Nook.

When we moved to Cowles Street the pressure was off. I could walk to the library three times a week if I desired. I could select books in a less rushed, more judicious fashion. If one librarian refused a request I could wait a few days and ask another. I loved the library—the smell of cheap paper, the random pattern of tan, blue, and black bindings, and the way the floor creaked loudly, perhaps from the weight of its contents, mocking the signs requesting silence. Mostly I loved reveling in worlds beyond Fairbanks—the English countryside with Toad, India with Kim, and North Africa with Lawrence.

The library's business counterpart was Adler's Book Shop, operated by our family friends David and Mary "Benji" Adler. It was a venerable business that lasted forty-three years in Fairbanks surviving fire (1948) and flood (1967). My slender allowance made me more a browser than a shopper, but I knew that Mr. Adler, a decorated World War I veteran with a limp and Groucho Marx eyebrows, was observant of my careful study of new children's books. He had a photographic memory for the location of any book in his store and a knack for guessing that when a customer asked for "Goodbye War" what she really wanted was *A Farewell to Arms*, shelved in the bookcase nearest the door—third shelf, left

David and Mary "Benji" Adler.
Fairbanks Daily News-Miner *file photo*.

side. As Christmas approached each year, my browsing became more ostentatious because after midnight Christmas Eve service we always joined my aunts, uncles, and cousins at a party in the Adlers' small house near the church. The adults drank sherry and told stories until 2 AM, perhaps hoping to exhaust their offspring to the point that no child ever reaches—sleeping in on Christmas morning. At the party we children each got to unwrap a gift from the Adlers, always a book, often a glorious book like my *Swiss Family Robinson* with its dozen slick colored pages illustrating the ecologically impossible fauna of the island.

Christmas may have been the high point of a child's winter, but most of our days during the long months of snow were spent in first- through twelfth-grade public classrooms at Main School on Cushman Street. In 1950 Fairbanks was not only crowded, but growing. Enrollment at the concrete building was 500 in 1940, 1,500 in 1950, and 2,500 in 1955. An addition to the building constructed in 1949 was overflowing by 1951. For three years, while new elementary schools were being built (two neighborhood schools and two military-base schools), grade-school pupils attended Main School in shifts—either mornings (8 AM to 12:15 PM) or afternoons (12:45 to 5 PM). High school pupils continued a full-day schedule.

The school principal was Mariette Shaw Pilgrim—Mrs. Pilgrim. I was afraid of her. Never mind that I loved books, and she had written *Oogaruk, the Aleut*. Never mind that she was the wife of Earl Pilgrim, my father's mining colleague. In my memory she wears black, her dark hair is drawn back into a bun, and she is so tall that it hurts my neck to look up at her, so I study the floor. The principal's paddle was hung up for good toward the end of my grade-school years, but a trip to the principal's office was always serious. Parents usually sided with the teachers and Mrs. Pilgrim when called to school to discuss their children's behavior. Suspension and expulsion were ultimate punishments dreaded by children and by families whose only recourse was the stricter, tuition-charging Catholic school.

The authoritarian rule of principal and teachers, answerable only to the school board, meant that public-school classrooms were orderly. It also meant that pupils were vulnerable to arbitrary actions by teachers. Most teachers were dedicated to students, but some held slow students up to ridicule, punished the shy for being tongue-tied, and kept whole classes in from recess in an effort to extort the name of a culprit. Teachers who indulged in favoritism, racism, and petty tyranny were feared; we took our weak revenge in mockery and minor sabotage.

Our classes were unsegregated by race, social class, and achievement. Upper grades had a range of ages. There were no special programs for the gifted or slow: children who excelled skipped grades, those who failed were held back.

Because our usual homework was light—a spelling list, twenty repetitive arithmetic problems, and a few sentences to diagram (an arcane but decorative exercise guaranteed to improve our grammar)—and because there were few organized after-school activities for grade-schoolers—just scout meetings or music lessons—we had plenty of after-school time to play at houses with families different from our own.

The range from rich to poor in those boom days was not broad. The rich were not very rich, and the poor not very poor. Most of my classmates lived in modest frame houses or log cabins in mixed neighborhoods where painted two-story homes with lawns sat next to cabins surrounded by half-repaired cars. A few of my friends had more exotic housing. One girl lived in an apartment with her aunt, and two boys lived in U.S. Geological Survey housing, a neighborhood of twelve nicely furnished World War II surplus Quonset huts.

Some of these houses had a startling lack of furniture and an exciting number of children. Meals in those houses seemed to stretch easily to include any playmates present, but ran heavily to macaroni eaten with spoons when there weren't enough forks to go around. I learned that some of my fellow third-graders were competent at taking care of toddlers, a responsibility from which I fled. In other houses the furnishings and number of children were more similar to my home, but the family makeup was different. Fathers disappeared at times, not into work, but into alcohol. I met a mother so strict, or perhaps so bitter, that she withheld her daughter's allowance and garnisheed all her Christmas gift money to pay for the child's dental fillings. In those prefluoride days, the mother reasoned ungenerously that cavities were caused by eating forbidden candy. In two other families the mother was chronically ill and the children helped with her care. Some households included loving or eccentric grandmothers and grandfathers, a novelty that contrasted with my own geographically and emotionally distant grandparents.

I understood that in all these welcoming homes I was to play according to household rules. I ate fish on Fridays with Catholics. I tried to mind Athabascan mothers whose expectations I did not always understand, although I grasped vaguely the notion that Indian respect for elders meant something more than the trepidation I felt when I visited my own grandparents or the affection I had for Judie Tweiten's Swedish grandmother and her delightful lace cookies.

In the small pond of Fairbanks, the darker side of families was also revealed. One friend's father was murdered, probably by his stepmother and her lover. Other children were physically abused under the righteous motto "spare the rod and spoil the child." In those days even mention of incest was taboo, but a high school classmate sexually abused by her father bravely turned him in to the police before her younger sister was injured. Another man, inadequate to the task of raising three young children after his wife flew out of town with a new love and no forwarding address, dropped the children with distant relatives and forgot to return.

In each home we played and absorbed what we saw, unconsciously learning the variegation of our town.

School was the place where we formally learned Civics—our responsibility to the democratic society into which we had been lucky enough to be born. We also learned civic fears. The Korean War had begun, McCarthyism was gaining steam, and "Red Commies" were dangerous, if vague, specters. Most of the time they seemed to be Bad Russians (not good White Russians like our friends the Ashurkoffs). At other times they seemed to be Bad (Mainland) Chinese, Bad (North) Koreans, or Bad Americans skulking through government offices. Exactly what did Alta and Jim think of Joe McCarthy and his blacklists? What did they think of the Korean War? I cannot say. Even when we had no guests, the dinner conversation rule held—no politics, no sex, and no religion. I was left to form my own conclusions. I knew my parents were patriotic because they were Republicans. I knew they were religious because they were Episcopalians. I knew they must have had sex for me to be conceived, but at age nine, I doubted they had done "it" more than once or twice. This opinion was reinforced by my mother's silence on the subject and my girlfriends' scandalous, and not entirely accurate, descriptions of the mechanics involved.

Perhaps because my parents had so little to say, the danger from Communist conspirators and North Koreans remained hazy in my mind. More frightening and easier to visualize were the A-bomb and its big brother, the H-bomb. Despite the school's and my parents' efforts to keep images of Hiroshima and the Holocaust from children, I had found searing photos from both Japan and Germany in the public library. Hitler was gone and Americans seemed to believe that genocide had ended with him. But they were less sanguine about the risk of atomic war. Even the powerful adults in charge of our lives feared the gargantuan weapons that had ended the War in the Pacific. In 1950, practice blackouts were resumed for the first time since World War II. National magazines and newspapers showed photos of private bomb shelters; however, I knew no one in Fairbanks sufficiently assured of their value to dig a hole into the permafrost. Our school held bomb drills where we dutifully ducked under our wooden desks, although even the teachers seemed to think it silly to use a desktop for protection from an atom bomb. Still, children are always glad of a little silliness to break up the school day; we whispered, pinched, and poked each other glee-fully under our desks.

Fire drills were different. We all knew people who had died in fires. Our parents and teachers had vivid memories of the explosive fire that burned the old wood schoolhouse to the ground one Sunday morning in 1932. Bob Taylor, clerk of court for whom my mother was deputy, died jumping from a third-floor win-dow when the Alaska Hotel went up in flames in 1935. The log church in which my parents were married burned in 1947; we attended its replacement.

By 1950 Fairbanks had two and a half times as many houses as in 1930, and fires were more frequent. The climate was dry, the city was built mainly of wood, and furnaces were stoked high during the long winter. Four or five lives a year were lost to smoke and flames. The year that we moved to Cowles Street the city suf-fered more than three hundred fires. The *News-Miner* published articles titled "No Fires for 6 Days" and even "No Fires for 36 Hours." When a fire started, the NC Company whistle blew a code signaling the section of town with the emergency so that volunteer firemen and householders could rush to the neighborhood.

Firemen fighting a blaze were usually surrounded by an audience of unhelp-ful spectators. We children ran to the site of excitement whenever possible. Fire chief Eugene Woodcox tried to shame spectators into better behavior by publish-ing a newspaper list of satiric suggestions for fire watchers: go to every fire, park carefully so you block the fire truck, don't let the firemen get in your way, back over the fire hose when you leave, etc. But the spectacle was irresistible; adults and children alike continued to watch the fires and the men who fought them. Tanker trucks carried water to the blazes; in winter, ice from the plumes of water coated equipment, the roadway, and unburned parts of the building. Big fires, like the 1952 Pioneer Hotel fire that killed five guests, were always at risk of spreading to other buildings, initiating a conflagration like the one that destroyed much of the central business district in 1906. Firemen worked hard and blessed the usually windless air.

Main School was constructed of concrete, a deterrent to fire, but its forty classrooms and maze of halls were trimmed out and furnished with wood. Sur-prise fire drills were staged throughout the school year. Our performance was judged by the principal and by the fire chief, who held a stopwatch and swept the building to be sure no one had been left behind in a lavatory. Each class had an assigned spot at which to muster; teachers called roll on a sidewalk well away from the building. Our evacuation time—usually less than 180 seconds—was often reported in the newspaper.

The greatest threats to children's lives, however, were those for which there were no drills. Twin epidemics hung over the lives of Alaskans: polio and tuberculosis. Each year the school nurse lined us up to vaccinate us against typhoid and smallpox. But there were no immunizations for polio or TB. And the miracle drugs, sulfa and penicillin, which had dramatically reduced deaths from pneumonia, were useless against the tuberculosis bacillus and the polio virus. Doctors could only try to treat symptoms while the diseases ran their course, and the survival of every victim was in question. For years nothing seemed to slow these scourges.

Epidemic tuberculosis came to Alaska with the Russians. The disease took its greatest toll on Eskimos, Aleuts, and Indians. In 1947 the TB death rate for Alaska Natives was nine times that of the United States as a whole, while the death rate for white Alaskans was twice the national rate. Dorothy and Florence Roth's older sister, Irma, contracted tuberculosis as a freshman at Fairbanks High School. Her mother took her to California for rest and warmth, but to the sorrow of her family she died at age seventeen. In the 1930s and 1940s TB was the most common cause of death in the Territory, outstripping accidents and all other diseases combined.

Tuberculosis epidemics elsewhere had been halted by campaigns to identify people with active disease and isolate them in sanatoriums with adequate food and plenty of rest. In Alaska money for sanatoriums and travel for patients was chronically scarce. And patients were often understandably reluctant to separate from their families and go to Seward, Sitka, or Seattle for prolonged, perhaps terminal care.

In 1947 the federal government allocated more money for finding and treating Alaskans with TB. In Fairbanks we were all invited to the Masonic Temple to have a free, modern chest X-ray taken by a hulking, one-and-a-half-ton machine hauled up from Anchorage in a railroad car. The mayor, Hjalmar Nordale, led the citizens by "posing" for the first film. This spurt of anti-TB activity produced improvement, but failed to halt the epidemic. The TB death rate among Natives fell from 673 to 459 (per 100,000 people) but did not approach the national rate of 151. Government funding for X-rays in the villages, for travel, and for treatment remained inadequate. Critics suggested that progress against tuberculosis was slow because the threat was greater to Native than to white Alaskans.

In 1954, a former surgeon general, Thomas Parran, produced a report highlighting these statistics and recommended a vigorous attack on the disease. Response to the Parran report finally made a difference. The Public Health Service took over rural health care, built a new hospital in Anchorage, and began using newly available antibiotics against TB. Federal funds improved housing, sewer, and water systems in villages, thus reducing transmission of bacteria from the sick to the healthy. New cases decreased, and most of the newly diagnosed were cured.

As a white child growing up in Alaska's second-largest city, it was polio, not tuberculosis, that frightened me and my parents. The disease struck abruptly and seemingly at random. A child at school one day might be in the hospital the next. In the fall of 1950, the year we moved to Cowles Street, David Osborne, our neighbor at the compound and high school student-body president, fell ill on Wednesday, was hospitalized on Thursday, entered the iron lung on Sunday, and died on Monday. In St. Joseph's Hospital at the same time another high school boy, Julian Rivers, son of the federal attorney Ralph Rivers, was recovering after several days in the iron lung. The newspaper story reporting David's death and Julian's recovery also mentioned that preparations were being made to transfer Jo Anne Wold, age twelve, to Children's Orthopedic Hospital in Seattle for treatment of profound paralysis caused by polio. Frightened parents circulated rumors: cases were more severe in athletes who had been exercising; children who had just had tonsillectomies were more vulnerable to coming down with polio; David Osborne had not received prompt medical care because his mother was a Christian Scientist. The first two statements were true, but the third allegation was false. David had been taken immediately to a doctor and had received the best medical care available in Fairbanks. Alta was indignant about this cruel rumor that circulated at the time of his death, but people clung to this and other tales that suggested ways they might protect their young. Don't let your child participate in sports; avoid tonsillectomy; get prompt medical care; change diet; increase sleeping hours; avoid movie theaters and swimming pools. Should these precautions fail and your child fall ill, medical bills could be devastating. In Fairbanks, as elsewhere, door-to-door salesmen offered polio insurance policies on children.

Everyone understood that polio was an infectious disease. Hospitalized victims had few visitors, and some nurses were reluctant to serve on polio wards. Health authorities tried to avoid panic. Official organizations often referred to polio by its alternate name—infantile paralysis, a venerable, polysyllabic term that seemed to dismiss the risk to teenagers and adults. It was true that adults were less likely to catch polio, but once ill they were more likely to be paralyzed or to die. In the fall of 1950, a nurse from the National Foundation for Infantile Paralysis visited Fairbanks and encouraged Alaskans to be calm: in the past two and a half months there had been only forty-five cases, with five dead and eighteen paralyzed. Alaska was no different from the States: "[M]ortality during an epidemic of the disease usually runs between five and ten per cent, while 50 to 60 percent have non-paralytic results."

Her assessment did not comfort my parents or the town. The newspaper described Fairbanksans as "staunch" in raising money to buy iron lungs and in taking up collections for stricken families who had lost a breadwinner, but "scared" would have been an equally accurate adjective. Paralytic polio had been a known disease for a long time. Franklin Roosevelt's legs were paralyzed by polio in 1921. But annual epidemics were a post–World War II middle-class phenomenon. Some years were worse than others. Nationwide the worst year for paralytic polio was 1952, with 59,000 cases. In Fairbanks 1950 and 1954 were particularly severe years. On November 3, 1950, when Bill Eagan, a high school freshman, was diagnosed as the fall season's twenty-first polio case and placed in an iron lung, Dr. Gorman, the city health officer, took action. He canceled well baby clinics, citizenship classes, and meetings of fraternal organizations. He shut down the movie theaters and told parents not to take children to church. He even closed the schools. Briefly, it seemed that schoolchildren had been given an unexpected vacation. But none of us were surprised when the stringent Mrs. Pilgrim announced that school might be closed but lessons would continue. Parents were directed to come to the school to pick up mimeographed outlines prepared by the teachers. One high school music class continued over the radio. After seventeen days had passed with no new cases, we were allowed to return to classes. Bill Eagan was out of the iron lung, the movie theaters reopened, and the polio season for the year was over. The epidemics disappeared after 1955 when the Salk vaccine became available, and we lined up in gratitude to receive our three shots.

By the time we received our immunizations in 1955 and polio lost its fearful mystery, my father's job had again changed. We had moved to a new Company house back on Garden Island. I was a bus student again, but I no longer felt like a Garden Islander. I had become a citizen of the town and was becoming a citizen of the world. I was a Fairbanksan because I knew my way around back streets and spent time in homes different from my own. And I was becoming a citizen of the world thanks to the books and magazines of the George C. Thomas Memorial Library.

LIFE IN THE
WHITE HOUSE

Jim Crawford, general manager, 1952.
Author's collection.

{13}

GENERAL MANAGER FOR ALASKA

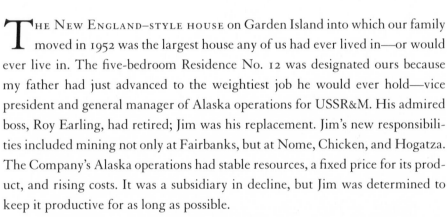

T HE NEW ENGLAND–STYLE HOUSE on Garden Island into which our family
moved in 1952 was the largest house any of us had ever lived in—or would
ever live in. The five-bedroom Residence No. 12 was designated ours because
my father had just advanced to the weightiest job he would ever hold—vice
president and general manager of Alaska operations for USSR&M. His admired
boss, Roy Earling, had retired; Jim was his replacement. Jim's new responsibili-
ties included mining not only at Fairbanks, but at Nome, Chicken, and Hogatza.
The Company's Alaska operations had stable resources, a fixed price for its product, and rising costs. It was a subsidiary in decline, but Jim was determined to
keep it productive for as long as possible.

Gold mining is a curious business. Gold in small quantities has use in dental
fillings, in jewelry, and in a few industrial applications. But the real value of the
metal is intangible—a cultural agreement that it represents wealth both to individuals and to nations. Governments accumulate stockpiles and sometimes adhere
to a gold standard in which the stockpile backs or at least defines the value of
government-issued paper bills and coins of cheaper metals. During essentially all
of the FE Company's existence, the U.S. dollar was tied to a fixed price of gold set
by the government. With a few exceptions for jewelers and dental-supply houses,
the federal government was the only legal buyer of refined Alaskan gold, and the
U.S. Mint was the Company's sole customer. Jim, a practical man who admired
usefulness above decoration, never wore a gold-encrusted ring or watchband; he
had no interest in the jewelry market. The nuggets that decorated my locket, my

mother's earrings, and our family dessert spoons came from small placer mines. The gold produced by dredges was not decorative but useful—useful to the mint and to the nation. The federal government's need was sufficient to justify the massive overturning and sifting of earth by USSR&M.

But Jim was an engineer, not a philosopher. It was not the "why" of gold mining but the "how" that deeply interested him. Clever engineering was required to extract the yellow metal deposited in prehistoric streambeds. My father thrived on solving the problems of "recovering" gold—a miner's term that suggests that gold, rightfully human property, was somehow after Eden lost deep in the earth.

The mines that Jim oversaw after 1952 were scattered across a 750-mile arc just south of the Arctic Circle. The task of management required frequent travel. Fortunately for him, aviation in Alaska had been making rapid advances. The federal government had just built Fairbanks International Airport with a six-thousand-foot runway to handle the DC-4s and later the DC-6s that would make daily flights to Anchorage, Juneau, and Seattle. The new airport was located six miles out of town, away from houses and traffic. During frigid weather, ice fog from smoke and exhaust rarely shut down the new runway. Fifty commercial aircraft and fifty-three private planes (one for every 150 Fairbanksans) were housed at the airport; during its second year of operation, officials counted 52,000 takeoffs and landings.

Weeks Field closed, but Fairbanks was still a two-airport town because Phillips Field had just opened northwest of the city center. Charter companies used this shorter runway to avoid higher fees charged at the international airport, which housed Pan American, Wien, Alaska, Canadian Pacific, Northern Consolidated, and other scheduled airlines. Airfields in Fairbanks and throughout the Territory were busy. By 1954 Alaska had 250 official airports and airstrips, and the Territory was dotted with dozens of other informal landing areas on beaches and river bars. During the summer, floatplanes set down on lakes, ocean inlets, and straight stretches of river. Ski planes carried traffic during the winter. By their teens, most Alaskans, especially those living in villages, were frequent flyers.

With all this flying, plane crashes were not rare, but my family adhered to the belief that most wrecks were caused by weekend pilots. Longevity in an airman was considered proof of flying skill. Jim placed great trust in experienced pilots like Sam O. White, who was in his seventies by the time he retired. Although my father took a dozen round-trip flights to mining sites each year, he knew each of his pilots, and we did not worry.

Of the mines for which Jim was newly responsible, the oldest was Nome. In 1899–1900, this harborless city was established at the site of Alaska's largest gold strike. By early summer 1900, Nome's census was about 21,000—a population never again reached. (The 2000 census lists Nome's population at 3,505.) Most early Nome miners worked the beach sand, which did not require elaborate equipment or a staked claim. A violent storm in the fall of 1900 destroyed part of the business district and most of the beach, where hand mining had nearly exhausted the available gold. Fifteen thousand men left before winter, the penniless taken out on army transport ships. After the influenza epidemic of 1918, the population dropped to a nadir of 600; only a few independent miners and small dredging companies were left to work the inland benches and creeks.

The largest of the dredging companies was Hammon Consolidated Gold Fields. This company had pioneered, although not perfected, cold-water thawing of frozen gravel, but it had been unable to make a profit. In 1924 Hammon was purchased by USSR&M. The team sent by the Boston office to make the Nome dredges profitable included O. J. Egleston and Roy Earling, the two men who preceded Jim Crawford as general manager of Alaska operations for USSR&M.

When my father became general manager, the Company's holdings at Nome included three dredges, a diesel power plant, and several outlying camps with bunkhouses, mess houses, and workshops. The main office, staff apartment building, gold smelter, and extensive warehouses were located in town. Nome was geologically different from Fairbanks. Its remaining placer gold was located not in ancient riverbeds but in ancient beaches, which over time had become inland benches standing sixty to eighty feet above modern sea level. As in Fairbanks, the gold-bearing gravel and the overburden covering it were frozen, and yearly precipitation was low (seventeen inches per year). To supply water for stripping and thawing and floating dredges, Hammon Consolidated had renovated three early-day ditches that stretched 110 miles over relatively flat land. Both the Territory and the Company built roads to the dredges, but the water-ditch camps were served until 1957 by a narrow-gauge railcar on the tracks of the old Seward Peninsula Railroad.

Nome was the third-largest gold-producing district in Alaska. Its paydirt rivaled that of Fairbanks, but Nome miners faced problems not found in the Interior. The mining season and the shipping season (when ships could anchor in the roadstead and send freight ashore in lighters) were both brief—four and a half months. This meant that Company garages, shops, and warehouses had to be unusually well stocked and that the Company had to be prepared to repair or remake a variety of dredge and power-plant parts. Many of the four-hundred-man summer workforce were Inupiat Eskimos. Jim appreciated the fact that an unusual number of these men had valuable spatial talent; they quickly grasped mechanical problems and were mysteriously able to stay oriented on snow-drifted tundra during whiteout conditions.

One of the general manager's prerogatives was bringing family along on summer business trips. This helped to mitigate the fact that no general manager could leave for vacation during the mining season. When I was eleven years old, Alta and I accompanied Jim to Nome. On the way we stopped for a three-day vacation in Kotzebue, but our stop in Nome was all business. We spent two long days in a Company car with the Glavinovich brothers—Carl, the general fore-man, and Walter, the Nome manager—driving over the gravel mining roads to visit claims and dredges. My father, Carl, and Walter held earnest discussions at each stop while my mother studied birds through binoculars and I tramped up treeless hills covered with blowing grass or strolled on beaches, gazing at gray breakers and imagining Siberia just beyond the horizon.

In town my mother read the Nome phone book. The population of the Territory was small enough, and Alaska phone books thin enough, that reading one was an efficient way to rediscover acquaintances who had once lived in Fairbanks. Of course, I had no interest in socializing with Alta's old friends. What impressed me in Nome was a lesson in arctic sanitation: where permafrost is continuous, waterlines, city sewers, and even outhouses are impractical. In the 1950s water was delivered by truck to a holding tank inside each house, where it was heated and pressurized to supply the faucets. Graywater from sinks and bathtubs was simply discharged into the backyard. For sewage, a honey-bucket collection company served even the finest houses of Nome. The company's collection wagon was pulled by Prince, loved by children in this one-horse town. Each bathroom had a small outside door through which the bucket could be removed. During our stay I repeatedly worried Mother with questions that boiled down to one horrid possibility: "What if the honey-bucket man opens that little door while I am sitting on the toilet?" I didn't think to ask, and no one else chose to discuss, where the collection company disposed of the honey-bucket contents.

Nome was not the only working vacation spot in Alaska for Jim and Alta. Chicken, near the Canadian border, was a cheaper and more convenient destination. Chicken could be reached from Fairbanks in one long day's drive in the Company Ford. The name of this town is said to have resulted from a spelling difficulty. Miners who rushed to the Fortymile District in the early 1890s initially called the site Ptarmigan Creek after the abundant local game birds. But when the camp grew and needed a post office, the inhabitants supposedly could not agree how to spell the name on the application so they switched it to an orthographically simpler bird. By 1906 Chicken was booming with four hundred residents, two saloons, two general stores, and a hotel. In the following decade miners left for new camps, and by 1930 the population was twenty. In 1935 USSR&M bought most of the claims in the area—including those underlying the town. The buildings became Company property, and by 1955 downtown Chicken was a Company camp with a census of thirty-four.

Alta liked visiting Chicken because it was the home of her special friend, Elvia Fisher, wife of the mine's superintendent, Jack Fisher. She would look forward to sitting in Elvia's cabin or flower garden exchanging news and drinking tea with Ann Purdy and other sourdough women. I looked forward to poking around in nearby streams because my father had shown me how to pan for garnets, which interested me more than flecks of gold. It was satisfying to find a few, even if they were so small that they got lost after a day or two in my pocket.

The Chicken dredge (Dredge No. 4) had previously been used on Pedro Creek in Fairbanks. When the Taylor Highway was built after World War II to connect Eagle to the Richardson Highway near Tok, the Company was able to scrap its plan to convert the little steam dredge purchased with the Chicken claims. Chicken was near the midpoint of the new highway; in the summer of 1959 Dredge No. 4 was trucked in pieces three hundred miles to its new pond in the Fortymile, where it was reassembled.

Chicken had the usual mess house, shops, and bunkhouse, but it did not have a full-scale smelter able to pour gold bars. Instead, the gold-mercury amalgam from the dredge was taken to a building with a small retort where the mercury was driven off and condensed back to liquid for reuse. The residual gold formed irregular lava-like chunks called gold sponge. The hardened sponge was cleaned with a wire brush and taken to the Chicken post office, which transferred it to the contract mail plane at the airstrip, which carried it as registered first-class mail to Fairbanks to be transformed into gold bars in the Gold Room smelter.

Lumps of gold sponge and gold bricks are heavy objects, but they could be mailed at the special Alaska gold rate of two cents per ounce (about $20 per gold bar). This rate, like the price of gold, remained stable for decades; it was probably the only stable expense the Company ever had. In the 1950s the average gold brick was worth about $30,000, but USSR&M employed no special guards in Chicken or in Fairbanks to transport sponge and amalgam or to protect the Gold Room. The Company's insurance policy required employees to carry rifles when they used an inconspicuous pickup truck to haul amalgam

USSR&M truck in front of the Hogatza post office at airstrip. *Author's collection.*

from the Creeks or gold bars to the post office. However, the likelihood of a major theft involving difficult-to-market sixty-pound bricks in a small town with limited egress was not high. The only Company gold thefts that I am aware of were two incidents of pilfering from a dredge. In the 1970s, Earl Pilgrim gave me a detective's account of one of these, which had occurred years earlier in Nome. My father employed Earl, an independent mining engineer, to investigate disappearing mercury and low gold returns at a Nome dredge. On Company dredges, the riffles were enclosed in a locked chain-link cage. Other than the dredgemaster, the only employee with a key to the cage was the panner, who "freshened" the mercury when the bucketline stopped briefly while the anchor spud was lifted and reset to move the dredge forward. Earl went undercover and signed on as an ordinary dredge worker. Within a few weeks he was able to tell my father that the riffle amalgam was disappearing into the panner's thermos. The other theft of Company gold was similar. In the days before the riffles were enclosed in a cage, a Fairbanks winchman gradually pilfered $500 to $1,000 worth of amalgam by tucking it into his clothing during shutdown for oiling.

Of all the USSR&M mines outside Fairbanks, however, it was neither Nome nor Chicken that most engaged my father. Jim had a special affinity for the one-dredge mine at Hogatza. Drilling at the site in 1940–41 had delineated an area suitable for dredging, but exploration stopped when Executive Order L-208 suspended gold mining during World War II. It was not until 1954 that my father returned to the problem of dredging the Hogatza claims.

Producing enough electricity to power a dredge at Hogatza was not feasible, so the Company purchased a diesel-fired dredge from the bankrupt Livengood Dredging Company near Fairbanks. In the summer of 1955, a convoy of trucks hauled this dredge in sections to a river landing on the Chena. The hull was reassembled in the river, loaded with equipment, and lashed to three Yutana Company river barges, which pushed it 750 miles—down the Chena, down the Tanana, up the Yukon, up the Koyukuk, and up the Hogatza. The following winter, Caterpillar tractors sledded the dredge sections from the Hogatza River landing to the new dredge pond for reassembly. By early spring 1957 the Company had not only rebuilt the dredge but, under the direction of Jack Boswell, had completed construction of an airstrip, camp, and corduroy road across swampy land between the river landing and the dredge pond. Most importantly, they had established a post office so that gold sponge could be shipped to Fairbanks by registered first-class mail.

Jim was on hand for the first Hogatza dredge cleanup on July 12, 1957. A photo of this smelting of sponge gold from amalgam shows frontier mechanics at work. The retort is located inside a fifty-five-gallon oil drum lined with firebricks. The heat source is an oil blowtorch. The mercury vapor in the collecting tube is being cooled by water brought by hose from a stream next to the retort. The whole outfit is outdoors, with Jim crouched in the gravel running the hose while Neil Rice from the Boston office and another man, perhaps master mechanic Ralph Norris, watch. Norris, whose special skills were needed at start-up, was both the first superintendent and first postmaster at Hogatza.

Jim returned to the mine several times each summer to consult with a series of superintendents who, during the eighteen years of operation, included Clay LaFon, Walter Glavinovich, and Jack Fisher. My father installed a new shortwave radio at home so that with the help of ACS he could talk to Chicken (KXL87) and Hogatza (KXC68) on evenings and weekends. The superintendents used code words to notify Fairbanks of dredge cleanups and gold shipments.

I was never invited to take one of the expensive bush flights to Hogatza, known locally as "Hog River," a nickname my father refused to use. I wanted to make the trip to see Susie, the camp's most famous denizen. Susie was a chocolate-brown black bear who had adapted remarkably well to the miners in her territory. She had begun by rustling in the garbage dump, then decided that she preferred fresher treats from the cans at the back of the mess house. The photographers in camp responded by placing tidbits in spots more photogenic than the garbage cans. Soon bear and man became accustomed to each other. The camp diet agreed with Susie; she was plump and her coat was sleek. Every other year she produced twins or triplets and brought them with her into camp. Eventually she learned to walk to the bank of the dredge pond and wait for the deckhand to lower the gangplank. Then she would board with her cubs to receive snacks, standing on her hind legs behind the winch handles while a photographer's helper dangled a treat above her nose. This resulted in widely circulated pictures designed to give the impression she was working the winches. Eventually some restrictions were placed on her access. The garbage cans were set on an electrified metal plate and she was directed to the dump. One day, as she tried to leave the boat, she was frightened by a dog at the shore end of the gangplank and leapt from the deck into the pond, causing fear for her safety amidst the machinery. After that day, the dredge gangplank was no longer lowered for her.

Alta did accompany Jim to Hogatza. In September 1965, she and Jim flew to the airstrip with Genevieve Parker Metcalfe and her husband, John Metcalfe, from the Boston office. While the three engineers toured the dredge, Alta visited Elvia Fisher, who had moved with her husband, Jack, from Chicken to Hogatza to become the settlement's postmistress. Susie the bear was nowhere in sight, but it was a satisfactory trip. The Koyukuk country in autumn was compellingly beautiful.

Alta understood Jim's special attraction to this mine. Jim had explored and helped develop the Chicken property at about the same time as Hogatza. But Chicken was on the road system, and the ground, like that at Fairbanks and Nome, had been already prospected and mined by sourdoughs. The problems of Hogatza were new. Instead of permafrost, the ground was so wet that water flowed through the dredge pond all winter. Moreover, the site was dauntingly remote, a challenge Jim liked. His original recommendation in favor of developing Hogatza was carefully worded and acknowledged unknowable risks, but he was gratified when the Company proceeded and proud when the dredging proved a success. The Hogatza dredge ran until 1974, seven years after all the other USSR&M dredges in Alaska had been shut down.

Despite Hogatza and other successes, my father's years as general manager were marked by omens that the Company would not be able to continue its operations for long. For instance, there was the matter of Patrick O'Neill. Pat had grown up in Alaska, graduating from the University of Alaska with degrees in geology, mining engineering, and the master's-level engineer of mines. In 1953, when he received the latter, he had already been working for the Company

for more than ten years and had risen rapidly in Company ranks to dredge superintendent. Jim may have envisioned him as the next general manager. However,
Pat's calculations showed that, at the current price of gold, the Company would
run out of profitable ground by 1963. Pat would then be in his late forties—too
young to retire and perhaps too old to easily start over. Gold had been $20.67
per troy ounce for almost a century before it rose to $35 an ounce during the
Depression. By the 1950s it had been set at $35 an ounce for only two decades.
Despite the optimism of some mining journals, Pat realized that the U.S. price
of gold might remain constant for the duration of his career. He resigned from
the Company to accept a job in Colombia—the first step in what turned out to
be a successful international mining career. For my father, Pat's departure was
a blow. So too, perhaps, was the fact that he could find no error in Pat's calculations. (In fact, all the Nome and Fairbanks dredges were shut down by the end
of 1964.) My father's diary entry on Pat's last day at work was, as always, terse:
"P. O'Neill left." However, it was one of only three entries circled in 1953–54; the
other circles marked the deaths a few months apart of Jim's mother and father.

The other omen was the uninterrupted rise of well-funded military industry, which competed with USSR&M for labor, fuel, and transportation. The
effect of defense projects and civilian construction was visible throughout the
city. Fairbanks's population rose by 76 percent in the 1940s, 130 percent in the
1950s. Subdivisions (Slaterville, Lemeta, Aurora, Island Homes, Hamilton
Acres, Westgate, Bjerremark, and a dozen others) at first surrounded the city
limits, then were annexed. The town sprouted sprawling apartment complexes
and two towering apartment buildings—the ten-story Polaris Building and the
eight-story Northward Building. Both advertised a distinctive northern luxury:
apartment windows above the fourth floor overlooked the low-hanging ice fog,
giving a view of the stars on even the coldest, darkest days.

Not only was the population burgeoning, but the city was becoming more
like small cities in the States. Local cash registers finally held more paper dollars
than silver ones, and the penny drawer was full. The *Fairbanks Daily News-Miner*
gushed economic good news. Echoing the confidence expressed in 1924, when
USSR&M came to town, the editor again proclaimed that Fairbanks would never
become a fading mining camp:

> With the border of Russia only a few hundred miles away, the United States
> will be forced to keep these ["vast military installations in the Interior of
> Alaska"] well-garrisoned for years to come. Therefore, Fairbanks' new-found

importance as a defense center is a status that is PERMANENT.... The city is taking on a distinctly modern appearance.... The inconveniences caused by the lack of paving and inadequate utilities will melt away.... The last vestiges of the log cabin and frame building construction of old Alaska will be erased in downtown areas, as new, fire-proof buildings are erected.... The future of the farthest north city on the American continent is assured.

In addition to Eielson Air Force Base, the "vast military installations" constructed soon after the war included Fort Greeley near Big Delta. The stated mission of the fort in the early 1950s was to train soldiers headed for cold-weather battle in Korea; the darker part of its mission, testing chemical and biological weapons, was not made public at the time. Later in the decade there was more construction at the fort when, as part of an experiment in remote power production, the army and its contractors built a small nuclear power plant.

The military building boom seemed to be as permanent as the *Fairbanks Daily News-Miner* had predicted. Each completed project turned out to be simply one more lap in a circular arms race with the Soviets. Russia tested its first atomic weapon in 1949. One year later the Canadians and Americans began construction of the Distant Early Warning (DEW) line, a seamless string of radar stations across the north and west coasts of the continent designed to detect enemy bombers flying the short northern route from Europe to North America. DEW line radars worked well, but the VHF radios used to relay warnings to the air force did not. As northern villagers knew, ionospheric interference often prevented radio communication for days. Therefore, in 1956 Fairbanks became the staging area for the hurried construction of the White Alice Communications System, a chain of seventy new-technology "tropospheric scatter stations" to replace the VHF radios. But six months before White Alice was dedicated in 1958, the Soviet Union launched Sputnik. The satellite broadcast radio signals around the world, in effect announcing the new age of communication satellites (the first of which was launched in 1962) that made the tropospheric scatter stations obsolete. Even the DEW line was out of date by that time because the threat of bombers had been replaced by the threat of intercontinental ballistic missiles. In 1959 at Clear, an Alaska Railroad stop just south of Nenana, a $360 million project began to construct a Ballistic Missile Early Warning System (BMEWS) station for North America.

Between 1940 and 1955 the federal government spent more than $100 million per year in Alaska, mainly on defense. Postwar military construction was rushed, providing cost-plus agreements for contractors and overtime for work-ers. Job seekers, like the early prospectors, came to the Territory hoping to make a bundle and return to a better life in the States. Independent gold miners and USSR&M, once large frogs in the small pond of Fairbanks, were now economic tadpoles in an enlarging lake. Prospectors of the 1950s carried Geiger counters, not gold pans. My father understood that times were changing, but he declined to be distracted. He continued to concentrate on the mining task at hand, recovering gold.

Jim's fourteen-year tenure as vice president and general manager of Alaska operations was founded on his record for meticulous work, loyalty, long hours, and engineering savvy. But he had another valuable asset in his job—an unusually capable helpmate. As Jim's career as an engineer advanced, so did Alta's career as a homemaker and hostess.

FE Company general manager's house, showing the backyard with greenhouse and garden.
Author's collection.

{14}

HOSTING COMPANY

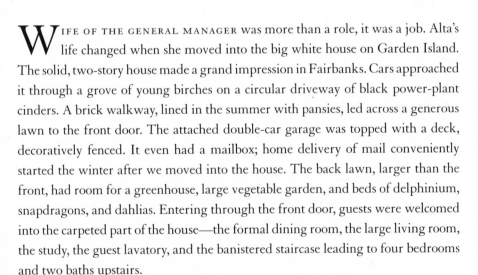

WIFE OF THE GENERAL MANAGER was more than a role, it was a job. Alta's life changed when she moved into the big white house on Garden Island. The solid, two-story house made a grand impression in Fairbanks. Cars approached it through a grove of young birches on a circular driveway of black power-plant cinders. A brick walkway, lined in the summer with pansies, led across a generous lawn to the front door. The attached double-car garage was topped with a deck, decoratively fenced. It even had a mailbox; home delivery of mail conveniently started the winter after we moved into the house. The back lawn, larger than the front, had room for a greenhouse, large vegetable garden, and beds of delphinium, snapdragons, and dahlias. Entering through the front door, guests were welcomed into the carpeted part of the house—the formal dining room, the large living room, the study, the guest lavatory, and the banistered staircase leading to four bedrooms and two baths upstairs.

The house also had private areas, rooms with wood or linoleum floors—the laundry and drying room, the back bathroom, the sewing room, the kitchen, two walk-in pantries, and a screened sleeping porch with three beds. In these work areas and in the garden my mother busied herself feeding and lodging a summer stream of official visitors.

The Company had designed and built this house in 1940 to accommodate not only the manager's family but overnight guests from the Boston, Nome, and San Francisco offices. Mary Earling, who had previously endeared herself to my mother for her support of Jane in the Christian Science Church, had been the only other general manager's wife to preside in the residence. Mary was a warm and well-organized hostess who had extended her hospitality to even non-Company visiting dignitaries during the postwar years when local hotels were crowded and sometimes raucous. Alta took her as a model.

Managing this new household was more complex than my mother's continuing occasional work as substitute teacher for the high school shorthand and typing classes. But management came easily to Alta, and the challenge was a welcome change. Moreover, she was not going to give up substitute teaching, curling, social clubs, or church committees just because she had new tasks at home. Instead she hired a cleaning lady or, more precisely, a weekly helper.

Laura David Anderson, my mother's contemporary, was a short, stocky, soft-spoken Athabascan with thick, silver-rimmed glasses. Laura spent one day a week helping Mother and one day helping my Aunt Audrey Loftus. She quickly became a reliable part of the lives of both families. She was a hardworking matriarch with one grown daughter. She supported her Norwegian-immigrant husband, Charlie, an "invalid" (my father's tone of voice supplied the quotation marks) fifteen years her senior, and a blind but alert nonagenarian mother. She also aided and encouraged numerous nephews and nieces, the children of her twelve siblings. In addition to English, Laura spoke an Upper Tanana Athabascan dialect. When asked, she

Laura Anderson with her century-old uncle at Tanacross.
Courtesy of Barbara Hale.

could teach Athabascan names of plants or the correct way to address an elder. She had been born upriver on the Chena the year after the town of Fairbanks was established. For a few years she attended an Episcopal missionary school, where she learned to write in the same clear penmanship as my mother. Her mother taught her Native skills including skin sewing, beading, and gathering plants for food and medicine. She knew how to drain sap from birches and how to trap molting birds for food. She made dolls dressed in Athabascan costume, sometimes trimming her own hair to provide tresses for a special doll.

I was allowed to call her "Laura" instead of "Mrs. Anderson," a familiarity that was forbidden with other adult women who were not considered relatives. The use of her first name suggested her role as a domestic employee but also designated her as someone privy to the family. Not surprisingly in our small city, we were connected in other ways. On Sundays Alta (wearing a stylish hat out of deference to St. Paul and to custom) and Laura (wearing a colored head scarf tied around her chin for the same reason) met at church. Laura was also coauthor with my Aunt Audrey of a small book sold to benefit St. Matthew's. *According to Mama* was based on Laura's translation of stories told by her elderly mother, Helen David Charlie, about life in the Interior when few whites had entered the country. Published in 1956 and bound with bead-trimmed moose-hide lacing, it was the inspiration for two subsequent booklets authored by Audrey and published in Fairbanks by the church. *According to Papa,* published in 1957, dealt with the same time period from a man's point of view as told to Audrey and Laura by David Paul, a village elder and church deacon in Tanacross. However, the third booklet, *According to Grandfather (The Medicine Man),* published in 1965, did not specify Audrey's collaborator(s). They may have declined to have their names listed. The church taboo against dancing and storytelling had withered, but feelings about sorcery perhaps had not. The introduction to *According to Grandfather* consists of three careful paragraphs about the history of shamanism in Alaska, a fourth paragraph about the role of superstition in European cultures, and a conclusion with a distancing dedication to "grandparents, whatever their beliefs and wherever they may be." My copy has a handwritten inscription by Audrey: "Alta and Jim—To encourage greater tolerance and understanding—Audrey Loftus."

Laura had no fixed tasks in our house. She worked alongside my mother, ironing, weeding, washing dishes, and vacuuming. She worked rhythmically, somewhat slowly, and according to her own methods. Everything was done thoroughly. Neither my father nor I were allowed to offer her any suggestions or direction. At noon, she ate when my father came home for lunch, companionably sharing the jalapeño peppers they both savored. On her days off during berry season, Laura and Alta would often drive to some favorite patch to pick for their respective families. The female bond was strong. Late in their lives, I remember taking Mother to visit Laura in a Fairbanks nursing home. We found Laura sitting cross-legged on her neatly made bed, infirm but as flexible as a young girl. She and Alta did not talk much, but we stayed for a long time.

Even with Laura's help, my mother was constantly busy. She rose early, whistling absentmindedly while making beds, cooking breakfast, and composing a shopping list in rapid, court-trained shorthand. In the half-awake state that came to me a few minutes before my alarm rang, I would often hear her faint whistle—perhaps "Lili Marlene" or a German lullaby her father used to sing.

Unlike my sister, Alta didn't listen to records or music on the radio while she worked, although she had innate musical talent. As a girl, in the days when the Tanner ranch was still making money, she had loved taking piano lessons. (The lessons were given by her godfather, whom she never forgot, but whose name I never knew.) Music in rural Montana, and perhaps always for my mother, was like curling—something one did with others, not something one just listened to or watched others do. The furniture of our new house included a shiny symbol of refinement and culture—a baby grand Chickering piano. Before we moved into the manager's house, the only keyboard instrument Alta had personally owned was a three-octave portable folding organ that she occasionally took to Harding Lake Girl Scout camp to encourage the girls to sing. On the baby grand she played by ear two-handed renditions of any song that she or my friends and I could sing. This enviable talent was not handed down to me. After we moved into the big white house, I reluctantly took three years of piano lessons. I never learned to play by ear and barely learned to read simple sheet music. My piano teacher, a man already prone to despair and anger, fired me, telling my mother that he could not in good conscience continue to accept her money. Alta was too prudent to waste money on a lost cause and acquiesced without fuss or recrimination, perhaps recalling Jane's disastrous dance lessons.

In summer Alta's days were spent tending greenhouse, garden, and guests. Beds, towels, and tablecloths constantly needed to be changed. They were laundered in our automatic washer, and then hung outdoors on the clothesline or indoors on rods that slid into a heated chamber in the laundry room. When the white cotton bedding was dry, Mother or Laura or I would fold it lengthwise and feed it between the warm rollers of our big mangle to iron it before it was stored with the towels in the linen cupboards. Tablecloths were starched, then ironed by hand with special ironing cloths to prevent scorching. As a teenager I not only ironed on Saturday afternoons with KFRB tuned to the Top 10, but helped keep our linens white by recharging the water softener. Twice a month I accomplished this necessary and satisfying half-hour task by opening and shutting valves in the proper sequence and adding fresh rock salt. Even the deep FE Company well water was tinged yellowish-brown by iron oxides.

Laura and I were useful to Alta in the laundry room, garden, and bedrooms, but neither of us was competent at or invited to join her in preparing food. Alta's guest meals were larger and slightly more elaborate than family meals, but cooking had recently been made easier by a shipping change. Refrigerated trucks now traversed the Alcan, and the railroad and ship lines had introduced containerized shipping. Goods no longer had to be reloaded and repacked between ship and shore. Perishables were fresher and prices lower. Dried eggs, along with canned butter and canned bacon, almost disappeared from grocery shelves. "Fresh eggs," consistently refrigerated and days rather than weeks in transit, competed with expensive "air eggs" in the stores. Alta quit "candling" eggs in front of a bright light to check for spoilage; she no longer had cake making interrupted by an egg with a "rubber ball" yolk from prior freezing. She could even choose to indulge herself by using a cake mix, although she never lowered herself to cookie mixes or unmotherly packaged cookies. The local dairies gradually folded, unable to compete with milk shipped from Washington in paper cartons. Commercial soda pop appeared, and we quit making root beer from sugar, root beer extract, water, and yeast. This not only saved the time required for mixing and bottling, but saved the sticky cleaning time that resulted every time a cork gave way under pressure while fermenting.

From the viewpoint of a picky eater, not all these changes were good. The new "fresh" grapefruit was sour to the point of bitterness compared to the canned variety. Winter salads of mealy tomatoes, waxy cucumbers, and almost chlorophyll-free lettuce were hard to stomach after our "real" summer salads. On the other hand, Spam no longer appeared in sandwiches.

Alta's meals for summer guests now contained beef and chicken instead of moose meat. But the type of meat was not the reason her meals appealed to our company. It was the hard work she had done in the garden. The vegetables she served—peas, beans, broccoli, cauliflower, potatoes, and carrots—were from plants she had planted or transplanted in late May. The greenhouse provided ripe tomatoes, cucumbers, peppers, lettuce, and green onions for salads. Her standard dessert of store-bought vanilla ice cream was topped with newly picked strawberries, raspberries, or rhubarb sauce.

Dining room, general manager's house. *Author's collection.*

When we had no guests, we ate in the kitchen breakfast nook off heavy everyday plates with painted roosters. In contrast, guest meals were served in the dining room beyond the swinging doors of the china pantry. In the dining room even a simple lunch of soup and sandwiches was eaten with silver flatware, etched glasses, and the Bramble Wedgwood china from Edmonton. Our large square kitchen contained a chest freezer but no dishwasher. Every guest meal meant thirty minutes of washing glasses, teacups, saucers, dinner plates, salad plates, serving bowls, dessert bowls, butter plate, gravy boat, knives, forks, salad forks, teaspoons, and dessert spoons. It was a two-woman job, and guests were not invited into the kitchen. I never helped Mother cook, but, unless Laura was available, I was her skilled though unenthusiastic dish dryer.

Of course our guests needed more than meals and clean bedding. They needed transportation, entertainment, and personal laundry. Most particularly they needed reassurance that when they were tired from travel, sleepless from excessive daylight, itchy from mosquito bites, and gritty with dust, they could take refuge in Alta's clean house and easy good humor.

Some of the people who stayed in our home also entertained us. The non-Company guests, in particular, often had interesting backgrounds. One was a blind world traveler, a Rotarian who must have been a guest in 1955 when my father was president of the Fairbanks Rotary Club. Although he told fascinating after-dinner anecdotes, I was more interested in his Braille watch, the ease with which he maneuvered his way around a strange house, and the tidiness with which he ate. (A private experiment with a plate of food and a blindfold showed that I could not match his skill.)

Two other guests who interested me were reporters for the David Brinkley television show. When they arrived at our house, Mother was out, and I was assigned to show them to their room. I was embarrassed when one of them asked me if I had ever seen their show. We had bought a television set soon after KTVF began broadcasting in Fairbanks in 1955, but I was a busy teenager and rarely watched. I had to confess that I had never seen *David Brinkley's Journal.* Curiously, the reporters seemed undismayed; they admitted that they also did not have much time to watch TV. (Had I been an educated watcher, I would have been less embarrassed because I would have known that tapes of *David Brinkley's Journal* were usually not mailed to KTVF or KFAR-TV for rebroadcast in Fairbanks.) Despite my ignorance, I was intrigued to realize that the reporters were paid to travel around, take movies, talk to people, and write about what they learned. It seemed a romantic profession, as suitable to a woman as to a man.

The downside of a reporter's job, however, was revealed the next winter. In January the David Brinkley program about Alaska was aired in the contiguous forty-eight states. Denunciations of its purported content occupied many column inches in the *Fairbanks Daily News-Miner* for several days in a row. The newspaper's editor, the head of the Chamber of Commerce, the governor, members of the congressional delegation, and several letter writers resented the description of Alaska as "the biggest, coldest, emptiest, and happiest state." Claiming that the program focused on the middle two adjectives, the writers described Brinkley in bitter terms. Governor William Egan called Brinkley "a two-week expert seeking the negative sensational" and asked the president of NBC for equal time to show the movie *Alaska! American's Brightest Star,* which "depicts an accurate image of Alaska's potential and development." (This Chamber of Commerce–sponsored film was unreservedly enthusiastic: the world's largest hydroelectric plant was soon to be built on the Yukon River at Rampart; the Japanese were bringing new money to the pulp mill in Sitka; Cook Inlet oil would make the state another Kuwait; and the variety of game in Alaska ranked it next to Africa.) The *Daily News-Miner* called on three Alaskans quoted in Brinkley's program—two mayors and an economist—to defend their comments. The mayors refused the bait and maintained silence. The economist added more column inches. One of the most stinging statements in Brinkley's narration was unattributed: "for every 16 cents Alaska pays in Federal taxes, Alaska gets back $1. In a sense, it is a ward of the federal government, and in its present state couldn't survive without it." I knew that my father had expressed this opinion to the reporters at the dinner table the previous summer. In January, however, he chose not to disclose this fact to indignant fellow civic leaders. Unlike my Aunt Dorothy Loftus (who ran unsuccessfully for territorial legislature in 1940) or my Aunt Audrey (a Republican who lost her seat on the university board of regents after serving for two years because a Democratic legislature refused to confirm her nomination by a Republican governor), Jim disliked being the outspoken center of public controversy.

Some of our Company guests, notably Genevieve Parker Metcalfe, repaid Alta and Jim by offering hospitality in Boston. The Company had a policy that every fourth winter, on a rotating basis, professional employees would be given four months' paid vacation. These sabbaticals were supposed to ease the "hardship" of a remote post like Alaska. Actually, Alaska employees were often less at home in the States than in the Territory, but all gladly took the vacation, usually crisscrossing the country to visit relatives. In first and in fifth grade I attended three different schools, moving in November from Fairbanks to Eugene, Oregon; in January from Eugene to Webster Groves, Missouri; and in March back to Fairbanks.

In my fifth-grade year Jim had the first of many annual business meetings in Boston, so we meandered our way from Missouri to Massachusetts, stopping to see Florence and Tommy Thompson in Washington, D.C. (posted there by the foreign service), Uncle Gus Crawford and his family in New Jersey, and Great-Aunt Katharine Anthony in New York City. At the latter stop I was struck by the difference between frail Grandmother Pearle in Missouri and her sister, Kate, in New York City. We had tea with my great-aunt and her good friend Jeannette Rankin, who lived in the same Greenwich Village apartment building. Aunt Kate was an outspoken lesbian feminist who knew arcane facts of history from her book research. Jeannette Rankin was a politician. As U.S. Representative from Montana, she had been the only member of Congress to vote against the country's entry to both world wars. In the latter vote, taken immediately after Pearl Harbor, she was the only dissenting member of Congress, holding to her pacifist principles in the face of enemy aggression. The tea was far livelier than any meal in the Webster Groves house, but it was an unfair comparison. My paternal grandparents were ailing; both died within the year, shortly after their sixty-third wedding anniversary.

As we moved from city to city, Alta was as cheerful and gracious a guest as she was a hostess. Her husband may have been tired and easily flustered by the frustrations of travel. Her daughter may have been shy and eager to withdraw into the nearest piece of reading material. But Alta was neither. She was probably the reason that so many people welcomed us warmly.

During the winter when she wasn't traveling, Alta could relax. Houseguests were rare; there was no garden to tend; her daughter was in school. Relaxing meant spending time on her favorite and useful avocation—sewing. Like many of her generation and upbringing, Alta was an accomplished seamstress. In the general manager's house she transformed the back bedroom into a sewing room. Her new 1953 Singer was handsome and built to swing up out of a walnut sewing table. It came with a box of clever attachments, including one that made buttonholes. Alta sewed everything from school clothes to formal dresses using Butterick, McCalls, or Simplicity patterns. Occasionally she would even tackle the more elaborate draping of a Vogue pattern.

In the fall, when Fairbanks fabric stores received new bolts of winter cloth, she would make a trip to town to study pattern books illustrated with colored drawings of finished garments. When I was young enough to appreciate special homemade school clothes, she would take me with her and let me choose one pattern I liked, perhaps a circle skirt that immodestly spun outward from my waist when I twirled. After careful study at the high, slanted counter supporting the big pattern books, Mother would select a pattern—perhaps a formal dress with sleeveless top and sleek lines—and the clerk would locate in the store's big file drawers an illustrated envelope containing the tissue-paper pattern in her size. Then Alta would search the store for fabric and for matching thread, hooks and eyes, bias tape, and other notions specified in the directions. Sometimes she would buy additional material for a tiny, short-sleeved jacket that she would trim with carved walrus-ivory buttons or buttons covered with fabric to match the dress. She never chose yardage of florid color or bold pattern, although she occasionally attempted a subdued print that required careful alignment at the seams. The fabrics she used had musical names that I loved: satin and sateen, moiré and faille, taffeta and velveteen. When I was in high school, Mother even made me a formal. The skirt was mint-green tulle; the bodice was brocade figured with gold thread. I loved the dress as much as the words that described it. The dresses

Alta made were nicer than those in the Sears or Montgomery Ward catalogs, and less expensive than those sold at the Northern Commercial Company or the women's apparel shops. Alta's creations also fit her more precisely than off-the-rack dresses because she altered the patterns to accommodate her short-waisted figure. She took courses given by the university's Cooperative Extension Service in the Bishop method of sewing to learn special techniques like pattern alteration and serging.

My sister and I and the girls of our generation were, like our mothers, supposed to learn how to sew formals and other clothing. But the charm of ready-made clothes, with their ever-changing styles, easily purchased in a non-Depression economy, subverted this goal. At home Mother tried valiantly to communicate the satisfactions of smooth darts, perfect pleats, and invisible bias binding. The school system got involved by requiring home economics for seventh-grade (cooking) and eighth-grade (sewing) girls. While the boys produced bookends and wood boxes in shop, my friends and I passed home ec, making gathered skirts and peasant blouses of the simplest imaginable design. My mediocre peasant outfit was a harbinger of my adult sewing skill, but in my twenties I was grateful that I had learned enough from Mother to enable me to machine-sew from commercial kits useful gear like duffle bags, tents, sleeping bags, and down parkas.

In those early days in the manager's house, Alta's efforts at directing her younger daughter to play piano and sew were unrewarded. But her good cheer and optimism were undaunted. Remarkably, she returned to the social education that had so pained Jane—the womanly art of attending tea parties. My memory of tea parties as both tension-filled and boring is similar to my sister's, but during one exceptional tea party, I received an unforgettable lesson that my mother had not set out to teach—but teach it she did, by example, during a dramatic pre-party incident. I no longer recall who was to be honored at this autumn event, but my mother was the hostess. The house had been vacuumed and dusted. The teacups and the teaspoons with gold nuggets on their handles were laid out. Tea appetizers, possibly my mother's tiny homemade cream puffs stuffed with canned shrimp and cream cheese, were enticingly arranged. The ladies, many of whom would park near the side door to our kitchen, would soon be walking up the pansy-lined front walk.

My mother, who was probably wearing a rayon dress with subdued flowers and a wide belt, was in my bedroom urging me out of jeans and into a white blouse and pleated plaid skirt for my required appearance to pass the cream puffs. My bedroom window overlooked the kitchen door with the garbage cans nearby. Mother glanced out the window and spied a rat on one of the can lids. Without comment, she went to her bedroom closet to get her single-shot .22. She put a round in the chamber, opened my window, and shot the rat. It was a tribute to her shooting skill that it was a clean kill and that there was no damage to the garbage can lid. She went downstairs, put the corpse in the can, cleaned the rifle, washed her hands, and returned to her task of hurrying me. I think she mistook my stunned look as sympathy for the innocent animal because as she quickly brushed my hair, she gave me a brief lecture on hygiene and rats—especially the one in question, which she assured me "had a sore on its tail." At that point the doorbell rang, and she descended, unruffled, to greet her first guest. She did not actually say it, but I understood that she was acting on her personal motto: "You do what needs to be done without making a fuss about it."

Stripping frozen muck off the gold-bearing gravel with a hydraulic giant.
Author's collection.

{15}

SCHOOLGIRLS ON THE CREEKS

Alta's mentoring in womanly arts suffered a hiatus when I was in the seventh and eighth grades. During those two winters she handed the job over to the nuns of an Episcopal boarding school in Portland, Oregon. The reason for my displacement was the crooked teeth I inherited from Mother. When Alta grew up in rural Montana, tooth arrangement was simply a personal characteristic like the color of one's eyes, the straightness of one's nose, or the extent of one's teenage acne—none of which could be influenced by the beauty aids of the day. But Dr. Howard Hughes, our dentist in Fairbanks, pointed out that in the 1950s teeth could be straightened. Perhaps there had been moments in Alta's life when the jaggedness of her smile distressed her. Perhaps she felt that the awkward, bookish tomboy she was raising was going to need the aid of modern dentistry to attract a husband—or even to get a date to the prom. In any case Alta and Jim decided to take advantage of their rise into the middle class and follow the urging of Dr. Hughes. This decision had consequences. There were no orthodontists in Fairbanks. I would have to be sent Outside for two school years so that braces could be attached to my teeth and tightened the requisite number of times. A Portland orthodontist was engaged, tuition was paid, and I was quickly baptized in a private Saturday-morning ceremony. My father had intended for me to make up my mind about baptism as an adult, but the decision to send me to a church school forced his hand. My beloved Aunt Audrey became my godmother, ratifying her already-established role as my second mother.

St. Helen's Hall was an exotic experience for a pupil from Main School in Fairbanks. I had never met nuns who were neither wimpled nor Catholic. The girls wore uniforms (navy-blue serge jumpers with white seersucker blouses), attended chapel on Sunday nights, and took classes in horseback riding, playacting, and French. The teachers were surprisingly demanding; I had to give up reading library books in class. For those two winters I survived sore teeth, nauseating homesickness, and potentially dangerous tutelage from boarding girls exiled from home for more dramatic reasons than crooked teeth.

Alta made it up to me when I returned each summer by following her dictum that time outdoors cured, or at least eased, social sadness. She took me to a cottage near the sulfurous outdoor pool at Circle Hot Springs, sent me to Girl Scout camp on the old Clegg homestead, and drove me to our cabin at Harding Lake, taking the dirt lanes of the bypassed Old Richardson Highway so we could spot birds. I hiked, kayaked, sailed, swam, and patiently crept close to muskrats, grouse, and (once) a lynx. I built memories to replay the following winter after dormitory lights-out. Most of these memories were the sort that are common to rural children from northern temperate zones. But some were uniquely related to being the daughter of a mining engineer. For outdoor adventures, I found the roiled ground of mining operations as rich as pristine wilderness.

On my best expeditions to the Creeks, I had peer company—not my working father, but my friends Christine MacDonald and Judie Tweiten. We were all daughters of mining men and had learned early to travel the FE diggings by walking the pipeline of the Davidson Ditch. The pipeline, varying from forty-eight to fifty-four inches in diameter, was supported where necessary on low spruce trusses to rise above tussocks, bogs, and small creeks. The right-of-way was kept clear of willows and wild roses. The dry, curved top of the pipe created a straight, rust-colored walkway through woods, across streams, and over thawing muck. Miners on the job also walked the pipeline with brisk, purposeful strides. We girls lingered, talked, and stopped to watch black and yellow warblers in a thicket or study a mossy hummock of vole holes. Sometimes we dared each other to walk backward, or we climbed down to eat berries and to pick slender-stemmed white anemones for our braids. Christine, as sure-footed as the rest of us in our thin Keds sneakers, disliked heights and occasionally froze halfway across above a small creek or gully. We solved this problem by analogy to the cure for carsickness: when moving forward, don't look down; keep your eyes on the horizon. We also learned to keep our own counsel about adventures. Christine and I, while walking a pipeline in our early school years, saw our first wolverine. Christine's mother was so excited by this news that she curtailed our walking privileges. Eventually other adults convinced her that there had never been a report of this largest member of the weasel family (famous for destruction of traplines and cabins) harming children, and we were allowed to return to our hikes.

Our most frequent destination on these pipeline walks were the stripping operations. Men doing stripping (called "pipers," "nozzlers," or "hydraulickers") worked from valley bottoms where creeks had eroded the permafrost down to gravel and bedrock. They directed huge arcs of water from "giants" (counter-weighted nozzles) at frozen bluffs of black muck towering over the streambeds. It took two or three hours to wash the surface of a section of bluff. The piper would then move to another giant, allowing the area he had just washed to melt in the sun. He would hose the new section, washing away the three inches of sur-face mud melted by warm air in the prior eight hours. Half a dozen men per shift could operate the three to four dozen giants needed to strip a valley. In its peak years the Company operated 150 giants at its mine sites around Fairbanks. Dur-ing the nightless months of summer, three shifts of men working continuously could remove nine inches from the surface each day. The relative boredom of this job was relieved by discoveries of curved mammoth tusks and other Pleistocene remains protruding from the surface as their icy casket melted away. Otto Geist, a paleontologist at the university in Fairbanks, made it a point to know all the hydraulickers. Wearing high rubber boots, he was a regular visitor at stripping operations. Discoveries of artifacts by miners were fairly frequent and, in some cases, spectacular. In 1949 the head and foreleg of a baby mammoth (with flesh, trunk, and skin intact) was uncovered. It had been torn almost in half by the water jet from the giant. Geist sewed it together with large black stitches (con-spicuous in the proud photo at the FE Company office), embalmed it, and sent it for exhibit in New York at the American Museum of Natural History.

Perhaps because of the incipient boredom of the job, pipers welcomed child visitors. Christine, a ringer for the young Elizabeth Taylor, was an especially popular guest. Once one of the men gave her a baby snowshoe hare he had found (which died despite, or because of, frequent feedings of sugar water from a baby bottle). When I visited the pipers with my friends, I spent only a few minutes in bashful talk with the men. What I loved about the hydraulicking site was watching the moving arcs of water decorated with rainbows on sunny days; smelling the enticing organic odor of melting ancient mud; seeing an old-timer's cribbed shaft rising into the air as the muck around it melted away; and most especially, searching for the magically out-of-proportion objects washed from the

Man with mammoth skull and other Pleistocene bones.
Author's collection.

muck—tiny horse hooves, huge grooved teeth of mammoths, and weighty skulls of broad-horned bison. These incidental treasures were more exciting to me than the gold that culminated the miner's efforts. I walked below the bluffs that the giants had carved and along the runoff rivulets, looking for artifacts missed by the hydraulickers, rarely finding anything. The wet muck that my friends and I called "quicksand" at unexpected moments sucked at my feet in a stomach-churning way, but I never sank in more than shin deep. In my imagination I conjured scenes I later discovered to be untrue: great and small animals of the past prowling through spruce and birch groves similar to the ones that now covered their bones. Later I learned that the Pleistocene climate in the vast unglaciated Interior of Alaska and Canada produced not forests but cold, grassy steppes.

When we were not walking the pipelines, Judie, Christine, and I poked about in the woods that surrounded the mines. Their ponds held tadpoles and larvae of various species: mosquitoes, dragonflies, and caddis flies with their manufactured sand cases. Water skippers moved magically over the clear film of a puddle's surface. We caught grasshoppers, tried to hatch butterfly pupae, and located birds' nests with pink-skinned chicks of uncertain species. We were not fooled by the grouse with her "broken" wing routine, although we rarely found the babies she was leading us away from. We harassed wildlife, daring each other to get close to a yellow-jacket nest or to a porcupine as it twisted to present its quilly back and tail. Once I remember chasing a red squirrel with Judie at her family's mine on Chatham Creek. We pursued it like excited puppies, shaking it out of the little black spruce trees into which it was desperately trying to escape. Finally it wreaked appropriate revenge by falling out of a spruce and scratching Judie on the face and arm as it escaped. When her grandmother finished treating her injuries with pink Mercurochrome, Judie was a striking figure and remained so for a week.

This outdoor play on the Creeks—ignoble and delightfully free of adult supervision—was deeply satisfying. It was probably healthier than playing in town at being eighth-grade sophisticates, attending *Superman* matinees, and drinking cherry Cokes at the Co-Op Drug Store fountain. Moreover, on the Creeks children were sometimes asked to stop playing to do real adult tasks. That was how I happened to make my first solo drive.

Prior to this important event, my grade-school driving experience was minimal. I had once been behind the wheel of my sister Jane's car on her farm in New York State. She had tried to give me a lesson, but I had burned out her parking brake while concentrating on simultaneously operating the clutch, gas pedal, and steering wheel. At the time of my solo I was spending a few days at Chatham Creek with Judie. The private gravel roads surrounding the placer mine worked by her father and grandfather were traversed by four or five vehicles a day. Somehow Judie's father, Oscar Tweiten, found himself at a mine building at a distance from the house with his daughter, me, and three pickup trucks that he needed to get home. Judie actually knew how to drive. She had been taught at a young age so that she could help at the mine in the summer. I told her father that I had "a little" driving experience. I don't know if he realized just how little this "little" was, but he must have had some suspicions because he started the truck for me, put it in neutral, and had me climb into the driver's seat. Of all my friends' parents, Oscar was my favorite. He had a calm, trusting disposition and a musical Norwegian cadence to his English. He showed no sign of concern as he instructed me to drive slowly, without changing gears or stopping until I reached the house, where I was to put on the brake. The clutch was to be let out slowly to start the truck moving, after which it, like the gearshift, was to be ignored.

Judie had already left confidently in her vehicle when he reached in from the passenger side, had me depress the clutch long enough for him to release the parking brake, put the car in low, and remind me to "give 'er a little gas and let out the clutch nice and slow." I started off, the truck bucking and jerking as he slammed the door and jumped aside. Amazingly, the vehicle settled voluntarily into to a steady 10-mile-an-hour pace, and I was off alone, the open road ahead and a small tail of dust behind. After five thrilling minutes, I turned the corner to the house. I put on the brake twenty feet short of the green margin of the yard. The truck shuddered to a stop, and the engine died. Despite my awkward parking, I had a deep sense of pride and relief. Only a schoolboy who learned to swim by being thrown into a deep pool could have been more pleased. I savored the moment through the next winter, my last at boarding school.

That June Alta and Jim came to Portland and photographed me on the lawn of St. Helen's Hall. In the photo I am wearing a white eyelet dress, showing my even teeth with a smile, and holding an eighth-grade diploma. I returned to the big white house in Fairbanks with the double garage that now held not only my father's black Company Ford, but a vehicle my parents had decided was more suitable for the manager's family than the monochrome Studebaker. To the astonishment of my sister, me, and probably the neighbors, they had purchased a two-toned, orange-and-white 1954 Buick Roadmaster with chrome porthole vents adorning the front fenders. I was back in Interior Alaska, at home and ready to become a member of the first class to spend all four years at the modern, just-constructed Lathrop High School. I was free of Main School, St. Helen's Hall, orthodontia, and drab family cars. I was fourteen, but I felt that my teenage years were just beginning.

{16}

NEW LATHROP HIGH SCHOOL

I WAS A FASHIONABLE FRESHMAN the day after Labor Day 1956 when I set out for brand-new Austin E. Lathrop High School. Gone were the blue serge jumper and white seersucker blouse required by St. Helen's Hall. I had no appreciation for the uniform that had spared me clothing competition with wealthier classmates. When I packed to leave boarding school, a friend and I had staged a dramatic burn of our well-worn outfits in the center of the playground, whereupon I learned my final lesson from St. Helen's: seersucker melts and serge just chars. In Fairbanks I climbed carefully into the school bus wearing white buck shoes, a short-sleeved sweater, and a straight, shin-length skirt that was as snug as my ninety pounds and my mother would allow. The skirt pinioned my knees into a "sexy" walk. Only the pleat in back allowed me to climb the metal steps of the bus.

Our new school had six hundred students and no cloakrooms. When I arrived that first morning, I was assigned a shiny metal locker in which to stow books and outdoor clothing. This narrow private space was comforting; it affirmed that I belonged. My modern nickname, "Sally"—the name on my report cards and diploma—also marked me as one of the crowd. Perky names ending in an "ee" sound were in. Of the seventy-three girls in my high school graduating class, more than a quarter had names ending in "y" or "ie"; five of them answered to "Judy." There were no old-fashioned "Sarahs" at Lathrop or any of the other schools I attended.

I was glad to be back in public school. My friends had not forgotten me. In the cafeteria we sat together and ate lunch without a nun or housemother at our table.

In contrast to St. Helen's Hall, most of my classes were easy. Although some of our twenty-six teachers, like Christine Smith for English and Jane Williams for biology, were talented and dedicated, in many classes I was back to the pleasant task of hiding an open library book on my lap. In spite of my sense of freedom, however, my life at Lathrop was constrained in ways that I never thought to question. The school district prescribed the classes required for graduation (two years of math, two of science, three of English, three of social studies, four of PE, etc.). Required classes occupied four or five periods of the six-period day. My parents, veterans of the Great Depression, prescribed most of my electives. They wanted me to be able to earn a living by the time I graduated from high school. And as my mother had discovered, secretarial skills could reliably support a woman until marriage. I was to take two years of typing, one year of double-entry bookkeeping, and one year of Gregg shorthand. This meant I could take only the minimum required courses in science and math. I acquiesced to two years of math but bargained for the fumes and Bunsen burners of Chemistry instead of Typing II, arguing that the business teacher, Lois Meier, would let me work ahead in Typing I. My parents were persuaded. Ultimately both typing and bookkeeping served me well, although my shorthand disappeared, accompanied by a few semesters of college Russian and Yup'ik Eskimo, into the foggy country of unused languages. As I was making up my schedule at Lathrop High, neither I nor my family guessed that I would later enroll in college physics, trigonometry, and calculus, facing painful catch-up study during the first month of each course.

My classmates and I were not only under the rule of our parents but also restrained by our remarkable principal, J. Ellsworth McCarthy. School discipline and order were respected and expected by the parents and the community. "Mac" was quick-tempered, humorless about misdemeanors, and energetic. A compact bachelor with a receding hairline and coarse features, he could appear in unexpected locations with alarming speed. On one memorable occasion he arrived at the door of a local pool hall in the middle of a school day, loaded a group of hooky-playing boys into a van, and drove them back to school without a word. He knew every student by name and reputation. He made the rules and dispensed the discipline. Stairs were one-way; gum was not allowed; tardiness produced detention; playing hooky or smoking or talking back to the principal could get a student suspended or expelled. Not surprisingly, Mac's mother (whom we suspected of having a sinecure since she substitute taught until she turned eighty-three) found the pupils at Lathrop more respectful than students in other schools. Mac helped several boys who needed serious guidance, but others—expelled without recourse after they were sixteen and no longer legally required to attend school—he probably harmed. GEDs were not available in those days, and lack of a diploma could be a lasting handicap. (Although it is true that some expellees simply thumbed their noses at the principal, went into skilled trades, and in those boom years soon made more money than their teachers.)

Mac had less interest in, and perhaps less need to discipline, girls. Although boys were more likely to be expelled, the ratio of male-to-female students remained one to one. Pregnant girls, even those who hastily married, were excluded from classes—a school policy that finally changed during my junior year. Our principal, a respected member of the Lions Club, Masons, Boy Scouts, Elks, and Safety Council, held great power over us, but I considered him capricious and tyrannical. Teenagers are sensitive to injustice; I seethed impotently when he meted out different punishments to me and my friend Christine for a joint infraction. My grades were good and my parents prominent; I received a warning. Chris received a monthlong suspension from extracurricular activities.

Mac's mental dossier about my good grades was correct; but good grades, especially for girls, were not "cool" during those years at Lathrop. My social life was already a little tenuous, depending as it did on my lively and more popular friends. I did not wish to call attention to anything that would endanger my position on the margin of this group. On the other hand I could not bring myself to write down wrong answers on tests. So when I was asked about my grades, I fibbed vaguely toward the median. In my junior year, I received comeuppance for these lies told in service to the girlish charm of nonachievement. To my surprise, one of my downgrades actually appeared on my report card. I knew I had gotten straight A's on my Chemistry exams, yet my final grade was a B. I consulted my parents, who suggested discussing it with my teacher, Mr. Ringstad. Myron Ringstad, white-haired, slightly bent, and nearing retirement, was not surprised at my question. He was kindly and paternal as he explained my B grade: "You scored A on your tests and laboratory work because girls are good at memorizing, but girls can't really understand chemistry the way boys like Mark and James do." My parents found his explanation amusingly old-fashioned. They simply laughed and shook their heads. As long as my Chemistry grade was a passing one, it was unimportant, especially for work in an office.

What was important, not to parents but to the student body at Lathrop High, were the Big Three that occupied us and our cool compatriots in California—sports, cars, and dating. However, the Big Three in Fairbanks did not refer to football and baseball, convertibles, drive-in movies and beach parties.

In the Territory, "high school sports" really referred to just one sport—boys' basketball. There were minor club sports—curling, bowling, dog racing, skiing—and a few other school teams like track and hockey. But by climatic necessity the premier school-year sport had to be one that could be played indoors in winter. By custom, it had to be played by the more athletic sex. Girls might play half-court basketball in after-school Girls' Athletic Association (GAA) contests, run long distance (maximum one-half mile) in a GAA track race, or play GAA softball during the few weeks between snow melt and school dismissal in May. GAA girls could even earn a white sweater with a gold and purple letter by accumulating 2,400 points as they "indulged in...basketball, baseball, volley ball, badminton, shuffle board, ice skating and hiking." But girls' athletic contests were local, unadorned by audiences except for a disorganized cluster of boys drawn to any activity involving girls in shorts.

Boys' basketball, by contrast, was serious business. Lathrop's games with teams from Seward, Palmer, and Anchorage were attended by the entire student body, townspeople who weren't even team parents, and a *Fairbanks Daily News-Miner* reporter with a flash camera. The starting five had no difficulty finding dates. Cheerleaders, waving purple-and-gold pompoms, urged the crowd to a sacrilegious frenzy: "1, 2, 3, 4, 5, 6, 7/All our boys will go to heaven/When they get there they will say/'Oooh, Anchorage, where are they?'" Song leaders, in short skirts and fitted sweaters, summoned the crowd in the bleachers to stand and sing our fight song, "Malemutes," while the band played. Our hearts felt a patriotic, or at least chauvinistic, stirring as we sang. In our and in every high school of the Territory, basketball was king.

Lathrop's only local basketball competition was from smaller Monroe Catholic High and the university's junior varsity team. Most of our rivals were located hundreds of miles south along the Railbelt, the strip of land served by the Alaska Railroad. The team, coach, and managers traveled down the tracks to away games. But when the Malemutes traveled to Anchorage for the Western Alaska Championship Tournament during the alternate years when it was not held in Fairbanks, the train also carried cheerleaders, song leaders, parent chaperones, and rooters who found or invented a role to fill. In my sophomore year, when the tournament was held in Anchorage, one of the Fairbanks song leaders committed an infraction at home so serious that her mother canceled her trip to the tournament. As appropriate to my status on the margin of the in crowd, I was an alternate song leader. I took her place on the train.

The train was a wonderful setting for a holiday from school—we walked freely from car to car, pausing on the open jointed platforms where noise and wind demanded shouted conversations. Inside the cars, show-off boys moved not only horizontally but vertically from floor to seat to sturdy luggage rack overhead. We gossiped, giggled, flirted, played cards, and eventually slept as the twelve-hour trip progressed. And of course we ate. Some of our food was portable and its remains probably the horror of the cleaning crew, but many of us bought at least one meal in the dining car. The prices in the car were high—as befitted white-linened tables served by waitresses in white aprons. (Prices were also influenced by the logistics of cooking hot entrées in the adjoining kitchen car and by the lack of competition.) The dining car had about eight tables, each seating four people, so those of us willing to spend our pocket money on fine dining had to eat in shifts. The setting had a subduing effect, doubtless to the relief of the few regular passengers who, through their failure to attend to the basketball schedule, had inadvertently bought tickets on "our" train. Rambunctiousness temporarily under control, we conducted ourselves as if the constant jarring of the train's bump and sway on the uneven railbed were the gracious roll of the *Queen Mary*, and we tried to keep our milk and soda from spilling onto the tablecloth.

Even when we were not in the dining car, our train behavior was never outrageous, since the penalty for serious misbehavior was to be sent home or not allowed to come on a subsequent trip. Only a teenager strongly driven to achieve recognition for daring would sneak onto the train the contraband drug of the fifties—alcohol. Official chaperones had power; the uniformed conductor had authority. We generally obeyed both them and the posted signs, never flushing the toilet onto the tracks while the train was at a station. Our return trip from the tournament took its tone from the outcome of the games. After a customary loss to Anchorage in 1958 we were as sleepy and subdued as we were jubilant in 1959 when, on our home court, Lathrop beat Anchorage for the Western Alaska Championship and then beat Mount Edgecumbe for the All-Alaska Championship.

Despite the excitement of basketball rail trips, the train was not our favorite transportation. We were smitten with the automobile. The cult of the car was as powerful for Lathrop students as it was for our contemporaries in the States.

In a sense we were becoming our southern contemporaries: 70 percent of my senior classmates had been born in the States, 30 percent had attended at least one year of high school elsewhere, and only three were Alaska Natives. In the 1950s both the absolute number and the proportion of Natives in Fairbanks and its school system decreased. Our senior class (2 percent Native, 4 percent black, and 92 percent white) mirrored the larger population. The reasons that Native students and their families were moving away from Fairbanks are doubtless complex, but one shameful truth is that Lathrop High was not a comfortable place for Eskimo and Indian students. Many teachers had low expectations for these young Alaskans. One former student recalls a teacher's surprise when she returned for her junior year: "Ah, you are still here." Fellow students sometimes expressed similar attitudes. In 1953, Ralph Amouak, originally from Point Hope, was the only Native in his high school class. He and another student worked at the school as janitor's helpers. In the yearbook, the class wag wrote a "prophecy" for the senior class, jocularly predicting greatness ten years hence for students like Richard Wien, scion of the Wien Airlines family: "Richard Wien, world famous aeronautical engineer, designed a plane so fast that it crashed into itself coming back." For Ralph Amouak, captain of an intramural baseball team, he predicted: "Ralph…is still pushing mops down the corridors of Fairbanks High School— between baseball seasons, that is." These expectations had little to do with the abilities of Native students—two of my contemporaries eventually served in the Alaska State Senate, and Ralph Amouak, according to the Internet, became a nationally respected authority in the field of alcoholism treatment. Attitudes like those of the surprised teacher and the class wag did not begin to change until the shift in power at the time of the 1971 Alaska Native Claims Settlement Act.

In the 1950s I was blind to what was happening to my classmates of color. My white classmates and I were dumb, distracted, and dazzled by other colors, by the brilliant shades that decorated the material world we were about to claim—colors like Torch Red, Tuxedo Blue, Surf Green, and Madeira Maroon that lacquered the finned cars being shipped north from Detroit, the cars we wanted to drive.

Two years after my solo in Oscar Tweiten's pickup, I was officially taught to drive by my mother because my father's impatience was not suited to repeated struggles with backing and parallel parking. Immediately after my sixteenth birthday I became a legal borrower of the two-toned Buick. I had no dreams of having my own car. In the 1950s, Fairbanks parents rarely purchased a second automobile for a teenager. Nevertheless, enterprising sons did sometimes buy their own vehicles. Summer and evening jobs were plentiful and well paid. Boys who were not saving for college used their earnings to buy old cars or pickups; they then spent hours in garages, repairing and customizing. In those days before automatic transmissions and computerized ignitions, some of these boys learned nearly all there was to know about cars. When automobiles belonging to relatives and neigh-

Three photos of Second Avenue taken from Cushman Street.
FROM TOP: Ca. 1930 (Jim's album). *Author's collection.*
Ca. 1948 (Jane's album). *Courtesy of Jane Crawford Tallman.*
Ca. 1958 (Sally's era). Polaris Building in view. *Courtesy of Barbara Hale.*

bors malfunctioned, certain boys were called for advice in much the same way that teens today are sometimes respectfully consulted about computer problems. It was an unspoken belief that mechanical skill was inherited on the Y chromosome. I remember only one girl who developed significant garage expertise. Girls, particularly beautiful girls, were presumed to be attracted to the owners of cars adjusted to display a raked angle, racing stripes, and rumbling pipes. There may have been some truth in this. It did seem that college-bound, slide-rule-carrying boys, who displayed their lack of style by driving borrowed family cars, were rarely observed transporting the head cheerleader or the prom queen.

During the summer we imitated Californians. In our own or in family cars we cruised the two main streets, hailing each other and listening to one of two local radio stations on our autos' tinny monaural speakers. Sometimes we parked at the new A&W Drive-In to order Cokes and stroll between cars. The old-fashioned Co-Op Soda Fountain was part of a childish walking past. Occasionally we risked our lives in those seat-beltless vehicles when the boy driving took out that talisman of maturity, his church key (beer can opener), to open his second or third beer, or when rivals agreed to a drag race on the mostly gravel roads.

But these all-American teen rituals were considerably curtailed by winter. The A&W closed, and intersections turned icy. Cars became cranky—especially cars without garages, cars whose drivers depended on headbolt heaters, battery warmers, and starter fluid to get them going. My family was grateful for our heated garage, although the rapid change from warm to cold promoted condensation of water vapor in the gas lines, causing the engine to miss. If water in the lines froze, the car was immobilized. We were careful to pour a can of Heet (a "drying" methanol additive) into the tank at each fill-up.

Cars designed for temperate winters were sometimes inadequate in truly frigid weather. Defrosters melted only tiny semicircles on the front windows. The driver or passenger riding shotgun had to scrape repeatedly, peeling off curls of frost that landed on laps and boots. The weaker the heater and the leakier the car, the greater the interior frost problem. Volkswagen bugs were famous for interior icing, but a friend of mine had a car that trumped even the VW for winter impracticality—a Citroen 2CV Deux Chevaux. How this thin-bodied vehicle with its rear-hinged doors had crossed the Atlantic and wandered so far north, I do not know, but it was so airy that during the winter it could not be driven by just one person; a copilot was required to provide continuous frost removal. Even clear windows did not solve all winter visibility problems. Daylight was brief; streetlights were limited; and, in deep cold, ice fog accumulated.

At 40 below even parking posed a problem. When a driver stopped to do an errand, she had three choices: finish the task before the engine had time to get cold, plug the headbolt heater into an electrical outlet, or leave the car running in neutral—further adding to the ice fog. Failure to take one of these precautions could mean the engine would refuse to start. When chilly parked cars did start, their stiffened tires, slightly flattened on the bottom, produced a disconcertingly bumpy ride. Once a car returned to its temperate garage, however, the ice would melt, the tires would soften, and the vehicle would regain the powerful and innocent appearance that so appealed to us.

Cars took teens out to meet one another, and they provided us with private space. These were important to our third preoccupation—dating. I use the term "dating" loosely because our rendezvous with the opposite sex were often loosely organized. Three or four girls would band together to go to a dance, each secretly intending to abandon the gang if the right boy offered a private ride home. The dances varied from brightly decorated, well-chaperoned proms in the school gym to sock hops at the YMCA to laxly monitored dances in dim venues like the Eagles Club or the Civil Defense Quonset Hut. Occasionally our destination was even murkier, a barely lit home where parents were out of town. In these racier locations, boys no longer in school, their Lucky Strikes rolled into their T-shirt sleeves, were in attendance. They contributed forbidden elements—beer and dirty dancing to Jerry Lee Lewis or Bobby Darin played full volume on the 45 rpm record player.

Dating and driving around in cars with boys held dangers that my parents preferred not to discuss, apparently counting on inherited conservatism to keep me safe. In my case and my sister's, this dubious approach did seem to work. Community values relating to "good girls" and "bad girls," plus the lack of any birth control other than unreliable condoms, also deterred sexual activity. The majority of my classmates were virgins at graduation. This does not mean that teenagers did not fall in love. Frequently a girl would put the world on notice that she was going steady by wearing her boyfriend's ring on a chain around her neck. Two of my classmates received real engagement rings as graduation gifts. Some girls, bolder than I, had sex with their special boyfriends. A few of these found themselves pregnant and "had to" get married, the accepted and traditional option for a pregnant teenager. These unplanned marriages were not necessarily less successful than planned unions contracted by other classmates five to ten years after graduation.

A few white pregnant girls did not marry but quietly went Outside to homes for unwed mothers, where they gave up their babies for adoption. A single teenager attempting to raise a baby was unusual; it was considered impractical and perhaps irresponsible to the child. Intrafamily adoption, which kept an infant within the extended family, was a more frequent solution for Native girls than for non-Natives.

Abortions were illegal and rarely discussed except with intimates. I recall knowing of only two in high school. In both cases the girls went out of town; one even went out of the country. But it was always whispered that abortions were available locally—for a price in money and sometimes in safety. In April 1961 a medical doctor, Carl Boswell, was arrested and indicted for performing an abortion. The doctor's first attorney quit, and he had trouble finding another. The trial was scheduled to start December 11, but when the judge discovered the defendant had no lawyer, he appointed an attorney for the defense and delayed the trial one day to allow for preparation. In one of those small-town oddities, the lawyer appointed to the defense, Warren Taylor, was the father of the prosecuting attorney, William Taylor. The doctor and Taylor Sr. prevailed. At the end of five days of testimony and five hours of deliberation, the jury found Dr. Boswell not guilty. The arrest and the trial made the front page of the newspaper in an article that included the name and address of each juror. Then as now, abortion raised passionate controversy. At the time of Dr. Boswell's arrest an articulate matron with five children wrote a letter to the editor predicated on his guilt: "For those who believe that to perform an abortion is a major crime, it is surely their right to act accordingly. But what of the others of us? ... In regard to Doctor Boswell there will be at least several hundred women in this town who will be sympathizing with him." She was apparently correct. Nine years later 698 Fairbanksans, mostly women, staged a pro-choice rally. One week later, on April 30, 1970, the legislature overrode a veto by Governor Egan, and abortion was legalized in Alaska two and a half years before *Roe v. Wade* legalized abortion throughout the United States.

But the great risk of those weekend nights in the 1950s was not sex; it was the historic bane of Alaska: alcohol. Although young and old alike understood that teenage beer drinking could lead to fistfights, auto accidents, and pregnancies, the attitude toward teenage drinking was tolerant and obtuse. "Boys will be boys" was the phrase as certain classmates of both sexes slid into binge alcoholism that would alter the rest of their lives. The laws against underage drinking, like the city curfew for those under the age of nineteen (10 PM on school nights, midnight otherwise), were rarely prosecuted. Instead, they were used to remand teenagers to parents who were expected to take a strong stand about future infractions after being called to the police station late at night.

The Territory led all the States in alcohol consumption per capita, and tolerance for alcohol misdeeds was not just directed at teens. Mac, our high school principal, was convicted of more than one DWI; these peccadilloes were ascribed to the stress of his position. The attitude toward functioning alcoholics—the housewife, the businessman, the algebra teacher—was a statement that trailed off with a falling inflection: "What a shame..." The shame was private. No intervention beyond the family or perhaps Alcoholics Anonymous was called for. But nonfunctioning adult alcoholics who disturbed the peace or passed out on the sidewalk were considered a public shame. The city fathers had these drunks hauled to jail to sober up and serve time. It was a dangerous arrangement. In 1953 two inmates died in the city jail in one week. Both were in their forties and employed in vigorous trades when sober. Their guard was Police Chief Skelton, who had read in a police magazine that inebriates were dehydrated. He forced each of them at tear-gas pistol point to drink huge quantities of water; both died before reaching the hospital. The coroner's jury referred the case to the grand jury, who recommended the chief be fired. Instead he was demoted to patrolman and resigned a few months later. His replacement, Chief Danforth, lasted seven months before another grand jury, citing "shocking laxity" and "unsavory conditions," recommended he also be fired. Stan Zaverl, a patrolman in the ranks, was then named acting chief. Zaverl had been a Fairbanks patrolman for less than a year, but he had served in the army as an MP and as a deputy U.S. Marshal in Nenana, Nulato, and Fairbanks. His wife was Athabascan-Irish, and he understood conditions in Alaska. Within a month he suspended two policemen for leaving an intoxicated man outdoors at forty below zero; the man was wearing bedroom slippers and had no hat or mittens. Zaverl was appointed permanent chief and remained in office for many years. A few months after his appointment, Richard Cooley's report describing the egregious conditions at the city jail was published. The public and city council reacted: the lives of inmates outweighed budget constraints and respectful deference to jailers pursuing their duty as they saw it. The jail, the drunk tank, and the police offices were moved from the cramped space over the fire station to the roomier old Cheechako Hotel with three times as much room for offenders. In the new location inmates were served three regular meals a day and the sick were referred for medical care.

But this public fracas passed me by. I was a self-absorbed teenager with troubles at home. I had finally found a boyfriend, Merton Keaunui, a delightfully humorous, non-nerdy Hawaiian close to my opposite. My parents were less enchanted with my steady than I was, and they became alarmed when Mert graduated with the class ahead of me without ending our relationship. Rational persuasion, historically an ineffective approach to a seventeen-year-old girl with a boyfriend, did not deter me. The rector of St. Matthew's sided with Jim and Alta for reasons related more to color sensitivity from his Southern upbringing than to the Gospel. I quit church in a self-righteous huff that I managed to nurture for twenty years. But in 1959 I was as unwilling to take a stand against my parents as I was to give up Mert. I resolved the problem by taking my romance underground with a tiring string of subterfuges and outright lies.

Worse yet, Grandmother Lillian had come to live with us. Widowed and no longer able to manage on her own or even to be left alone, she required complicated ladysitting arrangements involving me, Alta, and Aunt Audrey. Unfortunately, age had stripped from Lillian the respectable garment of conformity, and her curmudgeonliness had declined to paranoia. Jim had appreciated Alta's support when his parents were dying, but he called a halt to our experiment in three-generational living when scissors, a paring knife, and a hatchet were discovered under the mattress of Lillian's bed. He had never been his mother-in-law's favorite, and perhaps he was afraid he would be the first to go if a Lizzie Borden mood overcame her. Grandmother moved to an old-age home in Eugene, where she fell for a gentleman resident on whom she showered gifts and where she lived relatively peacefully for another five years.

My high school years were passing, and I needed a plan for leaving home. I discovered I could not picture myself as a secretary married to my forbidden boyfriend, who in any case had not proposed. I began to be serious about becoming a college student. I credit the First National Bank, of which my father was a director, with encouraging this ambition.

My parents did not believe in idle teenagers. They shared the community sentiment that high school students should work during the summer. There was no shortage of jobs, work was good for character, and most families could use the money. My first full-time job at age fifteen was babysitting two primary-school children while their parents worked. Hectic days of keeping the kids out of the trees and off the street while cleaning up our kitchen messes reinforced my confidential plan to avoid motherhood. My friend L'Marie Wagner was taking care of a larger family next door with verve and apparent enjoyment. Her talent with children later led to her own family of twelve children, two stepchildren, and three foster children. My lack of talent at childcare led to a change of jobs the next summer.

Probably through nepotism, I got a job at the First National Bank. My task was to file canceled checks in drawer pockets marked with the name of the account owner. In those days, canceled checks were returned to the owner with the monthly statement. Checks for First National Bank were generic; the bank was identified but neither the account number nor the signer's name was printed on the check. Only the signature identified the check writer, and some signatures consisted simply of swirled lines recognizable only by the cognoscenti. We filers were allowed to go home when the last check in our portion of the alphabet had been filed for the day. During my first few weeks on the job, the janitor had to let me out of the building at night, but eventually I memorized enough scrawls to be able to keep banker's hours. As my skill increased over the two summers that I worked at the bank, I realized that my ability could only lead me upward—to teller. The idea of counting out money every day excited me about as much as taking shorthand or becoming a competent housewife. Although I had no idea what I might major in or what I would do with a degree, the life of a college girl with access to a big library, a dormitory full of lively girls, and a campus load of young men suddenly had great appeal.

My parents joined me in planning my college career. It was a time of optimism for us all. The decade of the 1950s, with its Korean War and McCarthyism, was almost over. I would be graduating from high school in 1960 at the start of a new decade, and on the graduates' platform would be mounted a forty-nine-star flag. Alaska had just become the newest state in the union. Our territorial days were over.

Dorothy Loftus joins others to sign community thank-you letter to Congress for passage of the Alaska Statehood Bill, June 30, 1958. *University of Alaska Archives, Fred Machetanz Collection, 73-75-159.*

{17}

INTO STATEHOOD AND
OFF TO THE UNIVERSITY OF ALASKA

J IM CRAWFORD OPPOSED STATEHOOD for Alaska. In keeping with his character, he did not write letters to the editor or advertise this unpopular opinion in public, although he spoke strongly to family and trusted friends. In the August 26, 1958, plebiscite on statehood, he voted with the 16 percent of Alaskans who wanted to reject the long-sought offer from Congress to become the forty-ninth state. He was not swayed by the opinion of Bob Atwood, editor of the *Anchorage Times,* that

It would be unthinkable for good Americans to reject the traditional form of American government. Rejection by Alaskans would be a great victory for the Communists. Their leaders would point to Alaskans and say, "Even Americans don't want that form of government"... It is astonishing that... good Americans would place the prestige and dignity of the United States in jeopardy... [letting] their distaste for statehood overshadow their concern for the nation.... There were signs of coordination between the statehood saboteurs in Washington and in Alaska.... This insidious campaign has given Alaskans an indelible experience that should last a lifetime. They have lived under some of the conditions that prevail... in the new nations where Communists are engaging in subversion and infiltration.... The opponents [of Statehood have] been un-American and un-Alaskan. And what is more, they know it.

My father did not know it; he considered himself neither un-American nor un-Alaskan. His opposition to statehood was based on a rational financial calculation.

Without the $3.6 million territorial appropriation from the federal government, how could the state of Alaska with its 220,000 residents (50,000 of whom were military) support itself? Defense construction was decreasing, mining was in decline, logging was going nowhere, and salmon barons had overfished their resource. Even with a substantial state personal income tax, Jim did not think that Alaska could make ends meet. In making these calculations, Jim was not deferring to the USSR&M Company's desire to avoid more taxes on their already-marginal Alaska operations, although he certainly would have been accused of espousing Company interests had he been more public with his doubts. It was popularly, and probably correctly, believed that Outside lobbies with interests in Alaska (particularly the salmon industry) were largely responsible for Congress's reluctance to pass a statehood bill. However, the Boston office did not try to influence my father or to influence Jack Boswell, the Fairbanks operations manager, who was squarely pro-statehood. Boswell was an elected delegate to the Alaska Constitutional Convention held at the University of Alaska in 1955. The constitution formulated at the convention was based on model documents but addressed specific Alaskan issues like natural resources (including regulation of the salmon fishery) and the need for a strong, accountable executive branch. It was ratified by voters at a special election in April 1956 and used as part of the campaign to gain congressional votes for admission to the union.

It is ironic that as a mining engineer, my father did not include significant income from oil in his calculations of potential tax revenue. He shared the view expressed in a 1953 *Fairbanks Daily News-Miner* article titled "History of Oil Exploration in Alaska Is Frustration." The article documented all the oil discoveries that failed to yield economically viable fields: Oil Bay (1897), Katella (1902), Kanatak (1922), Cook Inlet (1936), Arctic Slope Naval Petroleum Reserve No. 4 (1944). As Alaska moved toward statehood, yet another discovery was being explored at Swanson River on the Kenai Peninsula (1957), but my father held little hope for it.

Jim's financial calculations for the new state were in fact correct—in the short range. Although the federal government provided transition funds, granted the new state 90 percent of resource revenues from federal land, and allowed the state to begin selection of 104 million acres of land for its own use, Alaska was in financial crisis by 1960. Administrative expenses of the new state were twice that of the territorial government, significantly exceeding projected revenue for 1961. But Jim's underestimate of oil revenue made him wrong in the long run. Swanson River and nearby offshore land under Cook Inlet saved the government. Leases on state land in Cook Inlet brought Alaska $22 million in 1961 (the equivalent of more than $120 million today). Oil revenue—largely from lease sales—made up a third of the state's general fund over the next five years. Then ironically, in the middle of the decade, federal disaster aid following the April 1964 earthquake helped Alaska stay in the black. Finally in 1968, the discovery of the Prudhoe Bay field on the North Slope created the next great Alaskan boom, bringing a bolus of income to the state that outdid the projections of the most enthusiastic statehood proponents. This was, of course, money that would have gone into federal coffers had there been no Statehood Act. In retrospect, my father admitted that Atwood was right to support statehood—although not for the reason of quashing Communist ambitions. Jim Crawford was wrong to oppose it—although not for choosing to consider the financial consequences; his error was underestimating oil. Had petroleum not saved statehood, Alaska might have had to file for bankruptcy or revert to territorial status.

But financial matters were not on my mind or on the minds of most Alaskans on June 30, 1958, when Congress passed the Statehood Bill that mandated the August plebiscite. When the siren wailed announcing the vote of Congress, I rushed to the Chena River Bridge with my friends to watch the spontaneous parade and a star labeled "49" rise to the end of its guy wires by the pull of weather balloons. Upstream from the bridge, dye was poured into the water. Through a miscalculation it colored the Chena a curious green rather than the gold of the stars on the Alaska flag, but it was dramatic anyway. My aunt Dorothy Loftus, white hair pulled into a graceful bun and face alight with youthful enthusiasm, was photographed by artist Fred Machetanz as she signed a community thank-you letter to Congress. Curfew was suspended for teens, and festivities continued deep into the night. Bars failed to close, creating a windfall of paper currency for owners who had prudently stocked up in preparation.

The celebration was more modest the following January, when President Eisenhower signed the official proclamation making Alaska the first new state in almost fifty years. Sirens announced the signing at 7 AM Fairbanks time, but the thermometer read minus eight degrees and no one danced in the streets. However, for Alaskans January 3, 1959, was an important date. It was Suffrage Day: for the first time citizens over the age of nineteen would be able to vote for their governor, congressional delegation, and the president of the United States. In that first year of statehood, few people in town skipped going to the polls to register their choice.

I was still six months short of my nineteenth birthday in November 1960. I longed to vote for Kennedy to counter my father's vote for Nixon. I discussed

Kennedy's strengths with my mother, nominally a Republican. She nodded and listened attentively, but neither I nor my father knew how she marked her ballot in the little cubicle behind the red, white, and blue curtain. She was a strong proponent of the secret ballot and of peace in the family. Although Kennedy won the presidency, Alaska's three electoral votes went to Nixon by a 4 percent margin.

In family matters, however, there were no secret ballots; all votes were exposed. We were unanimous in the matter of my going to college, but I wanted to fly to a glamorous university in the Lower Forty-eight (the post-statehood term for the contiguous states). My father held out for a probationary freshman year at the University of Alaska four miles from our house with a transfer to a distant college if I did well. My mother supported him; it was the same offer they had made to my sister more than a decade before.

And so my future was decided before high school graduation in May 1960. Friends who had accepted my minimized grade reports were surprised to discover I was valedictorian. My callow graduation speech unwittingly presaged the hippie ethos that would bloom later in the decade. I enjoined my classmates to admire the flowers instead of rushing after material success. This suggested, of course, that the generation before us, the proud parents in the audience, did not properly appreciate the beauty of life. My parents ignored this implied rudeness and presented me with a marvelous graduation gift creatively wrapped by my mother and ceremoniously presented by my father. The heavy, mysterious box contained a white portable electric Smith-Corona typewriter. It seemed too elegant to be a cousin of the bulky, gunmetal-gray manual Underwoods in my typing class. No longer would I have to worry about producing a heavy black **f, g, h,** or **j**; or with recording a barely readable *q, a, z,* or *p.* The keys moved easily, the hammers never jammed, and the manual carriage throw required only a gentle nudge. It was a gift full of hope for both my parents and me. From my point of view it would be invaluable, although not required in those days, for writing the college papers that would provide my escape from home, from the bank, and from the raw, impoverished State of Alaska. Moreover, I had absorbed my parents' pecuniary views. They and I both felt reassured that if times went bad, the white typewriter would be a portable tool to help me earn a living, at forty-five words per minute.

In the fall I moved into the women's dormitory at the university. The rules at Wickersham Hall were generous in comparison with St. Helen's, and the housemother was notably less attentive than Alta to my dress and behavior. Boys were allowed in the dorm's living room during respectable hours, and the curfew, although rigid, was pleasantly late—11 PM on weekdays and 1 AM on weekends.

Sally Crawford, high school graduation, 1960.
Author's collection.

But the great revelation of my freshman year at the University of Alaska had nothing to do with social life. I discovered that some professors had intellectual passions. I had always accepted an adage popular with miners, entrepreneurs, and mechanics: "Those who can, do; those who can't do, teach." I had modified this opinion to include teaching children as "doing" something, but I expected little from geologists who taught earth science because they were unable to locate a rich uranium lode or from English instructors who taught Shakespeare because they could not write plays. My freshman professors reshaped my thinking. I discovered that they researched, wrote knowledgeably, and spoke enthusiastically about their subjects. Brina Kessel taught Biology 101 illustrated with examples from an Alaska that I knew but had never analyzed. Michael Krauss, a linguistics PhD only a few years older than his students, taught French 201 to enrollees whose high school French credits indicated anything but competence. He ignored our deficiencies, refused to use English in class, and assigned novels by St. Exupery and Camus, dragging us forcibly upward. As an aside he revealed his fascination with Alaska's Native languages, several of which were headed toward extinction. English 101 was taught by Joe Meeker, a visiting professor with a master's in wildlife ecology and a doctorate in comparative literature. He insisted that a good student essay featured clear thought, imagination, and organization. He was remarkably uninterested in the correct use of the comma or in whether the writer spelled "judgment" with one "e" or two. I was extraordinarily lucky in my classes, and the experience changed my life in the next three universities I attended.

Not all of my fellow students found adjustment to college joyful, or even bearable. One of my roommates spent Christmas vacation with our family; she remained abed twenty hours a day trying to sleep her way out of a depression. Another friend, brokenhearted over a boy, consumed a bottleful of aspirin in a movie-theater restroom. She confessed to a roommate before lapsing into semi-consciousness and spent several frightening days in the hospital. I had no wisdom or even an inkling of how to deal with depression, but I knew it was dangerous and it frightened me. I had not forgotten the 1958 suicide of college student Quentin Johnson, the older brother of a classmate. He was sober and left no note when he shot himself at the family's Harding Lake cabin. Less than forty-eight hours later his former schoolmate, Bud Waxberg, left a card table where he had been drinking and playing bridge with his father and friends and similarly shot himself without explanation.

In the first half of the twentieth century, most victims of suicide in Alaska, as in the States, were elderly, powerful men who faced debilitating illness—men like Jim Huntington Sr. of the Koyukuk region and James Barrack of Fairbanks. Traditionally, older men were four times more likely to kill themselves than teens or young adults. But at the time of the deaths and near-deaths of young people during my high school and college years, the pattern was changing. Alaska's current epidemic of youthful suicide was taking off. Its causes were complex, but particularly in villages left behind during the construction and oil booms, young Alaskans were finding little rewarding work. Drug and alcohol use was rising, racism continued its toll on self-esteem, and hopes were falling.

My age-mates were also dying from illness and accidents. Marie Uotila, a college sophomore, died within a month of being diagnosed with leukemia; Judy Neff Blair was also carried off by cancer; Jim Cassady crashed a plane on Denali; Conrad Egowa drowned while swimming in a local gravel pit. My friends and I were not invulnerable.

While I was learning these lessons from life, Alta was celebrating her wintertime empty nest by signing up for short courses at the university and developing a keen enthusiasm for a subject rarely taken seriously by nonaficionados—birdwatching. So that she could use both hands on her binoculars, she sewed a clever cover with a wrist strap for her copy of *Birds of North America* by Roger Tory Peterson. She began checking off species on a life list. She even managed to stir mild birding interest in my father and me. But we were dabblers; Alta rapidly outstripped us. In 1968 she traveled to the Pribilof Islands with Roger Tory Peterson himself to view birds. Her respectful family stayed home and admired the photographs she brought back.

During the warm months, Alta continued to tend houseguests. In addition to the usual travelers, she hosted some longer-term guests. During the first summer of statehood, young cousins from opposite sides of the family stayed with us. Petite, blond Jackie Crawford, daughter of Uncle Gus, had just finished her first year at Harvard Law School. My father helped her find a summer job with some Fairbanks attorneys unusually busy with the change from territorial to state law. She moved into an upstairs bedroom for three months of work and adventure in Alaska. My dark-haired, muscular cousin Gale Weatherell moved into the downstairs bedroom vacated by his grandmother Lillian. He lived with us only half-time because as a brakeman on the Alaska Railroad, he commuted between Fairbanks, Healy, and Anchorage.

Gale's occupation was the result of a childhood encounter with an extraordinary railroad engineer, Otis Harrington, who, to Gale, looked just like Casey Jones. He wore a striped engineer's hat with matching striped coveralls, heavy gloves, and a red bandana around his neck. In his steam locomotive Harrington carried a bag with candy for children along his route. When his train pulled into Talkeetna, the kids would run down to greet him. Sometimes he would let them climb into the cab to blow the whistle or even pull on the throttle to move the train a short distance. Although as a teenager Gale frequently flew recreationally with bush pilot Don Sheldon, trains rather than planes took hold of his imagination. After he finished high school and satisfied the draft in the army, Gale dabbled with farm and factory work in New York State and took one or two community-college courses from instructors whose pay was significantly less than that of an Alaska Railroad brakeman. Then he returned to Alaska and to the railroad.

Jackie and Gale each regarded the other as exotic, shaped by hard-to-imagine experiences and full of strange competences. Gale understood sled dogs; he could imitate birds and run a riverboat. In turn Jackie could tell him what he needed to do to regularize his use of the name Weatherell although his ex-stepfather had never adopted him. (He did not act on her advice at the time because he had no need to document the name—which had seen him through school, work, and the army—until 2002 when Canada began to demand from Alaskans driving the Alcan Highway passports or birth certificates that matched their photo ID.) Mother was fond of both Gale and Jackie and enjoyed watching them step into adult work.

Two years later I imitated Jackie by finding a summer job related to my college major—biology. Instead of returning to the bank, I remained at the University of Alaska to work in a lab that I had largely to myself because of its pervasive odor. My assignment was to cut open caribou stomachs preserved in formaldehyde, remove the contents, and separate by size the lichens that the animals had eaten before being shot near Point Hope the previous autumn. The purpose of this task, which left my hands pale, shriveled, and pungent at the end of each day, was to allow a botanist to classify the lichens and check their strontium 90 content. This long-lasting radiation had entered the food chain, which stretched from lichens to caribou to man, via the prevailing winds from Soviet nuclear testing sites. My university salary was funded by the Atomic Energy Commission (AEC). Headed by Edward Teller, the AEC had responded to the 1958 nuclear testing moratorium by proposing a free public-works project for Alaska—an underground nuclear explosion to create a new harbor on the northwest coast near Point Hope.

The story of this ill-conceived plan, code-named Project Chariot, is well told by Dan O'Neill in his book *The Firecracker Boys*. The proposed harbor would be closed nine and a half months a year by ice. It would also be 250 roadless miles from the nearest shippable mineral (low-grade coal) and thirty-two miles from Point Hope, whose villagers were already concerned about the high level of strontium 90 recorded in their bones. My father was glad to see me employed, but astounded at the impracticality of this project. After attending the AEC meeting in Fairbanks promoting this coastal remodel, Jim could only speculate about the agency's rationale: "They seem to be rather anxious to get underway at an early date and it would appear that international prestige might be the underlying motive." Perhaps because Project Chariot rapidly became political and therefore off-limits for dinner-table conversation, he did not share his doubts with me. But rising local controversy penetrated even the aromatic isolation of my lab.

The editor of the *Fairbanks Daily News-Miner* supported the project. He had the American enthusiasm for spectacular science: a test bomb explosion had "a golden brilliance…a skyful of fleecy clouds invisible in the darkness an instant before, were momentarily printed with gold." He also had the Alaskan predilection for big land developments: "an opportunity for Alaska to have a $5 million earth-moving job done at no cost to the new state." And the usual patriotic/altruistic twist: "Alaska's yes vote on this vital project will result in incalculable benefits to all mankind." However, Tom Snapp, a *Daily News-Miner* reporter, ran a countering series of articles near the back of the paper detailing the views of Eskimos, dissident scientists, conservationists, and Alaska's congressional delegation (which opposed the Rhode Island–sized land withdrawal involved).

The year after I sieved lichens, the AEC quietly abandoned Project Chariot. The fallout from these unexploded bombs included the firing of several scientists at the university (my boss, Bill Pruitt, among them), the establishment of the Alaska Conservation Society, the rising Native political consciousness, and the founding of a statewide newspaper (*Tundra Times*).

But in the fall of 1961, when I left the lab, I was leaving Alaska and its controversies behind. My wish to fly away had come true. I left in style—no Sunday hat, no white gloves, no airsickness bags, no six-hour DC-6 flight. Fairbanks International Airport had recently lengthened its runway to 10,300 feet to accommodate Pan American's Boeing 707 jet planes. My nonstop flight to Seattle, the first leg of my journey to Middlebury College in Vermont, took only three hours. For the next four years I came back to Fairbanks to visit at Christmas and to work various summer jobs, but my Fairbanks childhood was over. Seven years would pass before I again lived year-round in Fairbanks. By that time Jim and Alta would have moved south, reluctantly leaving Alaska behind.

Fairbanks flood, 1967.
Alaska State Library, U.S. Bureau of Public Roads, PCA 229-3.

{18}

LEAVING ALASKA

JIM AND ALTA'S LIFE in Fairbanks between the declaration of statehood and Alaska's centennial in 1967 was marked by dredges being shut down, by Company property being sold off, and by natural disasters that shook and soaked Alaska's two leading cities.

The first of these natural disasters, the earthquake in south-central Alaska, had a great effect on the state, but little direct effect on Fairbanks. On March 27, 1964, I was in Oregon talking long distance to my father when he made a startled noise. A minor earthquake had shaken the house, but he made light of it. Fairbanks had experienced many earthquakes, including a notable one on July 22, 1937, which registered 7.5 on the Richter scale with an epicenter about forty-five miles south of the city. That earthquake smashed merchandise in liquor stores, cracked the Richardson Highway, and almost killed my uncle Ted Loftus.

In 1937 Ted and an FE Company crew were experimenting with a new method for mining rich but deep gravel at Ruby Creek near Chatanika. They drove a shaft through fifty-two feet of frozen muck, then thawed an additional 120 feet of gravel to reach bedrock. At bedrock they hollowed out a sixty-four-square-foot cave and thawed horizontal drifts radiating out from it. The crew installed floodlights and a sluice box in the cave and used a hydraulic giant to wash bedrock gravel through the riffles, hoisting the sluice box two hundred feet out of the shaft for cleanup. The crew and the sluice box were both on the surface when the earthquake hit. They were shaken but unharmed. After several hours they returned to inspect the mine. According to Ted, "It was pretty hard to find.... The whole ceiling had come down; there was nothing but black muck, frozen. If that had happened at any other time it would have literally squashed us.... We opened it up and continued mining."

But the early-evening earthquake of Good Friday 1964 that had seemed so mild to my father was the second-largest earthquake ever recorded—a hundred times stronger than the Fairbanks earthquake of 1937. It registered 9.2 on the Richter scale. The epicenter was less than a hundred miles east of Anchorage. In Anchorage, Valdez, Seward, and Kodiak 115 people were killed, mainly by tidal waves. Property damage was extensive, estimated at $580 million. The entire city of Valdez had to be rebuilt; a new site with better wave protection was selected. South-central Alaska recovered from this tremendous blow not only because of federal disaster funds, but because of the generosity of individuals and aid organizations throughout the nation.

The second disaster was the August 1967 Fairbanks flood. At the time of the flood, my parents were back living in Residence No. 7, one of the cottages in the Company compound. The only two FE Company dredges still running in Alaska were those at Chicken and Hogatza. The power plant and the big white manager's house had been sold. Jim Crawford was reduced to working for the Company as a contract consultant. It was the hundred-year anniversary of Alaska's purchase from Russia. My father was one of the citizens on the Alaska 67 Committee that had opened Alaskaland, a Fairbanks history theme park, as part of the celebration and as a long-term tourist attraction. But it had been a dismal summer. The city had already been soaked by a record of more than three inches of rain in July when it started to pour on August 9. Six inches fell in the next six days—two and a half times the usual amount for the month. The three-mile dike at Moose Creek Butte stood fast but it offered scant defense against the swirling brown water overflowing from the Tanana River on the south and the Chena River on the north, flooding a two-hundred-square-mile triangle upriver from their junction—the triangle designated on maps as Fairbanks and vicinity.

My mother and father were at Harding Lake when water washed out the highway to town. They listened to flood news and personal messages broadcast directly from the KFAR transmitter—the only AM radio facility on high ground. With telephones out, the station became a community message board; announcers read hundreds of hand-delivered notes to family and friends separated by floodwaters. They put out urgent calls for diapers and canned milk. Alta, knowing that the presses of the *Fairbanks Daily News-Miner* were flooded and all long-distance phone lines were out of commission, began composing a diary letter based on the news reports and the scene that greeted them when they were finally able to reach town. Hitchhiking in France, I heard the news on a car radio: *"desastre...* Fairbanks, Alaska... *inondation."* I thought my weak French had failed me. Spring breakup was the time for flooding. Thanks in part to the Moose Creek Butte dike built in 1941, there hadn't been an August flood since I was three years old.

But the radio announcers in France and in Fairbanks were describing the flood of a century. The water crested more than six feet above the banks of the river. East-west streets downtown became temporary channels for water streaming toward Nenana, which was also flooded. Waves and debris beat against the deck of the new concrete Chena River Bridge that had replaced the old bridge with its steel trestles. Only islands of high ground—among them the high school and the airport—were dry. Fifty private riverboats worked nonstop to rescue trapped people and pets, taking them to safety while avoiding underwater hazards like parking meters. The high school housed four thousand; its tightly packed evacuees published "The Water Log," a daily "newspaper" of information and anecdotes, including two reports of fish migrating up streets where water was flowing at ten knots. Another four thousand people reached the airport, which had one dry runway. Passengers were flown to Anchorage until air traffic slowed due to the airport's dwindling supply of aviation fuel. Army helicopters evacuated the residents of the newly opened Pioneer Home, depositing them directly to one of the university dormitories on College Hill. The pioneers, whose collective memory agreed that this was Fairbanks's largest-ever flood, joined seven thousand other refugees on campus. A temporary community developed, with a nursery for toddlers, a play area in the gym for older children, a veterinarian-run pet area, movies, and free typhoid shots. Potable water was in short supply; bathing and most toilet flushing was out. But the electricity was on and the university's FM station was broadcasting. The university power plant, which stood on lower ground than the other university buildings, had been kept in operation by a crew of six hundred volunteers. They worked for thirteen hours: some manned pumps fueled by gasoline siphoned from nearby cars while others built a huge sandbag dike to keep water out.

Seven people died in the flood. Damage to Fairbanks and the surrounding borough was estimated at $153 million. The federal government sent disaster aid to the city, and the Small Business Administration offered thirty-year loans to homeowners and businesses at 3 percent interest. The NC

Company extended six months of credit to Fairbanksans trying to get back on their feet. Damage repair resulted in some long-term improvements. Old St. Joseph's Hospital on the riverbank was replaced by a modern Fairbanks Memorial Hospital on higher ground. KTVF, off the air for four months, came back on broadcasting in color. Most importantly, the Army Corps of Engineers constructed the $275 million Chena River Lakes Flood Control Project with new levees and an upstream dam whose adjustable gates could control flow in the river.

Jim and Alta drove back to town three days after the river crested, stopping at a highway checkpoint near Fort Wainwright to receive clearance from state troopers. In town, they parked at the margin of the receding flood, and Jim donned high-top waders to walk seven blocks to the Fairbanks police to obtain a pass to enter his Garden Island neighborhood. Jim and Alta were pleasantly surprised that, although their yard was still full of water, their Company cottage was among the 5 percent of buildings inside city limits that had not been damaged. The compound houses had no basements. Instead they were built on elevated foundations with a large crawl space beneath. Water had reached just to the top step of the outside stairs. Jim and Alta's city water, electricity, and sewer were working. Their car had been parked on a high road at Harding Lake; unlike many automobiles it had not spent days full of silty water. The Crawfords were indeed fortunate. Jim set to work surveying damage to Company holdings and preparing a report for USSR&M headquarters in New York. Alta gathered up bucket, rags, and broom to help the Adlers, now in their seventies, clean out their bookshop where some two thousand volumes had been destroyed. Cleanup was urgent for everyone; freeze-up was on its way.

Alta also helped muck out the basement of the Kellum Street house Gray Tilly had built nine blocks from the riverbank. Canned goods stored on basement shelves had been bathed in floodwater contaminated by cesspools. Alta soaked cans in Clorox, then washed and reshelved them. When she finished, the cans shone but their labels were gone; Lola was left to guess at their contents. The Tillys, already retired, had spent five days marooned in their partly flooded home. Lola, like Alta, had composed a newsletter, which she sent to everyone on her Christmas list. The style was urgent, telegraphic: "Noted water in street. Coming in basement fast.... Just time to turn off furnace.... Eventually 6 feet in basement and garage.... Saved our car.... Phones out, electricity and heat off.... Declared nat'l disaster. National Guard moved in." The final line reads: "We are *not leaving*—Faith and Love, Lola and Gray Tilly."

Ted, Art, and Jule Loftus, 1957.
Courtesy of Barbara Hale.

Lola Tilly, Audrey Loftus, and Alta
Crawford, ca. 1955. *Author's collection.*

Surviving original
members of PEO,
Chapter B, ca. 1965.
Members arranged
in same order as 1945
photo, with Alta
Crawford seated in
center, Dorothy Loftus
standing far right, and
Audrey Loftus stand-
ing third from left.
Author's collection.

But my parents were leaving. They had overstayed the date of my father's retirement from USSR&M. Jim was sixty-three years old and probably at the height of his knowledge about dredging and placer mining in the North. His dedication to his profession extended beyond the FE Company. When he drove to the FE Company dredge at Chatanika, he would stop for a mining chat with Oscar Tweiten, who was running a profitable bulldozer/sluicing operation on Chatham Creek. When our family went to Chicken, Jim extended the mini-vacation by driving over the Top of the World Highway to Dawson to confer informally with Canadian engineers about their dredging problems. In the 1960s gold mining was on the wane—beset by high labor costs, a fixed price for gold, and rising demands for environmental protection. Men who had devoted their working lives to gold were no longer competitors but beleaguered brothers. Jim's early retirement in the fall of 1966 was not because he had tired of his work or because his earnings had made him wealthy, but because USSR&M no longer needed the services of an Alaska vice president and general manager.

The Chicken dredge had another year to run; the Hogatza dredge had eight. All the Nome and Fairbanks dredges were idle. The Davidson Ditch and the power plant had been sold to electric companies. By 1966 the whole Alaska subsidiary had only a hundred employees. This was a handful contrasted with 1940, when the Company in Fairbanks alone employed five hundred in the winter and twelve hundred in the summer—out of a city population of thirty-five hundred. In the late 1960s about half of USSR&M's Alaska employees were operating the Chicken and Hogatza mines; the other half were mothballing and selling equipment, and disposing of the corporation's considerable real estate. Exploration, stripping, and thawing were business of the past. On the East Coast, longtime family directors of USSR&M were being deposed in bitter proxy battles at annual shareholders' meetings. As a vice president, Jim owned stock, but his ten shares were insufficient to have any influence on decisions. The Company headquarters had moved from Boston to New York. In 1965 USSR&M acquired Mueller Brass Company and soon thereafter Federal Pacific Electric Company. In a few years United States Smelting, Refining and Mining Company's name would change to UV Industries to reflect its diversification away from mining.

It was time for my parents to move out of Company housing. They considered staying in Fairbanks like the Tillys, but Jim, ever careful with money, calculated the cost of buying a house and living in Alaska versus the cost of a home and upkeep on the West Coast. He decided that they could not afford to stay. He may have also been looking forward to freedom from shoveling snow and starting balky cars in winter. Moreover, Jim planned to consult for dredge companies in the North and perhaps elsewhere. The best location for his consulting business was the hub city for Alaska: Seattle.

Jim and Alta bought a house in Bellevue, a Seattle suburb, but kept their half-interest in the Harding Lake cabin for summer visits. Jim consulted for the Company and for other dredging companies in South America. He and Alta fulfilled dreams of travel to China, Russia, and Europe. Eventually he set aside engineering to devote himself to caring for Alta as her bright intelligence dimmed into dementia. However, during that first year of retirement, my parents remained in Fairbanks where Jim worked in the office, at Chicken, and at Hogatza for an hourly consulting fee.

In November 1966, at the time of my father's official retirement as the third and final general manager for USSR&M in Alaska, I had been living in Berkeley, California, for two school years. My hair was long and straight, my skirts were mini; I took the Pill, knew the difference between a beer and a joint, and strongly protested the war in Vietnam. Jim was a balding Republican supporter of the U.S. government, but there was no rupture in our relations. The family policy of silence on sex, religion, and politics stood us in good stead. I dressed in my best to attend my father's retirement party at a Fairbanks restaurant. Company workers and old friends gathered. He was presented with a memento—a miniature dredge bucket full of gravel and nuggets in epoxy. The bucket and a small plaque with his name and dates of service were mounted on a jade base. His bosses in New York sent a telegram acknowledging Alta's work as well as his: "to Jim and Alta our thanks for a job well done and our very best wishes for the future." Jim's faithfully kept diary for this date omits its usual entry about where and with whom he and Alta had dinner (guests and dinner invitations being frequent in those years). His diary entry for the following workday is simply marked by a new innovation—a marginal note on the number of billable hours spent as a contractor on each task he did in the office. The first day of Jim's retirement was a monument to denial and to his love for his job; he celebrated by working at his oak desk in the concrete-block office building for nine hours.

In the fall of 1967, when Jim's consulting work for USSR&M ended, my parents drove down the Alaska Highway to Bellevue. They were the last in their generation of our family to leave Fairbanks and the state. They continued to live in the Seattle area, traveling to Alaska each summer until age became a barrier.

Jim died in a retirement home in 1994 after a short illness. Alta passed away peacefully in 2001 at age ninety-eight.

We family members born in Alaska owe a debt to the balding young mining engineer and the dark-haired bursar's assistant, and to her sister, cousins, and in-laws, whose optimism and energy carried them north to work and to establish a family in Alaska. With ingenuity they made their living in new territory. By example they showed us a way to live.

Alta and Jim Crawford, 1968.
Author's collection.

ENDNOTES

Notes to Chapter 1

5 *When he established his own farm*: Henry Crawford, *Willow Hill*, ed. Elizabeth Bascom (privately published, 1979).

5 *His son, my great-grandfather*: James Garvin Crawford, *Dear Lizzie*, 1862–1865, ed. Elizabeth Bascom (privately published, 1978).

6 *Temporarily, in his words, "stymied"*: James D. Crawford to Jo Anne Wold, ca. February 1980 (in author's possession). Further quotes from letter in next three paragraphs.

6 *The wage was $4.50 per day*: This daily net pay is roughly equivalent to $30 in 2001 dollars. The 2001 value of a dollar in the 1920s can be approximated by multiplying by 10. For the 1930s the multiple is 12.5, for the 1940s it is 10.7, for the 1950s it is 6.5, and for the 1960s it is 5.5. These calculations are based on the average Composite Commodity Price Index for each period. John J. McCusker, *How Much Is That in Real Money?: A Historical Price Index for Use as a Deflator of Money Values in the Economy of the United States*, 2nd ed. (Worcester, MA: American Antiquarian Society, 2001), 57–59.

9 *In 1910, at the height*: Alden M. Rollins, compiler, *Census Alaska: Number of Inhabitants*, 1792–1970 (Anchorage: University of Alaska Anchorage Library, 1978), 1,930–35.

11 *He patented his process in* 1920: Clark C. Spence, *The Northern Gold Fleet: Twentieth-Century Gold Dredging in Alaska* (Chicago: University of Illinois Press, 1996), 60.

13 *The* Fairbanks Daily News-Miner *celebrated*: "DISCOVERED! ARE WE LOST, CAPTAIN?," editorial, *Fairbanks Daily News-Miner* [hereafter *FDNM*], November 29, 1924.

13 *In 1926 the winter population of Fairbanks*: John C. Boswell, *History of Alaskan Operations of United States Smelting, Refining and Mining Company* (Fairbanks: Mineral Industries Research Laboratory, University of Alaska, 1979), 43.

13 *The Ditch took three summers*: The Ditch continued in service under various owners until 1967, when flood destroyed a large section. The longtime USSR&M ditch superintendent was Leonhard Seppala, famed for his role in bringing diphtheria serum to Nome over the Iditarod Trail in 1925. In winter he patrolled the Ditch by dogsled. My sister remembers his Chatanika cabin, where he would let her play with his latest litter of husky puppies with rich names like Duska, Malinka, Togo, Czarina, Sneegourok, and Peluk.

16 *Ever attentive to detail*: Spence, *The Northern Gold Fleet*, 189.

Notes to Chapter 2

19 *The Tanner sisters and the Stanfield sisters*: Information in the first three paragraphs of this chapter comes in part from Audrey Loftus, "So Much for Papa" (manuscript, n.d., Jule Hurley Loftus private collection). The Stanfield family also included a son, John.

22 *Art was green*: Photos of the 120-foot *Maid of Orleans* and its dories can be found in Captain Ed Shields, *Salt of the Sea: The Pacific Coast Cod Fishery and the Last Days of Sail* (Lopez Island, WA: Heritage House Publishing Ltd., 2001), 25, 31, and 52.

24 *As soon as this schooling was over*: Details in these three paragraphs from Jule B. Loftus (untitled manuscript, n.d., Jule Hurley Loftus private collection).

24 *The construction camps*: With few exceptions these camps disappeared or became solitary section houses. Exceptions include Anchorage and Nenana—each just a cluster of cabins before the commission laid out a town site, auctioned lots, and provided several years' governance.

25 *The brothers cut*: Quotes are from Arthur Loftus, "A Homestead 'Frat' House," *Farthest-North Collegian* 2, no. 2 (June 1924): 10. In 1939 Jule sold the homestead to university president Charles Bunnell for $3 an acre. Bunnell to Jule B. Loftus, August 17, 1939 (Charles E. Bunnell Collection, Box 11, folder 215, University of Alaska Fairbanks Archives). Today a residential area overlying the site of the homestead includes a Loftus Road.

26 *According to Jule*: Jule Loftus, "Corralling Caribou—a Wilder West Sport," *Farthest-North Collegian* 2, no. 1 (February 1924): 20–21.

27 *In a reply Bunnell expressed*: Art and Jule admired Bunnell's generosity to students. After Art failed to graduate, Bunnell loaned him $2,000 to buy a Caterpillar tractor with just one question: "Let's see, do I have enough money in my account?"

28 *When Florence graduated from high school*: The "trolley" was a self-propelled, narrow-gauge gas-electric passenger car operated by the Alaska Railroad. It made five trips a day between Fairbanks and the college, using the first four miles of track that led to Nenana. The trolley used one of the standard-gauge rails and a second, narrow-gauge rail set between the tracks. In the 1930s it was replaced by a standard-gauge Brill car, and eventually by bus service.

29 *Alta stepped onto the platform*: Alta Crawford, "Excerpts from My Life" (manuscript in author's possession, 1978).

31 *Bone dry*: The Volstead Act of 1920 enforced the Eighteenth Amendment to the U.S. Constitution, which prohibited alcohol. Alaska and the rest of the country returned to legal drinking in 1933 when the Twenty-first Amendment repealed Prohibition.

32 *This quasi-legal "restricted district"*: "The Line," as this section of Fourth Street was called, was finally closed in 1953. "Line Closed, Police Chief Reports Here," *FDNM*, June 4, 1953.

32 *My mother did not approve*: Claire Fejes, *Cold Starry Night* (Seattle: Epicenter Press, 1996), 156. The matron quoted is Eva McGown.

32 *Eventually Alaska's state constitution*: Alaska Constitution, Article I, section 22, added by amendment in 1972.

Notes to Chapter 3

40 *Jule's wedding night*: Jule B. Loftus (untitled manuscript, Jule Hurley Loftus private collection, n.d.).

42 *On their third morning at Curry*: Alta wrote a detailed account of this delay in Alta Crawford, "A Brief History" (manuscript in author's possession, 1991).

43 *According to my parents*: In his diary entry for March 30, 1930, Wickersham was cheerful about the delay: "The larger snow plow is coming from Anchorage . . . & they say we will probably get away from here in two days more. In the meantime I am getting acquainted with a crowd of about 100 men who are going into the Interior." It was not a bad situation for a campaigner. James A. Wickersham, *Diaries (Alaska): January 1, 1900–April 27, 1939.* Juneau: Alaska Division of State Libraries, 1969.

Notes to Chapter 4

47 *In response the Company hired more men*: Spence, *The Northern Gold Fleet*, 98.

47 *The pages of legal advertisements*: "Fairbanks Was the Grandaddy," *FDNM*, November 13, 1963.

50 *She arrived in Fairbanks*: Lola Tilly, "Pedro Monument Rededication, July 22, 1984" (manuscript of speech, Lola Tilly Collection, University of Alaska Fairbanks Archives).

50 *The thirty-bed Richardson Roadhouse*: Audrey Loftus, "Alaskan Roadhouses" (manuscript, Jule Hurley Loftus private collection, n.d.).

54 *Girl Scouting had been strong*: Bloom was one of the suffragists gratified when, in 1913, seven years before the Nineteenth Amendment, the first bill passed by the First Alaska Territorial Legislature granted women the right to vote in territorial elections. (Neither men nor women in the Territory could vote in national elections.)

54 *Weeks Field, the town's sports*: The first flight from Weeks Field was actually a nine-minute biplane demonstration before a paying audience in 1913. The plane entered and left town aboard a steamboat. Eielson's flight initiated the practical use of air power in Fairbanks.

Notes to Chapter 5

60 *Frances and Glenn sold*: Frances Weatherell Sandvik (untitled manuscript, Gale Weatherell private collection, n.d).

66 *Soon the* Fairbanks Daily News-Miner *was able to brag*: "42 Passengers, 5 Planes to Seattle in 1 Day," *FDNM*, September 17, 1941. The five airplanes were three Electras and two new fourteen-passenger Lockheed Lodestars.

66 *Readers were urged to get their nets*: "Dike Baffles Salmon," *FDNM*, July 7, 1941.

66 *Even though the six-cent airmail stamp*: At first airmail letters to the States were flown to Juneau and transferred onto a steamship to Seattle, where they were reloaded onto a plane. However, within two years PAA received a contract to fly mail all the way to Seattle, and Fairbanks celebrated again.

67 *Maury Smith, an early KFAR employee*: Maury Smith, "KFAR Is on the Air," *Alaska Journal* 15, no. 4 (Autumn 1985): 12.

67 *By 1940 they had expanded the McCarty Mine*: Philip S. Smith, "Mineral Industry of Alaska in 1940," in *Mineral Resources of Alaska*, 1940, USGS Bulletin 933 (Washington, DC: U.S. Government Printing Office, 1942), 22.

68 *The Company also expanded*: James D. Crawford, "Report on Fortymile, Sixtymile, and Seventymile Districts: Examination June 24 to July 22, 1933" (report to Fairbanks Exploration Company, 1933, Mike Busby private collection).

68 *Based on what he saw*: For another view of the Hogatza claims, see Sidney Huntington, *Shadows on the Koyukuk* (Portland, OR: Alaska Northwest Books, 1993), 146–49.

70 *In consternation cabin builders*: Public land in the Territory was owned by the U.S. government. Congress was the only legislative body from which the squatters could seek redress.

71 *His summary*: Brian Garfield, *The Thousand-Mile War* (Fairbanks: University of Alaska Press, 1995), 60.

71 *In December 1941*: Garfield, *The Thousand-Mile War*, 73 and 81.

Notes to Chapter 6

73 *The volunteers*: Alaska Communications System (ACS), operated by the Signal Corps, provided wireless telegraph service for civilians and military. After the war, ACS also offered residents long-distance telephone service at their downtown office, but at breathtaking rates. Three minutes of conversation with Oregon relatives was $6, with Missouri relatives $7.50. My parents wrote out an agenda for each call and spoke in rapid, telegraphic English.

74 *He had been too young*: A limited draft for men 21 to 35 to serve for one year in North America was instituted in 1940. After Pearl Harbor a series of changes expanded the draft age to 18 to 38 (and, briefly, to 45) to serve wherever needed until six months after the end of the war. Men 18 to 64 were required to register with the draft board.

74 *When summer came*: "Governor Urges No Fireworks," *FDNM*, June 17, 1942.

74 *This may have reduced accidents*: Highway crashes increased during blackouts. The nation was on year-round Daylight Savings Time during the war to give workers an extra hour to drive home before evening blackout drills began. This made no impact at Alaska's latitude.

75 *The Civil Defense Committee*: "Volunteers Worked Out Defense Plan," *Jessen's Weekly*, January 23, 1942.

75 *In a fine misunderstanding*: "Winged Squadron Prepares for Takeoff at Ladd Field," *FDNM*, December 12, 1941.

76 *Susan, daughter of my father's sister*: Anthony had been christened Pearle Anthony but discarded her first name. Her mother, christened Mary Pearle, dropped "Mary."

77 *In a January 1942 editorial*: "Speaking of Civilian Morale," *Jessen's Weekly*, January 23, 1942.

78 *He testified*: "Change in Censor Law Expected," *FDNM*, December 14, 1942.

79 *The* Fairbanks Daily News-Miner *responded*: "This Alien Question," *FDNM*, January 13, 1942.

79 *On April 2, 1942*: "All Japanese Soon Will Be Sent Out of Alaska," *FDNM*, April 2, 1942.

79 *The only exception to this*: "Deadline on Jap Order Is Monday," *FDNM*, April 18, 1942.

79 *The previous February*: "Fairness to Alien Labor Is Advocated," *FDNM*, February 11, 1942.

80 *Three days after the internment order*: "Regret to Leave," *FDNM*, April 4, 1942.

80 *Territorial newspapers reported*: "Gruening Visits Japanese Camp," *FDNM*, May 2, 1942.

80 *Michael had been*: "Local Hoop Star Now Internee," *FDNM*, December 18, 1942.

81 *The newspaper reported*: "26 Drunks Sent Out By WMC," *FDNM*, September 5, 1944.

81 *One fall month*: Dermot Cole, *Fairbanks: A Gold Rush Town that Beat the Odds* (Seattle: Epicenter Press, 1999), 128.

81 *Spokesman Frank Pollack's plea*: "CAA Threatens to Close Down Alaska Flying," *Jessen's Weekly*, February 27, 1942.

82 *To the relief of civilians*: Timothy Rawson, "World War II through *The Alaska Sportsman* Magazine," in *Alaska at War*, 1941–45, ed. Fern Chandonnet (Anchorage: Alaska at War Committee, 1995), 255.

82 *At the time the Japanese government*: Stan Cohen, *Alcan and Canol* (Missoula, MT: Pictorial Histories Publishing Co., Inc., 1992), 2.

83 *In Fairbanks, more than a thousand*: "Warning Given As to Rumors," *FDNM*, June 27, 1942.

84 *The United Press reporter*: William Gilman, *Our Hidden Front* (New York: Reynal & Hitchcock, Inc., 1944), 53.

84 *The death rate of interned*: John Ellis, *World War II: A Statistical Survey* (New York: Facts on File, 1993), 229 and 254. When the Aleuts finally returned home, many found their churches desecrated and their houses ransacked by soldier souvenir hunters. U.S. Commission on Wartime Relocation and Internment of Civilians, "War and Evacuation in Alaska," in *Personal Justice Denied: Report of the Commission on Wartime Relocation and Internment of Civilians* (Seattle: University of Washington Press, 1997), 355–56. Interned Aleuts and Japanese Americans received a public apology and compensation from Congress in 1988.

84 *On October 8, 1942*: Only placer mines that processed less than 1,000 cubic yards of material or hard rock mines that milled less than 1,200 tons of ore in 1941 were exempt. Some mines closed by this order never reopened, including the FE Company's McCarty Mine.

84 *Jim joked*: James D. Crawford, "Dope Sheet—James D. Crawford, February 26, 1979" (résumé in author's possession).

85 *There were 273 fox:* The other furs included beaver, rabbit, lynx, land otter, muskrat, weasel (ermine), nutria, and fitch (skunk).

86 *Instead of coffee*: White margarine, new to us, was not actually a wartime measure. In response to the butter lobby, Utah was one of many states that had banned the sale of colored margarine.

Notes to Chapter 7

93 *She was hired*: En route to Boston, Genevieve Parker was introduced to President Hoover, also a mining engineer, who "extended his congratulations." "President Meets Genevieve Parker," *FDNM*, February 6, 1930. The next week a reporter interviewed Ernest Patty, dean of the School of Mines, "about Genevieve's accomplishments." Dean Patty hastened to correct any misapprehensions: "Mining engineering as a profession is generally closed to women.... [T]his is a field of endeavor to which women should not aspire ... but [Miss Parker] is not a girl who is easily discouraged.... No one reading [her thesis] would guess that the data was secured by a woman." "Dean Patty Speaks," *FDNM*, February 12, 1930.

94 *During an average mining season*: Spence, *The Northern Gold Fleet*, 74.

98 *One of his postwar frustrations*: James D. Crawford to Fred Mulock, February 18, 1957 (John Reeves private collection).

98 *The barman directed him*: Riz Bigelow, "Prospecting Alaska," in *Alaska's Oil/Gas & Minerals Industry*, Alaska Geographic vol. 9, no. 4, 90 (Anchorage: Alaska Geographic Society, 1982).

99 *No one pondered*: Thirty years later a study suggested an answer to this unasked question: fifty to several hundred years, depending on the amount of clay discarded with the waste rock. Kay Holmes, "Natural Revegetation of Dredge Tailings at Fox, Alaska," in *Second Annual Conference of Alaskan Placer Mining* (Fairbanks: Mineral Industry Research Laboratory, University of Alaska, 1980), 175–84. In the 1970s, when environmental questions gained prominence, Walter Glavinovich, in charge of FE property, expressed a view held by many miners: dredges and their tailing piles actually improved land where "permafrost, polluted bogs and pesty insects once thrived." Spence, *The Northern Gold Fleet*, 147.

100 *I don't remember*: James D. Crawford, "Report on Moving Dredge 5 from Cleary Creek to Little Eldorado Creek 1947–48" (report to FE Company in author's possession).

100 *Jack Boswell wrote*: Boswell, *History of Alaskan Operations*, 32. Jack Boswell began working for the Company while still a student in 1926. He was manager of Fairbanks operations from 1952 until his retirement in 1965.

101 *The* Fairbanks Daily News-Miner *headline read*: "They Huffed and Puffed But Dredge Bogged Down," *FDNM*, March 20, 1958.

102 *The* Fairbanks Daily News-Miner*'s article for the day*: "Operation Continues," *FDNM*, March 21, 1958.

102 *The* Fairbanks Daily News-Miner *was finally able to report*: "Tractors and Men Finish Dredge Moving Project," *FDNM*, March 24, 1958.

Notes to Chapter 8

104 *To the north, beyond a grassy field*: Men who qualified for Company housing were a mix of professional engineers, office staff (cashier, purchasing agent), and master tradesmen (chief electrician, master mechanic). A few wives worked outside the home (Alaska Linck for Pan American Airlines and Tanya Ashurkoff for Arctic Contractors).

105 *Favorite Recipes*: St. Matthew's Church Guild, *Favorite Recipes* (Fairbanks: St. Matthew's Church, 1944), 154–55 and 159–60.

109 *Butchered, packaged, and stored*: This commercial freezer rented lockers until being displaced by home freezers in the mid-1950s. Some families avoided locker fees in winter by hanging their moose quarter from a house eave and sawing off frozen roasts as needed.

114 *At the mines, mosquitoes*: In 1931 the FE Company hired an entomologist to do a mosquito study on the Creeks. Each timekeeper was required to expose his forearm for five minutes at 4 PM each day and to kill and package any attackers. Counts ranged from two (July 28 at Fox) to seventy-five (July 15 at Chatanika). The Company compounded a citronella/camphor repellent shown to work (for about thirty minutes) and distributed it to workers. George Tulloch, "Report of Mosquito Investigations Carried on at Fairbanks, Alaska During 1931" (Fairbanks: University of Alaska Archives, VSFM "Mosquito").

Notes to Chapter 10

128 *She was the daughter-in-law*: "Pet 4," a 22.5-million acre federal reserve near the Arctic National Wildlife Refuge, was created in 1923. Explored by Arctic Contractors between 1945 and 1953, the reserve was not developed (except for a small field from which natural gas was piped to the town of Barrow) because its oil and gas deposits were deep and widely spaced.

130 *Robert Linde, a veteran*: Patricia Monaghan and Roland Wulbert, "No Antifreeze, No Headbolt Heaters 'BUT WE KEPT 'EM GOING,'" in *The Alaska Journal: A 1981 Collection*, ed. Virginia McKinney (Anchorage: Alaska Northwest Publishing Company, 1981), 240.

130 *In 1949, when the gray Studebaker*: The Alcan, today called the Alaska Highway, opened to a few tightly regulated civilian vehicles in 1946–47. In 1948 it opened to general traffic for one month. In 1949 it finally opened permanently to general traffic.

131 *Consequently she carried*: Audrey Loftus, "15 Days from Lowell [Oregon] to Fairbanks," *FDNM Heartland Magazine*, September 20, 1992, H11–14.

Notes to Chapter 11

139 *In 1916 a successful miner*: Specifications included oak floors, a lawn, a fireplace, a double garage, hot water heat, porcelain fixtures, and six inches of sawdust in the walls. Jo Anne Wold, "Dream House," *FDNM*, October 21, 1978. Across Cowles Street was another historic FE residence built in 1904 by Falcon Joslin, chief of the Tanana Valley Railroad.

139 *The following year*: Mary Lee Davis, *We Are Alaskans* (Boston: W. A. Wilde Company, 1931), 159. The house photos appear between pages 160 and 161.

140 *The only drawback*: The new Municipal Utilities System incrementally took over telephone, water, steam, and electricity service from the NC Company between 1949 and 1953.

141 *The trapline*: For a series on Gale's stories see Ken Marsh, "Growing Up in Vintage Talkeetna . . . Gale Weatherell," *Talkeetna Good Times Newspaper*, 2003–4.

143 *The newspaper published pleas*: "Save Electricity," *FDNM*, May 23, 1950.

143 *Caterer Anna Schiek*: "Housewives Take Strike in Full Stride," *FDNM*, May 24, 1950.

143 *His loyalty*: Jim faithfully represented the Boston office in opposing union demands but also took up the part of individual employees, obtaining raises for Ray Niemi and Jack Fisher in the midst of Company cutbacks in 1964, and securing a pension for the widow of Ralph Norris, who died just before retiring. Crawford to John Metcalfe, October 31, 1964, and Crawford to Fred Mulock, February 1959 (John Reeves private collection).

143 *Eugene Swendsen*: "Miner Is Killed in Accident; Pinned Under Hydraulic Hose," *FDNM*, July 15, 1952. Swendsen was the last fatality in the half-century history of the FE Company.

144 *The Company's accident rate*: Spence, *The Northern Gold Fleet*, 184.

147 *With time athletes improved:* Winter Ice Carnival events also moved in later years because warm outfall from the city power plant and new houses along the riverbank thinned the ice.

148 *Some teams were not only powerful*: In Nome in 1913 Seppala was hired part-time to train Siberian dogs imported across the Bering Strait by Roald Amundsen, fresh from his successful trek to the South Pole and planning an assault on the North Pole. When World War I canceled the expedition, Amundsen gave the dogs to Seppala as payment.

149 *Joe Mills, Nenana's barber*: Pegg Parker, "Ice Pool History Is Recorded," *FDNM*, May 19, 1945.

149 *The ingenious clock-stopping*: "Tanana Ice Breaks 12:39 P.M.," *FDNM*, May 14, 1949.

149 *Territorial law forbade*: With statehood, territorial law became state law, which the first Alaska State Legislature set out to modernize. While legislators were laboring on a bill to legalize nonprofit raffles, lotteries, and bingo, it came to the attention of a Methodist minister that current law made (and had made for more than forty years) ice pools illegal. He filed a complaint, and police seized the newly printed tickets for the 1960 Nenana Ice Pool. The legislature immediately mobilized and passed a limited bill legalizing the Chena and Nenana Ice Pools. A dissenting legislator groused that "the judiciary committee gave this its careful and learned study, lasting about 40 seconds." "Bill Would Legalize 'Ice' Only," *FDNM*, February 23, 1960.

Notes to Chapter 12

152 *I remember nothing about the courtroom*: The Swinging Bridge spanned Noyes Slough to connect Garden Island to the cabins of Graehl. This pedestrian suspension bridge bounced underfoot and rocked with the wind as we swayed across without touching the cable railings.

152 *I knew about prisoners*: A glimpse inside the federal jail would not have shocked me, but a look at the city jail a few blocks away would have. A 1955 report on the overfilled city jail described the scene: "Plumbing for the entire cell block consists of

one toilet and one washstand. . . . Food for the general prisoners consisted of coffee, water and one stale roll each day, augmented by one full meal a week. Trusties were fed three meals a week." Richard Cooley, *Fairbanks, Alaska: A Report of Progress* (Juneau: Alaska Development Board, 1954), 26. Reform followed the report.

152 *Some of these women were teachers*: Until World War I, the Fairbanks School District required women teachers to be single. At the time I was in school, women teachers could be married but were expected to resign when a pregnancy became visible.

154 *Recognizing her vocation*: Several years later the Fairbanks City Council quietly terminated Eva's employment. *Jessen's Weekly* disapproved in an editorial ("Economy and Eva McGown," November 11, 1954). The *Fairbanks Daily News-Miner* published a front-page story and photo of Eva reading her letter of dismissal and smiling sadly ("Eva McGown Too Busy Serving Fairbanks to Worry About Job," November 12, 1954, and "Letter of Dismissal," November 13, 1954). Citizens wrote letters to the editor and to the council, which rescinded its action. Eva died February 22, 1972, in the Nordale Hotel fire.

154 *Longtime businessmen*: Leslie Nerland and Wally Burnett aided both Hulda Ford and Irene Sherman, described in the next paragraph. When weather was dangerously cold, they persuaded Hulda to stay in a free apartment in the Polaris Building. When the city council wanted to take Irene's appliance-adorned property for a bridge approach, they hired a lawyer for her.

155 *Irene Sherman, property owner*: At age six Irene and two younger children were locked inside the family home in Fairbanks while her feckless mother went dancing. It was winter; the children's attempt to start a fire in the stove went terribly wrong. Rescuers saved only Irene, who spent her childhood in hospitals and convents. She emerged from this childhood bibulous, opinionated, and convivial. She had a reputation for creative profanity, concatenations of oaths that no one attempted to perpetuate.

155 *It had been built in* 1909: Mr. Thomas responded with $7,000 to an appeal from St. Matthew's Church, which was curtaining off part of the nave so that fifty weekday patrons could sit and read from the several thousand books in the church's non-lending library. The new library was initially owned by the church, which sold it to the city in 1924 for one dollar. Janet Matheson, *Fairbanks: A City Historic Building Survey* (City of Fairbanks, 1978), 11; Arnold Griese and Ed Bigelow, *O Ye Frost and Cold: A History of St. Matthew's Episcopal Church, Fairbanks, Alaska, 1904–1979* (Fairbanks: St. Matthew's Episcopal Church, 1980), 23–24.

161 *Our parents and teachers*: "Several hundred persons . . . gathered to watch. . . . Suddenly the air was drawn into the building in a great volume and the flames burst out throughout the building. . . . It had all the effects of an explosion. Four men were lifted bodily off their feet and hurled through the air." "Meet Today to Discuss School," *FDNM*, December 5, 1932.

161 *The* News-Miner *published articles*: *FDNM*, January 2, 1952. In 1950 there were 313 fires; in 1951 there were 342. The city had only eight fire hydrants—all downtown. Cooley, *Fairbanks, Alaska*, 26.

161 *Fire chief Eugene Woodcox*: "So You're Going to a Fire! Chief Offers Few Hints," *FDNM*, November 8, 1950.

162 *Epidemic tuberculosis*: There is debate about whether tuberculosis existed in Alaska in endemic form prior to Russian contact. However, there is general agreement that the epidemic that devastated the Native population occurred after the arrival of infected Europeans. Robert Fortuine, *"Must We All Die?" Alaska's Enduring Struggle with Tuberculosis* (Fairbanks: University of Alaska Press, 2005), 1–3, 6–11.

162 *The disease took its greatest toll*: George Rogers and Richard Cooley, *Alaska's Population and Economy*, vol. 2 (College: University of Alaska, 1963), 7. The Native population of Alaska decreased rapidly after foreign contact due to smallpox, measles, and influenza. Tuberculosis was unlike these other killers in that it was a slow-moving epidemic, with victims living for many years after acquiring the bacillus. Its long affliction slowed recovery of the indigenous population. Natives probably did not reach precontact numbers until 1960.

162 *In 1947 the TB death rate*: American Medical Association report quoted in "Alaska Tuberculosis Problem 'Unbelievable,' Say Medicos," *FDNM*, July 30, 1947.

162 *The TB death rate among Natives*: The TB death rate for Native children under age fourteen was more than one hundred times the rate for children in the States. Alaska Health Survey Team (Thomas Parran et al.), *Alaska's Health: A Survey Report to the United States Department of the Interior* (Pittsburg: University of Pittsburg Graduate School of Public Health, 1954), III-12–14.

162 *In 1954, a former surgeon general*: Alaska Health Survey Team, *Alaska's Health*, VI-46.

163 *The newspaper story reporting David's death*: "Young Polio Victim Dies at Hospital," *FDNM*, October 30, 1950. Julian Rivers now lives in Anchorage. Jo Anne Wold returned to Fairbanks and, despite severe paralysis, became an award-winning author. She died in 1985.

163 *Alaska was no different*: "Alaska Polio Cases Follow U.S. Pattern," *FDNM*, October 31, 1950.

164 *But annual epidemics:* Better public and private hygiene after the war spared middle-class infants many serious illnesses, but it meant that these infants no longer encountered the polio virus while young enough to be protected by their mothers' antibodies. Polio with maternal antibodies is usually a flu-like illness that induces lifelong immunity to the virus. Polio contracted after maternal antibodies have waned is more likely to cause paralysis or death.

164 *Nationwide the worst year*: These statistics are based on cases of paralytic polio only, ignoring the much larger number of subclinical or minor cases. Sources drawn from *A Paralyzing Fear: The Story of Polio in America* (PBS Video, 1998) and *Polio History Pages* (http://www.cloudnet.com).

164 *In Fairbanks 1950 and 1954*: Gloria Park, "Thirty or More Years Ago," *Alaska Medicine* 34, no. 2 (April–June 1992): 198. In Alaska in 1950 there were 83 cases of paralytic polio; in 1954 there were 372. In 1954 the U.S. city with the highest number of polio cases per capita was Ketchikan, Alaska.

164 *The epidemics disappeared*: Nationwide in 1954 about 38,000 people were hospitalized with polio; in 1956 there were 15,000; in 1960 there were 3,000; in 1970 there were 30; and in 2000 there were none. *Polio History Pages*.

Notes to Chapter 13

168 *The mines that Jim*: Statistics in this and the following paragraph are from Cooley, *Fairbanks, Alaska*, 43–44.

169 *Nome was the third-largest*: Prior to 1980, Nome had produced 3.5 million troy ounces, Juneau 7.1 million ounces, and Fairbanks 7.4 million ounces. William Hunt, *Golden Places* (Anchorage: National Park Service, Alaska Region, 1990), 350.

172 *The other theft*: "FE Dredgeman Caught Stealing Gold," *FDNM*, October 23, 1933.

173 *The whole outfit is outdoors*: Boswell, *History of Alaskan Operations*, 95, fig. 4-37.

173 *I was never invited*: "Hogatza" had already been Anglicized from the Koyukon Athabascan *Hugaadzaatno'*, meaning "good food resource river." Personal communication, Eliza Jones, coauthor, *Koyukon Athabaskan Dictionary*.

175 *Local cash registers*: Pennies, introduced to Alaska in Cordova in 1927, only slowly worked their way north to Fairbanks. In 1940 the Piggly-Wiggly supermarket began selling 37¢ sweet relish and 43¢ Fig Newtons. However, pennies were still in short supply in 1948 when the first parking meters created a brief "penny crisis."

175 *Echoing confidence expressed in 1924*: "A Year of Progress," *FDNM*, November 15, 1951.

176 *Later in the decade*: The reactor ran for ten years. Bill Johnson, "Fort Greeley's Remote Reactor: Alaska's Experiment with Nuclear Power," *Alaska History* 11, no. 1 (Spring 1996): 30–31. Today Fort Greeley continues its role in the arms race. Nine missiles designed to intercept Asian warheads in outer space are currently being installed at the fort in underground silos.

Notes to Chapter 14

180 *She supported her Norwegian-immigrant husband*: Laura never complained about supporting her husband or any other member of her family. Charles Oscar Anderson died in 1965 and is buried in the Pioneers of Alaska plot at Birch Hill Cemetery. Laura died in 1974 and is buried in the general plot at Birch Hill Cemetery.

185 *The newspaper's editor*: "Alaska Is Described as Biggest, Coldest, Emptiest and Happiest State," *FDNM*, January 8, 1963.

185 *Governor William Egan called Brinkley*: "Egan Hits TV Show," *FDNM*, January 8, 1963, and "TV Furor Still Boiling," *FDNM*, January 9, 1963.

185 *This Chamber of Commerce–sponsored film*: Lowell Thomas Jr., *Alaska! America's Brightest Star* (film presented by Alaska Bankers Association and Alaska State Chamber of Commerce, ca. 1960–65).

186 *Unlike my aunt Dorothy*: In this convoluted 1955 political event, Audrey had replaced a Democratic appointee not confirmed by a Republican legislature. (Alaskans had a

knack for electing a legislative majority from the party opposite that of the appointed territorial governor.) In a previous brush with appointive office in the early 1930s, Audrey had held the conjoined titles of U.S. Commissioner, Justice of the Peace, Coroner, Notary Public, and Probate Judge for the Chatanika Precinct area. She resigned the position(s) after about a year not because of the nuisance of notarizing, or the trauma of certifying death, or the discouragement of fining drunks, but because of the unsuitable couples she was legally required to unite in matrimony. Audrey Loftus (untitled manuscript, Jule Hurley Loftus private collection, n.d.)

Note to Chapter 15

193 *In its peak years*: Spence, *The Northern Gold Fleet*, 98.

Notes to Chapter 16

197 *Our new school had six hundred students*: It also had no handicapped access. Jo Anne Wold, who lost a few years of school after being paralyzed by polio in 1950, graduated with my class but did her course work at home.

198 *Not surprisingly, Mac's mother*: Jeannie Take, "Mrs. Mac Enjoys Sub Teaching," *Paystreak* [high school newspaper], May 1956; Joyce M. Tice, "Fritzsche—Vesta McCarthy," *Tri County Genealogy & History: Union Cemetery, Liberty Township, Tioga County, PA Obituaries* at http://www.rootsweb.com. I am aware of one other octogenarian who later substituted at Lathrop. Lola Tilly supplemented her university retirement (based on her highest three years of salary) until she turned eighty-six. Lola Tilly, "Pedro Monument Re-Dedication Speech," July 22, 1984.

200 *GAA girls could even earn*: *The Cache* [high school annual] (Fairbanks School District, 1953), 95. In 1957, Lathrop did make an initial attempt at a girls' varsity basketball team. Unlike the boys' junior varsity team and the cheerleaders, the team never acquired uniforms or a travel budget. It lasted five years.

201 *We gossiped, giggled, flirted*: With rapid diesel engines replacing steam power in 1956 and Anchorage replacing Seward as the main southbound passenger destination, trains no longer overnighted at Curry. The once-luxurious Curry Hotel burned to the ground in 1957 and was never rebuilt.

202 *Our senior class*: *The Cache* (1960), 17–33; U.S. Bureau of the Census, *Census of Population: 1960, vol. I, Characteristics of the Population, Part 3* (Washington, DC: Department of Commerce, 1961), 28. Two percent were Filipino or other minority.

202 *In the yearbook, the class wag*: *The Cache* (1953), 42.

206 *At the time of Dr. Boswell's arrest*: Joan Koponen, letter to the editor, *FDNM*, May 3, 1961.

207 *His replacement*: "Police Chief Danforth Replies to Grand Jury," *FDNM*, November 25, 1953. "Laxity" referred to investigation of businessman Cecil Wells's murder, "unsavory conditions" to the jail.

207 *A few months after his appointment*: Cooley, *Fairbanks, Alaska*, 26.

208 *I quit church*: My indignation was opportune; church services were boring compared to the drama of my love life. After a few decades of hard lessons from life, I found the Gospel considerably more compelling and returned.

208 *Widowed and no longer able*: My aunt Frances was not available to help. She had left Talkeetna and George Weatherell after the marriage degenerated in alcohol and abuse. In Anchorage she married Jim Sandvik but was widowed four years later when he and five others disappeared in a plane flying toward Kodiak. At the time of Lillian's crisis, Frances had taken her grief and moved to an island off Florida.

209 *Alaska had just become*: The new flag that we were so proud of, with its staggered seven rows of seven stars, did not officially change until almost a year after Hawaii was added as the fiftieth state in August 1959.

Notes to Chapter 17

211 *He was not swayed*: Robert Atwood, "Subversion Fails to Lure Alaskans," editorial, *Anchorage Times*, August 25, 1958.

212 *He shared the view*: "History of Oil Exploration in Alaska Is Frustration," *FDNM*, November 19, 1953.

212 *Administrative expenses of the new state*: Gordon Harrison, "Thirty Years of Statehood," *Alaska Daily News*, December 11, 1988.

213 *My aunt Dorothy*: Dorothy and Art moved to Oregon in 1955 but drove to Fairbanks each summer in a homemade camper that preceded factory models.

213 *It was Suffrage Day*: Voting age was changed to eighteen a decade later in response to the irony of young draftees being required to fight in Vietnam yet denied the vote.

213 *In that first year of statehood*: In 1960, Election District 19, of which Fairbanks was the center, had 8,735 registered voters; 8,664 of them cast presidential ballots. *State of Alaska Official Returns, General Election* 11/8/60 (Juneau: Secretary of State, 1960), 1, 29.

216 *Alaska's current epidemic*: W. Gary Hlady and John P. Middaugh, introduction, *The Recording and Epidemiology of Suicides in Alaska* (Anchorage: Epidemology Office, Division of Public Health, 1986). Between 1960 and 1974, suicide by fifteen-to-twenty-four-year-olds in Alaska almost tripled.

218 *The story of this ill-conceived plan*: Dan O'Neill, *The Firecracker Boys* (New York: St. Martin's Press, 1994).

218 *After attending the AEC meeting*: James Crawford to Fred Mulock, July 17, 1958 (John Reeves private collection). Teller's actual motive was probably to continue underground testing disguised as an Atoms for Peace project.

218 *He had the American*: "Brilliant Light Seen as Atom Bomb Blasts," *FDNM*, April 5, 1953.

219 *He also had the Alaskan*: "Alaska Can Have Massive Nuclear Engineering Job," *FDNM*, July 17, 1958.

219 *And the usual patriotic/altruistic twist*: "Atomic Harbor O.K. Vital," *FDNM*, January 10, 1959.

Notes to Chapter 18

221 *According to Ted*: Audrey and Ted Loftus interviewed by Phyllis Movius, June 15, 1992, University of Alaska Fairbanks Oral History Department, H93-05-01. The underground hydraulic mining experiment proved uneconomic and was abandoned in 1938. Philip S. Smith, "Mineral Industry of Alaska in 1938," in *Mineral Resources of Alaska: Report on Progress of Investigations in* 1938, USGS Bulletin 917 (Washington, DC: U.S. Government Printing Office, 1942), 46.

224 *Lola, like Alta*: Lola Tilly, "Flood Bulletin in Lieu of Annual Xmas Letter, September, 1967" (Lola Tilly Collection, University of Alaska Archives, Fairbanks).

226 *This was a handful*: Boswell, *History of Alaskan Operations*, 43. Ted Loftus was no longer among these employees. He and Audrey had retired in 1963 to Oregon, where Jule and Claire and Art and Dorothy Loftus lived.

227 *His bosses in New York*: USSR&M New York staff to W. A. Glavinovich, telegram, October 28, 1966, in author's possession.

227 *His diary entry for the following workday*: James D. Crawford, *Diary* 1966, entry for November 1, 1966, in author's possession.

227 *They were the last in their generation*: The five young couples married at St. Matthew's between 1926 and 1930 maintained close ties. All celebrated golden wedding anniversaries: the three Loftus couples in Oregon, the Thompsons in Florida, and the Crawfords in Washington.

WORKS CITED

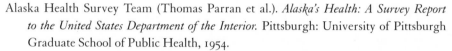

Alaska Health Survey Team (Thomas Parran et al.). *Alaska's Health: A Survey Report to the United States Department of the Interior.* Pittsburgh: University of Pittsburgh Graduate School of Public Health, 1954.

Anderson, Laura David. *According to Mama.* Fairbanks: St. Matthew's Episcopal Church, 1956.

Atwood, Robert. "Subversion Fails to Lure Alaskans." Editorial. *Anchorage Times*, August 25, 1958.

Bigelow, Riz. "Prospecting Alaska." In *Alaska's Oil/Gas & Minerals Industry.* Alaska Geographic vol. 9, no. 4, 88–117. Anchorage: Alaska Geographic Society, 1982.

Boswell, John C. *History of Alaskan Operations of United States Smelting, Refining and Mining Company.* Fairbanks: Mineral Industries Research Laboratory, University of Alaska, 1979.

Bunnell, Charles E. Collection. University of Alaska Archives, Fairbanks.

Cache [High school student annuals]. Fairbanks: Fairbanks School District, 1951, 1953, 1957, and 1960.

Cohen, Stan. *Alcan and Canol.* Missoula, MT: Pictorial Histories Publishing Co., Inc., 1992.

Cole, Dermot. *Fairbanks: A Gold Rush Town that Beat the Odds.* Seattle: Epicenter Press, 1999.

Cooley, Richard. *Fairbanks, Alaska: A Report of Progress.* Juneau: Alaska Development Board, 1954.

Crawford, Alta. "A Brief History." Manuscript, 1991. In author's possession.

———. "Excerpts from My Life." Manuscript, 1978. In author's possession.

Crawford, Henry. *Willow Hill.* Elizabeth Bascom, ed. New Jersey: private printing, 1979.

Crawford, James D. Diaries, 1965–67. In author's possession.

———. "Dope Sheet—James D. Crawford, February 26, 1979." Résumé in author's possession.

———. Letter to Jo Anne Wold, ca. February 1980. In author's possession.

———. Letters to John Metcalfe, Fred Mulock, and others, 1956–64. John Reeves private collection.

———. "Report of Chicken Creek, Forty Mile District." Report to Fairbanks Exploration Company, May 1940. Mike Busby private collection.

————. "Report on Fortymile, Sixtymile, and Seventymile Districts: Examination June 24 to July 22, 1933." Report to Fairbanks Exploration Company, 1933. Mike Busby private collection.

————. "Report on Moving Dredge 5 from Cleary Creek to Little Eldorado Creek, 1947–48." Report to Fairbanks Exploration Company, 1948, in author's possession.

Crawford, James D., and J. C. Boswell. "Dredging for Gold in Alaska: Fairbanks Operations." *Mining and Metallurgy* 29, no. 502 (October 1948): 574–79.

Crawford, James Garvin. *Dear Lizzy*, 1862–1865 [letters to Mary Elizabeth Wilson]. Elizabeth Bascom, ed. New Jersey: private printing, 1978.

Davis, Mary Lee. *We Are Alaskans*. Boston: W. A. Wilde Company, 1931.

Ellis, John. *World War II: A Statistical Survey*. New York: Facts on File, 1993.

Fejes, Claire. *Cold Starry Night*. Seattle: Epicenter Press, 1996.

Fortuine, Robert. *"Must We All Die?" Alaska's Enduring Struggle with Tuberculosis*. Fairbanks: University of Alaska Press, 2005.

Garfield, Brian. *The Thousand-Mile War*. Fairbanks: University of Alaska Press, 1995.

Gilman, William. *Our Hidden Front*. New York: Reynal & Hitchcock, Inc., 1944.

Griese, Arnold, and Ed Bigelow. *O Ye Frost and Cold: A History of St. Matthew's Episcopal Church, Fairbanks, Alaska*, 1904–1979. Fairbanks: St. Matthew's Episcopal Church, 1980.

Harrison, Gordon. "Thirty Years of Statehood." *Anchorage Daily News*, December 11, 1988.

Hlady, W. Gary, and John P. Middaugh. *The Recording and Epidemiology of Suicides in Alaska*. Anchorage: Epidemiology Office, Division of Public Health, 1986.

Holmes, Kay. "Natural Revegetation of Dredge Tailings at Fox, Alaska." In *Second Annual Conference of Alaskan Placer Mining*. Fairbanks: Mineral Industry Research Laboratory, University of Alaska, 1980.

Hunt, William. *Golden Places*. Anchorage: National Park Service, Alaska Region, 1990.

Huntington, Sidney. *Shadows on the Koyukuk*. Portland, OR: Alaska Northwest Books, 1993.

Johnson, Bill. "Fort Greeley's Remote Reactor: Alaska's Experiment with Nuclear Power." *Alaska History* 11, no. 1 (Spring 1996): 27–34.

Koponen, Joan. Letter to the editor. *Fairbanks Daily News-Miner*, May 3, 1961.

Loftus, Arthur. "A Homestead 'Frat' House." *Farthest-North Collegian* 2, no. 2 (June 1924): 9–10.

Loftus, Audrey. *According to Grandfather (the Medicine Man)*. Fairbanks: St. Matthew's Episcopal Church, 1965.

————. *According to Papa*. Fairbanks: St. Matthew's Episcopal Church, 1957.

————. "Alaskan Roadhouses." Manuscript, n.d. Jule Hurley Loftus private collection.

————. "15 Days from Lowell [Oregon] to Fairbanks." *Fairbanks Daily News-Miner Heartland Magazine*, September 20, 1992.

————. "So Much for Papa." Manuscript, n.d. Jule Hurley Loftus private collection.

Loftus, Audrey and Ted. Audiotape interview by Phyllis Movius. Fairbanks: University of Alaska Oral History Department, June 15, 1992.

Loftus, Jule B. "Corralling Caribou—a Wilder West Sport." *Farthest-North Collegian* 2, no. 1 (February 1924): 20–21.

————. Untitled manuscripts, approximately 150 pages, n.d. Jule Hurley Loftus private collection.

Ludwig, Richard F. "Sled Transportation: Heavy Single Loads in Interior Alaska." Unpublished report, 1958.

Marsh, Ken. "Growing Up in Vintage Talkeetna...Gale Weatherell." *Talkeetna Good Times Newspaper*, July 2003, August 2003, November 2003, December 2003, January 2004, February 2004.

Matheson, Janet. *Fairbanks: A City Historic Building Survey.* City of Fairbanks, 1978.

McCusker, John J. *How Much Is That in Real Money?: A Historical Price Index for Use as a Deflator of Money Values in the Economy of the United States.* 2nd ed. Worcester, MA: American Antiquarian Society, 2001.

Monaghan, Patricia, and Roland Wulbert. "No Antifreeze, No Headbolt Heaters 'ʙᴜᴛ ᴡᴇ ᴋᴇᴘᴛ 'ᴇᴍ ɢᴏɪɴɢ.'" In *The Alaska Journal: A 1981 Collection*, ed. Virginia McKinney. Anchorage: Alaska Northwest Publishing Company, 1981.

O'Neill, Dan. *The Firecracker Boys.* New York: St. Martin's Press, 1994.

Park, Gloria. "Thirty or More Years Ago." *Alaska Medicine* 34, no. 2 (April–June 1992): 197–99.

Parker, Pegg. "Ice Pool History Is Recorded." *Fairbanks Daily News-Miner*, May 19, 1945.

Polio History Pages. http://www.cloudnet.com/~edrbsass/poliohistorypage.htm.

Public Broadcasting Corporation. *A Paralyzing Fear: The Story of Polio in America.* PBS video, 1998.

Rawson, Timothy. "World War II through *The Alaska Sportsman* Magazine." In *Alaska at War*, 1941–45, ed. Fern Chandonnet. Anchorage: Alaska at War Committee, 1995.

Rogers, George, and Richard Cooley. *Alaska's Population and Economy.* Vol. 2. College: University of Alaska, 1963.

Rollins, Alden M., compiler. *Census Alaska: Number of Inhabitants*, 1792–1970. Anchorage: University of Alaska Anchorage Library, 1978.

St. Matthew's Guild. *Favorite Recipes.* Fairbanks: St. Matthew's Church, 1944.

Sandvik, Frances Weatherell. Untitled manuscripts, approximately 200 pages, n.d. Gale Weatherell private collection.

Shields, Captain Ed. *Salt of the Sea: The Pacific Coast Cod Fishery and the Last Days of Sail.* Lopez Island, WA: Pacific Heritage Press, 2001.

Smith, Maury. "KFAR Is on the Air." *Alaska Journal* 15, no. 4 (Autumn 1985): 9–15.

Smith, Philip S. "Mineral Industry of Alaska in 1938." In *Mineral Resources of Alaska: Report on Progress of Investigations in* 1938. USGS Bulletin 917, 1–114. Washington, DC: U.S. Government Printing Office, 1942.

————. "Mineral Industry of Alaska in 1940." In *Mineral Resources of Alaska*,1940, 1–102. USGS Bulletin 933. Washington, DC: U.S. Government Printing Office, 1942.

Spence, Clark C. *The Northern Gold Fleet: Twentieth-Century Gold Dredging in Alaska.* Chicago: University of Illinois Press, 1996.

State of Alaska Official Returns, General Election 11/8/60. Juneau: Secretary of State, 1960.

Take, Jeannie. "Mrs. Mac Enjoys Sub-Teaching." *The Paystreak* [Lathrop High School student newspaper], May 1956.

Thomas, Lowell, Jr. *Alaska! America's Brightest Star.* Alaska Bankers Association and Alaska State Chamber of Commerce, ca. 1960–65. Film.

Tice, Joyce M. "Fritzsche—Vesta McCarthy." *Union Cemetery, Liberty Township, Tioga County, PA, Obituaries.* In *Tri County Genealogy & History.* http://www.rootsweb.com, n.d.

Tilly, Lola. "Flood Bulletin in Lieu of Annual Xmas Letter, September, 1967." Lola Tilly Collection, University of Alaska Fairbanks Archives.

———. "Pedro Monument Rededication, July 22, 1984." Manuscript of speech. Lola Tilly Collection, University of Alaska Fairbanks Archives.

Tulloch, George. "Report of Mosquito Investigations Carried on at Fairbanks, Alaska, During 1931." Report to FE Company, Fairbanks. VFSM "Mosquito," University of Alaska Fairbanks Archives.

U.S. Bureau of the Census. *Census of Population: 1960.* Vol. I, *Characteristics of the Population, Part 3 Alaska.* Washington, DC: Department of Commerce, 1961.

U.S. Commission on Wartime Relocation and Internment of Civilians. "War and Evacuation in Alaska." In *Personal Justice Denied: Report of the Commission on Wartime Relocation and Internment of Civilians.* Seattle: University of Washington, 1997.

USSR&M New York staff to W. A. Glavinovich, October 28, 1966. Telegram in author's possession.

Wickersham, James A. Diary entry for 3/30/30 in *Diaries (Alaska): January 1, 1900–April 27, 1939.* Juneau: Microfilm by Alaska Division of State Libraries, 1969.

Wold, Jo Anne. "Dream House." *Fairbanks Daily News-Miner*, October 21, 1978.

INDEX

Page numbers in *italics* refer to figures.

abortion, 206
According to Grandfather (Loftus), 181
According to Mama (Loftus and Anderson), 181
According to Papa (Loftus and Anderson), 181
Adler, David, *157*, 157–58, 224
Adler, Mary "Benji," *157*, 224
Adler's Book Shop, 152, 157, 224
Alaska Agricultural College and School of
    Mines, 25, 27, 49, 55, 93, 234
Alaska Railroad, 29
    building of, 12–13, 25, 59
    and Curry Hotel, 40, 240
    and Gale Weatherell, 217
    passenger lists, 32
    snowbound, 42–43
    and Toonerville Trolley, 230
    towns serviced by, 20, 28, 49, 60, 62, 65, 176, 200
Alaska Statehood Bill, 210, 213
Alaska Steamship Line, 28, 32, 60
Alcan (Alaska-Canada Military Highway)
    construction of, 82–83
    Crawfords' 1949 trip, 130–35
    opens to public, 88, 235
    and Ted Loftus, 84–85
alcohol
    absence of, at Crawford wedding, 40
    bootlegging, 31
    Jim Crawford and, 37
    laws against, 31, 37, 60, 230
    as social problem, 206–7
    in Talkeetna roadhouses, 60
alcoholics, 32, 80–81, 207
Aleutians, battle for, 83–84
Aleuts, 84, 162, 233
Alien Enemy Act, 78–79
Ames, Charlotte, 112
Amouak, Ralph, 202
Amundsen, Roald, 236
Anchorage Times, 78, 211

Anderson, Charlie, 180, 239
Anderson, Laura David, 107, *180*, 180–82, 184, 239
Anthony, Katharine, 4–5, 126, 186
Asai, Mitzi, 80
Ashurkoff, Boris, 85–86, 100, 104, *138*, 160
Ashurkoff, Peter, 104, *118*
Ashurkoff, Tanya, 85–86, 104, 160, 234
Athabascan Indians
    booklets about, 181
    in Fairbanks, 16, 79
    Laura Anderson, 107, *180*, 180–82, 184
    as sled dog racers, 148
    in Talkeetna, 59, 62
    at Winter Ice Carnival, 147
Atomic Energy Commission (AEC), 218–19
Attla, George, 148
Atwood, Robert "Bob," 78, 211, 213

Baker, Hertha, 92, *138*
Barrack, James, 49, 216
berry picking, 43–44, 62, 104, 106–7, 182
Bigelow, Charles "Riz," 98
Blair, Judy Neff, 216
Bloom, Jessie, 54, 231
Booth, Jewel (later Boswell), 38, 85–86, 103
Boswell, Carl, 206
Boswell, Jack, *138*, *234*
    courts Alta, 37, 38
    FE Company operations, 100, 173
    life in FE Company compound, 103, 105, 106
    pro-statehood views, 212
    in Salt Lake City, 85–86
Boswell, Jewel (née Booth), 38, 85–86, 103, 105
Boswell, John, 103, *118*, 234
Boswell, Marian, 103, *118*
Boswell, Robby, 103, *118*
Bramstedt, Al, 67
Buckner, Simon Bolivar, 76–77, 79, 82
Bunnell, Charles, 27, 230

Burnett, Wally, 237
Butler, Ruthie, 145

Campbell, Susan, 76, 87, 114
Campbell, Tom, 76, 87
Campbell, Tommy, 76, 87
cars
    and high school students, 201, 202–3
    owned by Audrey, 131
    owned by Frances, 59, 60
    owned by Jane, 195
    owned by Jim and Alta: 1936 Ford Sedan,
        65, 86; 1941 Studebaker, 86, 88; 1949
        Studebaker, 130–35; 1954 Buick
        Roadmaster, 198, 202; Model A Ford, 49
    use of, during blackouts, 74–75, 232
    in winter, 204–5
Cassady, Jim, 216
Charlie, Helen David, 181
Chatanika mining camp, 15–17
Chicken, 68, 170–71, 173, 174, 222, 226
Christian Scientists, 63–64, 87, 125, 163, 179
Civil Aeronautics Authority, 65, 70, 81
civil defense, 73–81
censorship, 77–78, 83–84
Civilian Conservation Corps (CCC), 65
Clegg, Cecil, 54
clothes
    for afternoon tea, 128–29
    Alta's fur coat, 48
    for at-home afternoons, 44–45
    for church, 181
    for curling, 146
    for formal dances, 33–34
    for honeymoon, 41
    for office, 92
    for school, 197
    for wedding, 39–40
    See also costumes; sewing
Co-Op Soda Fountain, 152, 204
constitution, Alaska state, 32
construction camps, 24, 230
Cook Inlet oil field, 212
cooking, 56, 108–11
Cooley, Richard, 207
Copper River and Northwestern Railroad, 7
costumes, 113–14, 141
Crawford, Alta (née Tanner), *18, 21, 46, 56,
    113, 225*
    cares for Lillian, 208
    courtship, 35–38
    death, 228
    domestic activities, 111; cooking, 108–11;
        gardening, 86, 103–4, 182, 183;
        housework, 140, 182–183; sewing, 34,
        49, 146, 155, 187–88

employment: as schoolteacher, 21; at
    courthouse, 31; in bursar's office, 22;
    substitute teaching, 43, 49, 55, 180
    as hostess, 144, 179, 180, 183–84, 188–89
    Montana origins, 21–22, 85
    as mother: adopts Jane, 62–63; and Sid
        Tallman, 135; of Sally, 83, 108, 202;
        childrearing philosophy, 114–17;
        diagnosed infertile, 53; pregnancy, 71,
        73; role as family peacemaker, 144; sews
        costume, 141; social training, 127–29
    moves: to house at Sixth and Cowles, 53; to Salt
        Lake City, 85–88; to Staff House, 68–69
    and 1967 flood, 222–24
    opinions: on polio rumors, 163; on
        prostitution, 31, 32; political views, 214;
        religious views, 39
    outdoor activities: at Harding Lake, 55–57,
        64–65, 70; berry picking, 43–44, 104,
        106–7, 182; Girl Scout camping, 54–55;
        mushroom picking, 107–8; riflery, 21, 36,
        109, 189
    pastimes: birdwatching, 217; curling, 145–
        47; ice pools, 150; music, 182
    rents cabin with Gladys Welch, 29–31
    social life: dances, 32–34, 44, 112–14, 145;
        PEO Sisterhood, 111–22
    trips: Alcan Highway trip, 130–35; arrival
        in Alaska, 28–29; following Jim's
        retirement, 227; honeymoon, 40–43; to
        States, 186–87; Richardson Highway
        trip, 49–51; to Hogatza, 174; to Nome,
        170; to meet in-laws, 47–48
    wedding, 39–40
Crawford, Anthony "Toni," *4*, 76
Crawford, Ernest Augustus "Gus," 6, 65, 186
Crawford, Henry, 5
Crawford, Jackie, 217–18
Crawford, James Donald "Jim," *2, 3, 138, 166*
    childhood, 3
    and curling, 145–47
    death, 228
    domestic activities: helps slaughter pig, 106;
        operates furnace, 140; makes costumes,
        114; cooks pancakes, 111
    early employment, 6–9
    education, 4, 5–6
    family life: and Jane, 62–63, 135; and Lillian
        Tanner, 208; and Sally, 73, 108; BILs,
        111–12
    and FE Company: as chief of engineering,
        68; as consultant, 222, 227; as dredge
        superintendent, 88, 91–96, 102; as head
        of mineral exploration, 51; as manager
        of Alaska operations, 164, 167, 173–74;
        as manager of Fairbanks operations,

135, 139; Eugene Swendsen and, 143–44;
  summer with, 14–17; income, 6, 8,
  49, 51, 55, 103, 143; personnel issues,
  96–98, 142–43, 172, 236; promotion, 36;
  transferred, 84–88
 at Harding Lake, 55–57, 64–65, 70
 marriage of: buys house at Sixth and Cowles,
  53; courtship, 35–38; honeymoon, 40–43;
  trip to meet in-laws, 47–48; wedding, 39–40
 and 1967 flood, 224
 opinions: on Lola Tilly's cooking, 56; on
  Project Chariot, 218; on statehood, 186,
  211–13; political affiliation, 213, 227;
  religious beliefs, 39, 87
 retirement, 226–27
Crawford, James Garvin, 5, 16
Crawford, James Marion, 4, 5, 48, 175, 187
Crawford, Jane (later Tallman), 58, 72, *118*, *124*
 adolescent activities, 126–27
 adoption of, 62–63
 Alcan Highway trip, 130–35
 driving skills, 129–30, 132, 133
 early life, 60–62
 education, 123, 125–26, 135
 finds Jim's sword, 74
 marriage of, 135
 on PEO Sisterhood, 111–12
 and Sally, 73, 108, 195
 in Salt Lake City, 86–87
 upbringing: attends afternoon tea, 127–29;
  religion, 63–64, 87, 179; waters roads, 116
Crawford, Pearle, *4*
 appearance, 5, 38–39, 48, 76, 186
 gift from Jim, 65
 illness and death of, 175, 186, 187
 interest in genealogy, 5, 146
Crawford, Sarah Anthony "Sally" (later Isto),
  72, *133*, 197, *215*
 birth, 73, 83
 boyfriend of, 207–8
 childhood friends, 159–60
 clothes sewn by Alta, 187
 deaths of peers, 216
 driving lessons, 195–96, 202
 education: Lathrop High School, 197–99,
  214, *215*; Main School, 158–59, 160–61;
  St. Helen's Hall, 191–92, 196, 197;
  University of Alaska, 214–16
 explores downtown Fairbanks, 151–52
 and father, 91–93, 144
 games played by, 119–23
 jobs: as teenager, 208–9; at university, 218; at
  library, 151, 155–57, 164
 trips: on Alcan Highway, 130–35; to Anchorage, 200–1; to Creeks, 93–96, 192–96; to
  Nome, 170; to States, 186–87

upbringing: childhood lessons, 114–17; food
  rules, 108; religion, 208, 241
 as young adult, 219, 223, 227
Cremeans, Lola. *See* Tilly, Lola
crime, 31, 159–60, 172
curling, 145–147, 180
currency, 175, 213, 239
Curry, Charles, 40
Curry Railroad Hotel, 40–43, 240

dances
 Alta's fondness for, 32–34, 44
 Jim's presence at, 17
 Sourdough Dance Club, 112–14, 145
 teenagers at, 205
Danforth (Police Chief), 207, 240
Davidson Ditch, 11–12, 13, 192, 226, 229
Davidson, George, 11
Davis, Mary Lee, 139
Dellage, Dick, 19
Dellage, Norma (née Stanfield), 19, *21*, 131
Depression, Great
 Alaska shielded from, 36–37, 47, 48, 98
 economic effects, 45, 53, 55, 108, 198
 effect on fashion, 39, 85, 188
 lifts, 65, 70
Dimond, Anthony J. "Tony," 78
dogs, sled
 for Davidson Ditch patrol, 229
 for hunting, 24
 for planned North Pole trek, 236
 for racing, 147, *150*, 200
draft, military, 232
dredging, *90*
 draglines, 98–99
 as observed by Sally, 94–96
 technical challenges, in Alaska, 10–12
 in temperate zones, 10
 transfers, 11, 13–14, 99–102, *101*
 worker shortages, 96–98
Dutch Harbor, 83

Eagan, Bill, 164
Earling, Mary, 64, 179–80
Earling, Roy, 65, 96, *138*, 167, 169
earthquake of 1964, 213, 221–22
Egan, William, 185, 206
Egleston, O. J., 169
Egowa, Conrad, 216
Eielson Air Force Base, 97, 176
Eielson, Ben, 54, 231
Eisenhower, Dwight, 96
electric power plants
 FE Company, 142–43, 235
 NC Company, 74, 77, 143, 235
 University of Alaska, 223

Eskimos, 79, 98
  employed by FE Company, 98, 169–70
  in Fairbanks, 16, 79
  and tuberculosis, 162
  at Winter Ice Carnival, 147
evacuations, wartime, 73, 75, 76, 77
  of Aleuts, 84
  expulsion of undesirables, 80–81
  internment of Japanese Americans, 78–80

Fairbanks Curling Club, 145–47
Fairbanks Daily News-Miner
  and Associated Press, 35
  censorship announcement in, 83
  editorials: alien internment, 79, 80; David
    Brinkley program, 185–86; economy, 13,
    175–76; expulsion of undesirables, 80;
    Project Chariot, 218–19
  human-interest stories: basketball games, 200;
    Eva McGown, 237; fashion, 39; Nenana
    Ice Classic, 149; personal information, 32
  income from patent advertisements, 47
  news items: air travel, 66; dredge transfer,
    101–2; duck migrations, 54; fires, 161;
    Harding Lake lots, 69; road extensions, 65
  and 1967 flood, 222
Fairbanks High School, 125, 126, 141–42, 202
Farm Depression, 20, 21, 125
FE (Fairbanks Exploration) Company
  decline of, 167, 174–75, 177, 222, 226
  Garden Island facilities (*See* Garden Island,
    FE Company facilities on)
  Gold Room, 51–52, *52*
  holdings: Chicken, 68, 170–71, 173, 174, 222,
    226; Hogatza, 68, 167, 172–74, 222, 226, 227,
    239; Nome, 10–11, 167–70, 172, 175, 226
  mineral exploration department, 51
  offers meat storage space, 86
  personnel issues: death of Eugene Swendsen,
    143–44; pay cuts, 55; worker shortages,
    96–98; strikes, 142–43; theft from, 172
  staff photo, *138*
  and World War II: antisabotage measures,
    74; censorship, 76; closure, 84, 233
fires, 157, 161, 237
Fisher, Elvia, 171, 174
Fisher, Jack, 171, 173, 174, 236
flood of 1967, *220*, 222–24
Ford, Hulda, 154, 237
Ford, Sheldon, 154
Fort Greeley, 176, 239
Fortymile, 51, 68

gambling, 149–50, 236
Garden Island, FE Company facilities on, *139*
  housing: cottages, 103–4, *105*, 222; general

manager's house, 164, 167, *178*, 179–80,
    184; Staff House, 68–69, *70*, 84, 103
  offices, 14, 92
  utility services to, 31
gardening, 86, 103–5, 182, 183
George C. Thomas Memorial Library, 60, 151,
    155–57, *156*, 164, 237
Girl Scouts, 54–55
Glavinovich, Carl, 170
Glavinovich, Walter, 170, 173, 234
gold
  fever for, 53, 61
  government use for, 167–68
  panning, 97–98, 171
  placer mining, 9
  price of: and FE Company decline, 167, 171,
    175; increase of 1933–34, 47, 67; postwar
    stagnation, 98; stability of, 9, 37
  smelting of, 51–53, *52*
  stripping operations, *190*, 193
  weighing of, at roadhouses, 50
  World War II and, 84, 233
Gorman (health officer), 164
Gruening, Ernest, 70, 76, 78, 80

Haggland, Margaret, *112*
Hagiwara, Michael, 80
Hall, Esther, *112*
Hammon Consolidated Gold Fields, 11, 169
Harding Lake, 54–55, 64–65, 69–70, 192, 227
Harding, Warren G., 12, 54
Harrington, Otis, 217
Hess, Harriet, *112*
Hoeckle, Martha "Mardy," 152–53
Hogatza, FE Company operations at, 68, 167,
    172–74, 222, 226, 227, 239
  origin of name, 239
Holt, Bill, 39
Hoover, Herbert, 6, 47, 234
Hoover, Herbert Jr., Mrs., 128
Hoover, J. Edgar, 78
Hufman, Kay, 147
Hughes, Howard, 191
hunting
  by Alta, 36, 109
  by Frances Tanner, 61
  by Jim, 36, 51, 109
  by Lola Cremeans, 50
  on Harding Lake, 54–55
  in Talkeetna, 60
  and World War II, 81–82
Huntington, Jim, Sr., 68, 216
Huntington, Jimmy, Jr., 68, 148
Huntington, Sidney, 68, 232
Hurley, Cinderella Belle "Dill" (née Holston), 22
Hurley, Eleven, 22

Hurley, Isaiah, *21*
Hurley, Lillian. *See* Tanner, Lillian
Hurley, Sarah Frances (née Holston), *21*, 22

ice breakups, 148–50
ice service, 29, 30–31, 81
Immel, Gene, 130

Jackson, Nels, 67
jails, 152, 207, 236–37, 240
Japanese Americans, internment of, 78–80, 233
Jessen, Ernie, 77
Johnson, Andy, 68, 69
Johnson, Quentin, 216
Joslin, Falcon, 235
Juneau Empire, 79

Keaunui, Merton, 207–8
Kelly, J. J. "Codfish," 22
Kennecott Copper Mine, 6–9, *8*
Kessel, Brina, 215
KFAR radio station, 66–67, 73, 222
Kokrine, Andy, Jr., 148
Koponen, Niilo, 143
Korean War, 160
Krauss, Michael, 215
Kristoferson's Dairy, 6

L-208 (executive order), 84, 85, 88, 172–73
Ladd Field, 71, 75, 82
LaFon, Clay, 173
Lathrop, Austin E. "Cap," 66
Lathrop High School, 196, 197–202
Lavery, Bill, 67
Linck, Alaska, 103, 234
Linck, L. E. "Jack," 103, *138*
Linde, Robert, 130
Livengood Placers, 85
Loftus, Arthur "Art," *23*, 225
  and Charles Bunnell, 27, 230
  costume of, 114
  and Crawfords' adoption of Jane, 62
  early employment, 22–25
  at Harding Lake cabin, 70
  helps slaughter pig, 106
  marriage, 27, 39
  moves to Oregon, 241
  sends money to family, 49
  wartime activities, 85
Loftus, Audrey (née Stanfield), 24, *46*, 225
  community activities: afternoon tea, 128–29;
    booklets authored by, 181; costumes,
    113; PEO Sisterhood, 111, *112*; serves on
    university board of regents, 186, 239–40
  and Crawford family: adoption of Jane, 62;
    godmother to Sally, 191; cares for Lillian,

208; meets Alta at station, 28
  domestic activities: appliance owned by, 110;
    Laura Anderson, 180; organizes potluck,
    135; pig raised by, 105–6
  family activities: marriage, 22, 27, 39; Nancy,
    53, 83
  family of origin: childhood, 19–20, *21*; sends
    money to States, 49
  purchases Harding Lake lot, 70
  retirement, 242
  trips taken by: Alcan Highway, 131;
    Richardson Highway, 49–51
Loftus, Claire (née Stanfield), 24
  adopts children, 64
  childhood, 19–20, *21*
  marriage, 22, 27, 39
  meets Alta at station, 28
  sends money to family, 49
Loftus, Dorothy (née Roth), 27, 225
  and Alaska Statehood Bill, *210*, 213
  children of, 53
  and Crawfords' adoption of Jane, 62
  education, 25, 26, 27–28
  at Harding Lake cabin, 70
  on internment of Japanese Americans, 80
  marriage, 27, 39
  moves to Oregon, 241
  and PEO Sisterhood, 111, *112*
  runs for territorial legislature, 186
  sends money to family, 49
  wartime activities, 75, 85
Loftus, Jule (brother of Ted and Art), *23*, 225
  adopts children, 64
  arrival in Alaska, 24
  and Charles Bunnell, 27, 230
  homestead of, 25–26, 230
  marriage, 22, 27, 39, 40
  moves to Oregon, 85
  railroad and hunting work, 24–25
  sends money to family, 49
  takes classes, 25
  veterinary career, 26
Loftus, Jule (son of Audrey and Ted), 103,
    105–6, *118*, 131
Loftus, Nancy, 83, 103, *118*, 131
Loftus, Theodore "Ted," *23*, *138*, 225
  arrival in Alaska, 24
  costumes of, 113–14
  and Crawfords' adoption of Jane, 62
  during Richardson Highway trip, 49
  education, 26
  home in FE Company compound, 103
  marriage, 22, 27, 39
  and 1964 earthquake, 221–22
  pig raised by, 105–6
  purchases Harding Lake lot, 70

Loftus, Theodore "Ted," *continued*
retirement, 242
sends money to family, 49
wartime activities, 84–85
Lombard, Roland, 148

MacDonald, Christine, 145, 151, 192–94
MacDonald, Donald, III, *138*
Machetanz, Fred, 213
Mackey, Marie, 56, 154
mail service, 66, 231
and censorship, 78
for gold, 171, 173
transit time in 1930, 16
Main School, 58, 145, 158–59, 160–61
Mammy (caretaker), 3, 5
Mary Lee Davis House, 139–41, 144, 145, 151, 222
Masonic Lodge, 34
McCarthy, J. Ellsworth "Mac," 198–99, 207
McCarthyism, 160
McComb twins, 25
McGown, Art, 153
McGown, Eva, 32, 230, *113*, *153*, 153–54, 237
Meeker, Joe, 216
Meier, Lois, 198
Metcalfe, Genevieve Parker, 92–93, 174, 186, 234
Metcalfe, John, 93, 174
Migawa, Frank, 79–80
Mikami, Flora, 79
Milepost, The, 132
Miles, John, 11
military installations
Chilkoot Barracks, 70
Eielson Air Force Base, 97, 176
Ladd Field, 71, 75, 82
Missouri School of Mines and Metallurgy, 4, 5–6
Moody, Jim "Jimmy," 103, *118*
Moose Creek Butte dike, 66
Mormons, 87
Murie, Olaus, 26
Murray, Clara, 147
Musjerd, Frank, 29–30

Natives, 98
at Lathrop High School, 202
teen pregnancy among, 206
and tuberculosis, 162
See also Aleuts; Athabascan Indians; Eskimos
natural disasters
fires, 157, 161, 237
1964 earthquake, 213, 221–22
1967 flood, 220, 222–24
NC (Northern Commercial) Company, 30, 31, 77
and 1967 flood, 223–24
electricity, 74, 143, 235
and fire alarm, 161

and ice pools, 149
steam, 140, 235
water, 30, 31, 235
Nenana Ice Classic, 149, 236
Nerland, Leslie, 237
Nerland, Mildred, *112*
Newcomb, Simon, 79
Niemi, Ray, 236
Nome, FE operations at, 10–11, 167–70, 172, 175, 226, 239
Nordale, Hjalmar, 35, 162
Nordale Hotel, 153, 237
Norris, Ralph, *138*, 173, 236
North American Championship Dog Derby, 148
Northern Commercial Company. *See* NC Company
Northern Pacific Railroad, 60
Noyes, Fred, 69
nuclear power, 176, 218–19, 239
nuclear threat, 160–61

O'Neill, Dan, 218
O'Neill, Patrick, *138*, 174–75
Odd Fellows Hall, 34, 112, 145
Ogburn, Robert "Bert," 96
Ogburn, Ruth, *113*, 131
Ohlson, Otto, 42
oil, 6, 212–13, 235
oilers, 97
O'Neill, Patrick, *138*
Oogaruk, the Aleut (Pilgrim), 158
Osborne, Cap, 103, *138*
Osborne, David, 103, *118*, 162
Osborne, Eddie, 104, *118*, 122
Osborne, Margaret, 103

Pacific Alaska Airways (PAA), 65–66, 231
Parker, Genevieve (later Metcalfe), 92–93, 174, 186, 234
Parks, George, 51, 70
Parran, Thomas, 162
Patty, Ernest, 234
Paul, David, 181
Pearl Harbor, 70, 186
PEO Sisterhood, 111–12, *112*, 225
Petersburg fox farm, 85
Peterson, Roger Tory, 217
Phillips Field, 168
Pilgrim, Earl, 111, 150, 172
Pilgrim, Mariette Shaw, 150, 158, 164
polio, 162–64, 238, 239
post office, 152
pregnancy, 199, 205–6, 237
Prohibition, 31, 37, 60, 230
Project Chariot, 218–19, 241
prostitution, 31–32, 230

Prudhoe Bay oil field, 213
Pruitt, Bill, 219
Public Works Administration (PWA), 65
Purdy, Ann, 171

Quigley, Fannie, 44

radio broadcasts, 66–67, 76, 173, 183
railroads
  building of, in Alaska, 12–13
  Copper River and Northwestern, 7
  Loftus brothers' employment on, 24–25
  Northern Pacific, 60
  Tanana Valley, 14, 15, 25
  Union Pacific, 29
  White Pass and Yukon Railway, 49
  See also Alaska Railroad
Rankin, Jeannette, 186
Rayburn, George, 112, 144
Rayburn, Gina, 144
Residence No. 12, 164, 167, *178*, 179–80, *184*
Rice, Neil, 173
Richardson Highway, *46*, 49–51
Ringstad, Myron, 199
Rivers, Julian, 163
Rivers, Ralph, 80, 163
roadhouses
  on Alcan Highway, 132–33
  Burwash Landing Lodge, 134
  Canyon River, 24
  on Richardson Highway, 50–51
  in Talkeetna, 60
Roe v. Wade, 206
Roosevelt, Eleanor, 85
Roosevelt, Franklin, 47, 65, 79, 164
Root, Billy, 112
Roth, Ada, 27
Roth, Dorothy. *See* Loftus, Dorothy
Roth, Florence. *See* Thompson, Florence
Roth, Irma, 162
Roth, Rinehart, 28

salmon industry, 212
Sandvik, Frances. *See* Tanner, Frances
Sandvik, Jim, 241
Schiek, Anna, 129, 143
Seeliger, Al, *138*, 143
Seppala, Leonhard, 33, 148, *150*, 229, 236
sewing, 34, 49, 146, 155, 187–88
Sheldon, Don, 217
Sherman, Irene, 155, *155*, 237
Signal Corps, 65, 75, 232
Skelton (police chief), 207
sled dogs. *See* dogs, sled
Smith, Christine, 198
Smith, Maury, 67

Smith, Murray, 29, 30–31, 81
Smoke, Horace "Holy," 148
Snapp, Tom, 219
Sourdough Dance Club, 112–14, 145
Spell of the Yukon, The (Service), 78
St. Helen's Hall, 191–92, 196, 197
St. Louis Post-Dispatch, 65
St. Matthew's Church, 39, 161, 181, 208, 237
Staff House, 68–69, *70*, 84, 103
Standard Oil, 6, 73
Stanfield, Audrey. *See* Loftus, Audrey
Stanfield, Claire. *See* Loftus, Claire
Stanfield, Elma (later Stiers), 19, *21*
Stanfield, John, *21*
Stanfield, Leslie, 19, 20, 21, 22, 39
Stanfield, Norma (later Dellage), 19, *21*, 131
Stanfield, Pearl, *21*
Stanfield, Romeo, 19
statehood, 209, 211–13
Stiers, Sid, 19
Strom, Ralph, 96
Studebaker, 86, 88
Suffrage Day, 213
suicide, 216, 241
Swanson River oil field, 212
Swendsen, Eugene, 143–44, 236

Talkeetna, 59–60
Tallman, Sid, 135
Tanana Valley Railroad, 14, 15, 25
Tanner, Alta. *See* Crawford, Alta
Tanner, Frances (later Thompson; later
    Weatherell), *21*, *60*
  childhood, 21
  children of, 53, 63, 141
  difficulties in Idaho, 48, 59
  later life, 241
  marries George Weatherell, 64
  marries Jim Sandvik, 241
  moves, 60–62, 85
  and Sid Tallman, 135
Tanner, Frederick, 20–21
Tanner, Lillian (née Hurley), *20*
  absent from Jane's wedding, 135
  and Alta's wedding, 38–39
  and birth of Sally, 83
  moves in with Jim and Alta, 208
  moves to Talkeetna, 48, 59–60
  retirement, 85, 125
Taylor, Bob, 161
Taylor, Warren, 206
Taylor, William, 206
teachers, 158, 237
telephone service, 32, 50–51, 65, 144, 232
television, 185–86
Teller, Edward, 218, 241

Terao, Robert, 79–80
thawing, 9, 11, 15, 43, 169
Thomas, George C., 155, 237
Thompson, Florence (née Roth)
  children of, 53
  education, 27–28
  marriage, 27, 39
  wartime activities, 49, 76
  in Washington, DC, 186
Thompson, Gale. See Weatherell, Gale
Thompson, Glenn, 60–61, 63, 64
Thompson, Jane. See Crawford, Jane
Thompson, Tommy, 38, 39, 49, 76, 186
Tilly, Gray, 56
  enlists in military, 75
  and Gray Wangelin, 64
  at Harding Lake, 55–57, 64–65
  and 1967 flood, 224
Tilly, Lola (née Cremeans), 46, 56, 225
  friendship with Alta, 111
  Girl Scout camping, 54–55
  and Gray Wangelin, 64
  at Harding Lake, 55–57, 64–65
  and 1967 flood, 224
  Richardson Highway trip, 49–51
  substitute teaching, 240
  University of Alaska and, 75
Tonseth, Shirley, 131–32
tuberculosis, 162–63, 238
Tundra Topics, 67
Tweiten, Judie, 96, 114, 145, 192–95
Tweiten, Oscar, 96, 195, 226

Union Pacific Railroad, 29
unions, 142–43, 236
United States Smelting, Refining and Mining
  Company (USSR&M), 10–12, 212, 226
  See also FE Company
Uotila, Marie, 216
USSR&M. See United States Smelting,
  Refining and Mining Company

Van Winkle, James, 59, 60, 61, 125
Volstead Act, 31, 37, 60, 230
voting, 213–14, 231, 241

Wagner, L'Marie, 208
Wangelin, Gray "Yarg," 64

War Manpower Commission, 80
War Production Board, 84
water services, 29–30
Waxberg, Bud, 216
We Are Alaskans (Davis), 139
Weatherell, Frances. See Tanner, Frances
Weatherell, Gale, 141
  birth, 53
  lives with Crawfords, 140–42, 217–18
  moves from Idaho, 60
  name change, 64
  wartime moves, 85
Weatherell, George, 64, 85
Webb (honey-bucket man), 29–30, 31
Weeks Field, 54, 77
  1951 cold snap, 145
  antisabotage measures, 73, 74
  closes, 168
  first flight from, 231
  threatened closure of, 81
Welch, Gladys, 29–31, 37, 39
Weller, Rosamund, 64, 154–55
Wells Fargo & Company, 3, 4
White Alice Communication System, 176
White, John, 113
White, Sam O., 168
Wickersham, James A., 42–43, 231
Wien, Richard, 202
Wilcox, Helen, 112
Williams, Jane, 198
Wilson, Woodrow, 12
Winter Ice Carnival, 147–48, 150, 236
Wold, Jo Anne, 163, 240
World War II
  battle for Aleutians, 83–84
  censorship, 77–78
  Congressional vote on, 186
  end of, 87–88
  expulsion of undesirables, 80–81
  internment of Japanese Americans, 78–80
  Lend-Lease and, 82
  local measures, 73–77
  preparations for, 70
  shortages, 81
  suspension of gold mining, 84, 85, 88, 172–73
Wright, Gareth, 148

Zaverl, Stan, 207